A Falkland Islander's Wartime Journal

A Falkland Islander's Wartime Journal

Surviving the Siege

Graham Bound

Pen & Sword
MILITARY
AN IMPRINT OF PEN & SWORD BOOKS LTD.
YORKSHIRE – PHILADELPHIA

First published in Great Britain in 2022 by
Pen & Sword Military
An imprint of
Pen & Sword Books Ltd
Yorkshire – Philadelphia

ISBN 978 1 39908 867 1

A CIP catalogue record for this book is available from the British Library.

Printed and bound in the UK by CPI Group (UK) Ltd, Croydon, CRO 4YY

Pen & Sword Books Limited incorporates the imprints of Atlas, Archaeology, Aviation, Discovery, Family History, Fiction, History, Maritime, Military, Military Classics, Politics, Select, Transport, True Crime, Air World, Frontline Publishing, Leo Cooper, Remember When, Seaforth Publishing, The Praetorian Press, Wharncliffe Local History, Wharncliffe Transport, Wharncliffe True Crime and White Owl.

For a complete list of Pen & Sword titles please contact

PEN & SWORD BOOKS LIMITED
47 Church Street, Barnsley, South Yorkshire, S70 2AS, England
E-mail: enquiries@pen-and-sword.co.uk
Website: www.pen-and-sword.co.uk

Or
PEN AND SWORD BOOKS
1950 Lawrence Rd, Havertown, PA 19083, USA
E-mail: Uspen-and-sword@casematepublishers.com
Website: www.penandswordbooks.com

Dedicated to all who sheltered at the Upland Goose.
Good night, God bless,
wherever you are.

Contents

Introduction

Before dawn on the morning of 14 June 1982, an Argentine Air Force officer burst through the main entrance of the small hotel in Port Stanley where my family and many of our friends were sheltering. He told us that the British troops who had besieged Stanley for weeks were now massed on the outskirts of town and would soon be among us. He and his men were retreating. We would, he said, 'soon be free'.

That was just one of the dramatic encounters, experiences and conversations that I recorded obsessively in old ledgers, desk diaries and exercise books from the earliest days of the crisis. I did not know what I would do with this record, if anything. I probably played with the idea of using my notes as the basis for a book. But I was then just twenty-four years old, and at that age focusing my thoughts and efforts long enough to write a book would have been a very tall order.

So my eyewitness records of 1982 were put in a box file and then into a cupboard; not forgotten, but put aside. In the decades that followed, every time I moved house, or even moved country, the journals went with me. For a lengthy period the large box file acted as a doorstop. I once saved it from destruction as my apartment was flooded.

Very occasionally, I opened the journals and read a few of the slowly fading lines on pages that were yellowing with age. I always valued my journals. Now, at last, I have done something with them.

By the time this is published, almost 40 years will have passed since the war ended. In that time, the Falklands War has become a potent historical icon for those Britons who tend to look back on empire and even colonialism with nostalgia. While Britain has lost more wars than it has won since 1982, the Falklands War was a clear victory and has often been held up as an example of how the country can walk tall on the world stage if it has the will to do so. At least in 1982 it showed that it could repel foreigners and look after its own.

According to the fine print of that narrative, the Argentines were entirely to blame. They launched a surprise attack, which no one could have anticipated, on a tiny population which enjoyed the normal benefits of British citizenship and democracy. These people deserved to have their freedom restored.

The truth, which I hope emerges from these pages, is much more nuanced. Some readers (mainly the type described above) may not like that. My cynicism about some prominent British politicians, for example, may ruffle feathers. After the shock of invasion some referred to us as close 'family'. In the years preceding that, however, the same politicians regarded us as embarrassing country cousins, to be kept at arm's length in case we visited and emptied the liquor cabinet.

I take a chance with your judgement, therefore. But perhaps not a great one. I hope readers will remember that there is always a rawness and honesty about journals. Otherwise, what is the point of them?

If my text sometimes reads as a paean to the BBC, and especially the World Service, there is a good reason for that. WS (to use the acronym which I apply throughout the book) was our vitally important information lifeline. We trusted BBC journalists because they sought the truth like terriers. They had no time for jingoism or propaganda from either side.

The Argentines were very aware of our dependence on BBC WS, which was why they attempted to jam it. This action contravened the International Declaration of Human Rights and showed the Junta's contempt for the truth.

Have we not seen enough Falklands War memoirs and journals? I think we cannot have enough. No single memoir will be completely accurate, as authors write from different viewpoints and with different biases. But historians can draw on them all, attempting to build up a composite picture that is accurate and trustworthy.

There is another reason why I would encourage people to explore, interpret and, if possible, publish their journals (or their memories, if they wrote nothing down at the time). The act of reading and editing is therapeutic. Before I started this work, aspects of my experiences in 1982 still bothered me. This was not full-blown trauma, but too often I would revisit disturbing memories and images and question aspects of my own youthful character. Since completing this manuscript, I feel better about 1982. It is less of a presence in my life story. That is undoubtedly a good thing.

My wife is a psychologist and she was not surprised when I told her about this. She explained that weaving difficult memories into narratives is a recognized therapeutic technique. It helps both the subconscious and conscious mind make sense of events that are very out of the ordinary. As part of a story, those events have causes and consequences. I would encourage anyone to undertake this process.

There are two principal ideas that I would like this book to convey. Firstly, people on all sides made bad decisions; sometimes wilfully wicked decisions. As a result, some people did bad things. But on all sides there were also people who made good decisions and did good things. The full panoply of humanity was to be seen in that conflict.

Secondly, all of us who found ourselves in the Falkland Islands during those awful months of 1982, regardless of place of birth, were victims of an invasion, an occupation and a war that should never have happened.

Graham Bound
August 2021

PART I

SECRETS AND SUBTERFUGE

Chapter 1

Pawns in the Game

(16 February–11 March)

Tuesday, 16 February 1982

So, here we go again. Government House has just announced that the latest round of talks with Argentina is to resume in New York on 26 and 27 February. They get us nowhere, except perhaps more deeply into the mire of the dispute. But they go on anyway. The British team will be made up of diplomats Luce, Williams, Fern, Bright and Creswell. There will also be two of our representatives there.

Of course Buenos Aires doesn't recognize that we are grown-up enough to talk about our own future, so our people will be attached to the UK diplomatic delegation. The local reps will be [Councillors] Tim Blake and John Cheek. On the Argentine team will be Ross, Ortiz de Rosas, Blanco and Ortini.

GH [Government House] has issued a downbeat statement which suggests they are about as excited at the prospect as they would be by a wet winter Sunday in the Falklands – and believe me, that can be pretty boring.

The statement reads, 'The talks will be held at the request of Argentina, so the British will be attending to see what proposals they have.' It was reiterated (stifling a yawn, I suspect) that no decision will be reached that is not acceptable to Falkland Islanders. I suppose that the attendance of two councillors will help to ensure this is so. They might have signed off with, 'Move along; nothing to see here'.

The LADE F28 arrived today.[1] No British mail on board. That's very frustrating and it has happened too often lately. I wonder if this is a veiled message from Buenos Aires reminding us how they can tighten the screws on us whenever they want.

Wednesday, 17 February

[Local pilot] Eddie Anderson and a FIGAS [Falkland Islands Government Air Service] mechanic left by LADE yesterday. They plan to pick up the Governor's [Rex Hunt's] personal Cessna 172 and fly it across the water to Stanley. It seems that the ferry pilot had taken it as far as Rio Gallegos. It then developed some kind of electrical trouble, and although it seemed this could be fixed easily enough there, the pilot decided that he did not like the look of the few hundred miles of open South Atlantic. I can't say I blame him. All credit to Eddie and the mechanic.

Friday, 19 February

The Governor's shiny little Cessna plane arrived this afternoon. Apparently, LADE loaned Eddie and the mechanic survival equipment for the flight, which was good of them.

I overheard a conversation in the West Store between people who would know that Ronnie Lamb [the Chief Police Officer] had borrowed a Marines or Defence Force pistol last week when he travelled to North Arm to arrest a Chilean worker who had, it seems, suffered a mental breakdown and was behaving in an alarming way. I'm sure that he was more of a danger to himself than to anyone else, but Ronnie Lamb seems to have a dramatic approach to situations. Some weeks ago, he waded into a Marines v Locals brawl at a dance in the Town Hall and was sent flying with a punch to the head. Not particularly good policing, I'd say, but I suppose he has some nerve.

Work on the Youth Club building has been completed. We [I was on the committee] just need to tidy it up and then we can have the grand opening tomorrow.

Another Polish man has jumped ship and applied for asylum. That brings the total of refugees in Stanley to six.[2]

Saturday, 20 February

Governor Hunt officially opened the new Youth Club building this afternoon. There were plenty of kids there, and I think we can all feel proud of the work done. The general public were invited to look at the building, and people who had helped in any way at all to complete it received a special invitation. There were about forty people there and they were all given coffee and tea.

We held an opening disco in the evening. I was the DJ and it seemed to go well enough. Aunt Ning [King], who is the Chair of the committee, along with Alison and Barbara [King], Paul Howe and Shelley Livermore supervised. About fifty kids joined the club today.

Sunday, 21 February

Life cannot be easy for the Poles who've taken refuge in Stanley. One, a nice guy called Roman, had a disagreement with his landlord and left the house with his few possessions in a plastic bag. Alison, Barbara and I found him looking very lonely and depressed on Victory Green and we tried to persuade him to come back to the

Upland Goose with us. But he just didn't want to be helped. It seems to me that these guys need to move on to a country where they will have a better chance of finding a new life. Eventually, one of the other Poles persuaded Roman to go back to his lodgings.

Monday, 22 February

The [British Antarctic Survey ship] RRS *Bransfield* arrived this morning. Camp sports week began at Goose Green and Pt Stephens.

Tuesday, 23 February

The LADE F28 arrived with two weeks of mail, and [Postmaster] Bill Etheridge kindly kept the Post Office open late so that we could get our mail.

Wednesday, 24 February

Councillors John Cheek and Tim Blake left for the talks in New York on today's LADE plane. I hope no one slips anything into their coffee while they're enjoying the flight.

Mavis Hunt [the Governor's wife] spent a few hours at the Goose Green sports today. Presumably she didn't have a go at the steer-riding.

Thursday, 25 February

Interesting – one or possibly two unidentified aircraft were seen near Goose Green on Tuesday. Having a look at the sports? I doubt it. Government House contacted the LADE people in Stanley for an explanation, correctly assuming the plane was theirs, and were told that it was a Learjet on a mission to calibrate the beacon near Stanley airport. But no permission had been sought for this flight, and that makes me wonder whether calibration was really what they were up to. There was no explanation why the second plane was flying around. My guess is that both were involved in reconnaissance.

The Argentine Learjet antics continued into today. One was seen over Stanley at about 1.15pm. I rang up Government House to see whether permission had been sought for this flight but I couldn't get any comment. GH's default position is not to comment on anything vaguely sensitive. As usual, the tone of voice suggested that *Penguin News* should wind its neck in.

There was a car crash in Stanley today. A Land Rover ran into a Hillman Imp. No one was badly hurt but, not surprisingly, the Imp came out worse from the encounter. That's not much of a story, even for *Penguin News*. I wish I could report that the Learjets have been taking reconnaissance photos of Stanley. We'll give it (and GH's refusal to comment) a mention anyway and let readers fill in the gaps.

Friday, 26 February

Last evening on [BBC World Service's] Radio Newsreel, Harold Briley reported on the coming Argentina/UK talks.[3] He reflected that there seems to be more tension about this round, perhaps even a degree of threat. He actually asked Argentine officials attending the talks if they would invade. 'Good God, no!' they responded. 'We've waited 150 years and we wish to resolve the matter peacefully.'

I was a bit shocked by this report. I think secretly we are all afraid that the situation might lead to an invasion (and those strange Learjet flights need to be seen in that context). Addressing the elephant in the room, as Briley has done, is good but it also means that the subject is much harder to avoid now. I think we have avoided talking about invasion locally because it is a scary thing to contemplate, and we know we would be powerless to stop it.

Yesterday at about 6.00pm HMS *Endurance* left for South Georgia. On board were Lord and Lady Buxton, who will visit their daughter Cindy. She is making wildlife films on the island for British TV. Also on board is [the Philatelic Bureau's] Lewis Clifton, who will be preparing collectors' covers. Hell of a job, Lewis, but someone has to do it.

Another Polish sailor has jumped ship. The new refugee is said to be a doctor. That means that we now have seven Poles in Stanley who have chosen refugee status rather than martial law. I admire them.

No news yet about the outcome of the talks in New York. They were supposed to have ended yesterday, but neither side seems to be saying anything.

Two Marines received minor fines for what was described as 'indecent exposure' in the Victory Bar. No more details available, but there's been a good deal of sniggering. The Marines have a penchant for getting their clothes off when they've had a few drinks.

The good weather means that mushrooms have been popping up on the green areas around Stanley. The King girls [Anna, Alison and Barbara] and I went mushrooming at Yorke Bay. That's Saturday's breakfast sorted.

PC Bryson tried to sort out another melee on Friday night in one of the pubs. Apparently, he clouted a Marine over the head with his truncheon. The Marine was hospitalized. I don't think they're supposed to whack people over the head.

Monday, 1 March

Barely a squeak of information about the talks today. At 10.00am the Governor issued a typical non-statement, saying that the Argentine proposals had been discussed in detail in New York. We are none the wiser about what went on, so nothing to report in *Penguin News*, which I have to put to bed soon. But I will make the point that we are being deliberately kept in the dark about our own affairs. We really are pawns in this game.

Argentine Radio is reporting that the Junta will be meeting tomorrow to discuss the dispute in the light of the New York talks. The generals in Buenos Aires clearly have something to chew over.

Tuesday, 2 March

The Italian Ambassador to Uruguay, a Dr Martino, arrived for a one-week visit. He is also the Italian Consul for the Falklands. I shouldn't think that work keeps him very busy, so I guess this visit is a perk of the job.

Ken Gaiger received a three-month jail sentence yesterday. He had been charged with violent behaviour, for which he has something of a track record. Gaiger was apparently so upset about his sentence that he started throwing chairs around the court. He received a further fifteen days for that.

Argentine Radio is reporting that, following the meetings in New York, there is a proposal to hold monthly talks about the sovereignty of the Islands. This is a lot more than our government has told us.

The Falklands delegation returned from New York today. We await news from them. No doubt they have been sworn to secrecy by the Foreign and Commonwealth Office, but perhaps their sense of duty to us will encourage them to feed us a few crumbs. Perhaps!

Two more Polish fishermen jumped into the port agent's launch today and have requested asylum. The skippers of the ships are behaving quite reasonably and some are sending the crewmen's property ashore later.

Wednesday, 3 March

Something stirs. There was a joint Executive and Legislative Council meeting today at Government House chaired by Rex Hunt. After a lengthy debriefing of the two councillors who went to New York, both councils retired to draft their response for the government in London.

No public statement yet, however, and no leaks, which I had hoped might enable us to put something other than speculation in *Penguin News*. There is a feeling that we are entering an important phase and yet we are being kept in the dark.

Thursday, 4 March

Joint Councils reconvened to discuss the talks. Rumours (credible, I'd say) suggest the meeting was very stormy. There were sharply differing views about whether the full list of points – perhaps demands and threats – made by the Argentines would be released to the public. Governor Hunt eventually lost his temper and walked out. I'm not that surprised. He can have an easy way with people, but in his eyes at least, Governors can be expected to govern.

Later: the story has developed. I'm told that [Councillor] Terry Peck invited his colleagues Tony Blake, Mary Jennings and Ron Binnie to continue the meeting unofficially at his house, and that meeting went on late into the night.

Almost simultaneously, the radio station conducted a discussion programme with [Councillors] Tim Blake and John Cheek, who were, of course, at the talks in New York. They were questioned quite hard by Patrick Watts and a few others on the interview panel, but they refused to divulge any details.

What we can safely assume is that the talks were difficult and dominated by Argentine demands for progress, perhaps with thinly veiled threats. I find it all interesting and exciting to a degree, but also hugely annoying. We are being treated patronizingly by London and Government House.

I'm also worried, and that sometimes verges on fear. If threats are being expressed by BA's far-right Junta, which has been totally ruthless with the opposition in its own country, then it's dangerous. The *Buenos Aires Herald*[4] routinely discusses the 'disappeared', the murders and the torture.

BBC World Service was particularly difficult to hear tonight, but through the static we picked up that Luce, representing the Foreign Office, had spoken of the 'need to resolve the dispute'. He seems to favour increasing the frequency of Argentine/British meetings with pre-established agendas.

There was also a report suggesting Argentina might apply economic sanctions against the UK. I don't think punitive tariffs on corned beef and Bovril exports will upset London too badly, but they *might* have in mind sanctions against us here in the Islands. As (thanks to London) they control fuel supplies, flights and even medical care, they could make our lives very uncomfortable.

Friday, 5 March

Finally! The Governor has issued a statement about the talks. It's a meandering statement, not saying much that we don't know already about the state of relations with Argentina. But Rex Hunt said that the councillors have now completed their debriefing of the two councillors who attended the New York meeting, and it is now up to the Falklands Government to prepare a statement to London expressing their view on whether the talks should even be continued, and if so where, when and covering what issues. He referred to 'inaccurate statements' made by the Argentine press and radio and urged Islanders to disregard them.

The governor concluded by saying there would be another meeting of councillors in a fortnight, during which a statement of their views will be finalized and then communicated to London. So what more do we know now? Precious little, except that the Argentines appear to have put us in a bind.

Saturday, 6 March

A break from politics today. The annual Horticultural and Home Produce Show was held today in the gymnasium. Great turnout as usual, with keen competition between flower and vegetable growers and makers of cakes, bread, jams and any other food that can be created with a peat-fired range.

The auction of produce this evening was a lot of fun and I came home with a fair amount of bargains. The big prizes: Best Vegetable Garden, Fred Cheek. Best Flower Garden, the Upland Goose Hotel.

Sunday, 7 March

As the remains of the Horticultural and Home Produce Show were being cleared away in the gymnasium, something rather strange happened in the sky over Stanley. At about 15.40, a Lockheed Hercules of the Argentine Air Force appeared overhead, circling the town briefly before heading for the airport, where it touched down successfully. This is not normal. These large planes did use the airport very briefly a few years ago when they brought in components for the kit house that LADE built for its manager, but otherwise there is no need for them to come to Stanley.

As I understand it, there was minimal warning that the plane was about to land. I'm assuming that LADE office knew, but I haven't been able to find out whether the authorities here had any warning at all. As it's a Sunday, there would have been no one in the terminal or the control tower.

LADE says the Hercules was on its way to Marambio base in the Antarctic and was returning to Rio Gallegos after a fuel leak was discovered. LADE has aviation fuel tanks here so the story is not illogical. However – massive 'however' – people who went to the airport to have a look at the plane said it was showing no signs of losing fuel. Wouldn't it have been trailing a stream of fuel as it approached and taxied along the runway? Gerald Cheek, the Director of Civil Aviation, who went to the airport, told me later that there was no sign of lost fuel.

In any case, the Hercules left Stanley again, ostensibly for Rio Gallegos, at 18.20. What was all that about, *really*? Could that have been an intelligence gathering mission?

Monday, 8 March

Strong winds last night, and today, gale force plus. A wind speed of 62mph was recorded at midnight. There was remarkably little damage around town.

It's Commonwealth Day today. As usual, Governor Hunt read the Queen's message to the school kids. Then the usual half-holiday was declared and the kids ran off happily, probably thinking very little about the state of the empire today and what it means to be an unloved colony 8,000 miles from the mother country.

Tuesday, 9 March

The First Secretary at the British Embassy in BA arrived by LADE flight today. No indication why he is here, but it's reasonable to assume he'll be briefing Rex Hunt about attitudes in Argentina and taking the political temperature here.

Wednesday, 10 March

The Polish defectors have been offered sanctuary in the annex to St Mary's Church. Most, if not all, are Catholic, so this seems to make sense. I suppose Monsignor Spraggon is pleased to have his congregation expanded.

The airmail service is becoming increasingly sporadic. We speculate, of course, that this is LADE silently saying, 'We can make life difficult, you know', but there's no proof of that. Anyway, a great backlog of parcel mail made its way up from the airport to the Post Office today, including watches and jewellery for the shop[5]. Always enjoyable helping Mum and Dad open such goodies.

Councillor John Cheek and his family left for the UK via BA. John only returned from the New York talks last week.

Thursday, 11 March

Governor Hunt has been having a good day. He spent several hours practising landings and take-offs in his new Cessna plane. It's been very sunny and warm, so he must have enjoyed it. Certainly much more fun than trying to keep the lid on whatever happened in New York and the stressful aftermath.

Councillors representing East Falkland have been visiting some camp[6] settlements to consult with their constituents. I haven't spoken to them, but I have it from reliable sources that they are asking those they represent for permission to go back on the election promise made by every councillor not to talk to the Argentine Government about Falklands sovereignty. This is important because it suggests that the Argentines took a very hard line in New York and we are contemplating caving in to them.

The pressure to concede will be coming from London as much as it is from Buenos Aires. I do not trust London any more than I trust Buenos Aires, and I'm not alone in that feeling.

Friday, 12 March

Sweltering temperatures today (for the Falklands). This afternoon the mercury reached 21.4°C in Stanley. Chartres experienced 24.5°C, which must be very near the highest temperature ever recorded here. We are sub-Antarctic, after all!

The new school hostel, where children from the camp were to live, was officially condemned today. Not a single schoolchild has been through the door. This bunker-like building was constructed at great expense using an experimental concrete-spraying method. Apparently, the sheer weight of the roof makes it unsafe. What an embarrassment.

More positively, we're pleased that the new Youth Club is being enjoyed. Lots of kids turned out for the disco this evening. It's good to feel that something is being done to relieve the boredom of growing up in Stanley. No fights and no sign of drinking, although I expect there were tins of beer hidden in the gorse bushes outside.

Chapter 2

Tit for Tat

(15–29 March)

Monday, 15 March

RRS *John Biscoe* arrived from the Antarctic today and berthed at the Public Jetty at about 8.00pm. She will be on her way back to UK soon after the Antarctic season. She's looking like a very old ship now.

Tuesday, 16 March

Governor and councillors returned to the stormy subject of the New York talks today. Let's see if this leads to them coming clean about it all. They again discussed the outcome of the meeting and reached a decision about their proposed next step in diplomacy. The First Secretary at the British Embassy in BA is still here, and I strongly suspect he will have attended the meeting advising of the consequences of defying the Argentines' demand for substantive talks. In fact, that is probably *why* he's here.

I need to get something to put on the front page of *Penguin News* other than the Land Rover v Hillman Imp crash ('Horror on John Street, Not Many Injured'). I've been holding back the latest edition in the hope that I can get a good story, but I may have to let it go soon. I called Government House and asked to interview Governor Hunt. To my surprise he agreed, and I went up to GH late in the afternoon.

Mr Hunt was friendly, as he always is, but he seemed stressed. The conversation went like this:

Bound: 'We know the discussions have been difficult and you and the councillors have been having a tough time. But you must know too that we are frustrated by the lack of news. What's going on, Sir?'

Governor (sighing): 'I know what the feeling is locally. The problem is that these talks are confidential. What I can tell you is that at the meeting with councillors today we agreed unanimously on the message we will send to Her Majesty's Government, and our position has now been communicated to the Foreign and Commonwealth Office.'

Bound: 'That's very interesting. What did you tell the FCO?'

Hunt (sighing again): 'I'm sorry, Graham, but I can't tell you. As I said, the talks were confidential.'

Bound: 'I appreciate that the talks were confidential, but surely our response as a community isn't. Are we saying that we are prepared to concede to Argentine demands (whatever they are) or are we stonewalling them and prepared to take the consequences?'

Hunt: 'I'm sorry but that's confidential.'

It was the most unsatisfying interview I have ever conducted, but I did feel that Hunt would have liked to have said more. He's hobbled by London. I swallowed the remains of my coffee, thanked the Governor for his time and left. No scoop there.

The LADE plane arrived late today with forty-five bags of mail. They will be opened tomorrow. Also on the aircraft were ten employees of Gas del Estado. This was unexpected, it seems, but the Argentines say that the men will be refurbishing the storage plant at the east end of Stanley.

Friday, 19 March

Today there were more suspicious aerial goings-on over Stanley and its hinterland. A Learjet of the Argentine Air Force circled the area for an hour or so. A call to LADE office produced the explanation that the aircraft was testing the navigation beacon on the ridge to the east of Stanley. Again? We expected it to land, but it didn't and eventually flew off to the west. Previously, LADE has used propeller planes to check the aviation electronics. What other purpose might a Learjet have? Aerial photography maybe?

HMS *Endurance* is evidently in the area, as at midday her helicopters were buzzing around. The ship herself steamed through the Narrows at 2.00pm. She is coming back from what may be her final Antarctic trip of the season.

I'm leaving at 5.00pm for the Malo huts with Alison and Anna [King], Paul [Howe] and Walter [Felton]. I feel a fishing trip is what I need now. We'll be away for just one night. Hope they're biting.

Saturday, 20 March

Back from the Malo this evening. No drama on the track, mainly thanks to Walter, who picked his way slowly and carefully through the bogs. A nice 24 hours or so away. No great catches, but I caught a nice 3lb trout and two mullet over 12lbs.

More dramatic things appear to have been happening in Stanley. At about 6.00am, while Walter was brewing tea at the huts and the rest of us were still snoozing, the Governor was picked up by *Endurance*'s boat and taken out to the ship to discuss a developing situation on South Georgia with the ship's Captain, Nick Barker. None of this is official, but I've gleaned it from a few official sources.

No one would want to be having a meeting at the crack of dawn, so it seems to suggest that the situation is becoming a bit serious.

The story emerging from South Georgia is this. It seems the Argentine Navy's support ship *Bahia Buen Suceso* arrived at Leith Harbour on Friday afternoon and disembarked about forty men who intend to dismantle the old whaling station and ship the scrap back to Buenos Aires. However – and this seems to be a very big however – the ships should have stopped at King Edward Point first, where it would have been cleared by the authorities.

This is the first we have heard of this scrap metal mission. It's hard to know what to make of it, if anything. It's not hard to imagine that the captain of the ship arrived in South Georgia believing that as (in the Argentine view) the island belongs to them, they had no reason to tip their hats to a Brit and get him to rubber-stamp their documents. This does seem a rather petty matter, though, so I expect it will be resolved with one or two face-saving measures soon.

Later in the day: more reports filtering onto the streets of Stanley suggest this is a little more serious than I had thought. The BAS [British Antarctic Survey] field party near Leith Harbour, which had originally reported *Bahia Buen Suceso*'s arrival, also heard about five shots fired. I've no real idea, but I wonder if they were presenting a salute of some kind during a flag-raising ceremony (which would be serious), or perhaps shooting reindeer for a barbecue. But the fact that they have weapons on board? Not good.

On a more mundane level, Stanley took on *Endurance* at football this afternoon and got a thrashing at the hands of the matelots. The score was 6-1 to *Endurance*. Usually Stanley wins the annual match, so something clearly went wrong.

There was a dance in the Town Hall this evening, the usual boring, dry event, with Betty Ford blowing the dust off records that belong in the museum. I didn't go but now wish I had, as at around 11.00pm all the Marines who were there were summoned away, loaded into one of their trucks and taken back to [their barracks at] Moody Brook. Word quickly went around the Town Hall that this is to do with South Georgia.

PN is nearly ready to be run off now, but I'm holding off for just a little longer as this potentially important story develops. *What's happening at South Georgia?*

Sunday, 21 March

Endurance sailed early this morning for South Georgia. It will take the best part of three days for her to get there. She had been scheduled to go to Montevideo, where she was to pick up the new detachment of Marines. She would then return to Stanley with them, before sailing north to Montevideo again with the departing detachment. But that's off now, and this situation is starting to look complicated. There are thirty or so Marines stranded in Uruguay and a similar number stuck here, although I think at least some of the Falklands Marines are now on *Endurance* as she steams south.

Rex Hunt spoke on the radio at 8.15 this evening about the situation on South Georgia. He said that, at his request, the Leith Harbour scientific party formally advised the captain of the *Bahia Buen Suceso* that he had landed illegally. Any personnel on shore must return to the ship with all their equipment. They must not remove anything from Leith or interfere with any BAS activities.

The captain was also to be told that he must take his ship to King Edward Point, where she would be formally received by the authorities. The crew were told that no firearms can be taken ashore.

The captain 'acknowledged' the message and offered the BAS team a meal on board the ship. Apparently, they dined on venison. I guess that suggests that the shots heard the previous day involved some reindeer going to meet their maker.

The Embassy in Buenos Aires has made an official complaint to the Argentine Government and pointed out that the *Bahia Buen Suceso* must go to King Edward Point for those all-important rubber stamps.

This is all very well, but there is no one in South Georgia to enforce the message, and there won't be until *Endurance* arrives in the middle of the week. I get the feeling that everything has been done as courteously as possible, in the hope that the Argentines will feel they have made their point and can now beetle off back to BA, dignity intact. That's a bit of a gamble, though.

Monday, 22 March

The Argentine supply ship *Isla de los Estados* has been in port for a few days, almost certainly on an innocent visit to deliver bottles of gas and equipment for the refurbishment of the Gas del Estado depot.[1] The ship sailed about 10.00pm.

On South Georgia, however, and even in Stanley, things are happening. Last night, someone forced their way into the LADE office on Ross Road, although there was no sign of damage to the door. The Argentine flag was left in place within the building, but it was covered with a Union Jack, and the words 'Tit for tat, you buggers' were scrawled across a surface. (I think I know who the two burglars are but I'm not going to note it here).

The LADE office incursion did not surprise me. I've spoken to a few people today who were building up a real head of steam about (to use one description) the 'cheeky Argie bastards'. Some people are demanding real action, insisting that *Endurance* uses force to evict the *Buen Suceso* and her personnel, who may include soldiers.

I must admit that I feel a little bit that way myself. It has always annoyed me that Britain gives in to almost all Argentine demands in return for an easy life. But that's just made them bolder and bolder. Now they're ignoring Falklands authority[2] in South Georgia and they're taking pot shots at our reindeer. Using *Endurance* to draw a line in the South Georgia snow might be a little dangerous, but it could send a good message to BA: 'This far and no further'.

Tuesday, 23 March

Yesterday evening, Government House released a statement saying that the BAS party at Leith Harbour had observed *Buen Suceso* weighing anchor and leaving. That's good news, but this is not: apparently there are still at least six men on shore, and they have a small launch. Government House said the FCO has been advised and a further strong protest is being lodged through the Embassy in BA.

The LADE F28 arrived today. As usual, the plane will stay overnight before returning to Comodoro Rivadavia. In the light of the 'tit for tat, you buggers' break-in, the LADE staff in Stanley are clearly worried about their plane. They have told the authorities here that the aircraft must be guarded throughout the night, or it will fly out before nightfall. This has been accepted, and as I write this late on Monday night, four (presumably armed) Marines are guarding the plane.

As it happens, Mum and Dad are due to leave on the plane tomorrow. They will be going to BA first, then across to Montevideo, where they'll see old friends and have a break.

Wednesday, 24 March

I drove Mum and Dad to the airport today, and the F28 took off at about 8.00 am. Before they went through to the departure area, Dad and I had a surprisingly serious conversation. I think we both were feeling that the situation here is becoming worrying. He tried to reassure me that they did not plan to be away for very long. But that was not what I wanted to hear, I told him, more earnestly than I have ever said anything to my father, 'Please promise me that if anything bad happens here while you are away, you'll continue to Britain. Buenos Aires would not be a good place to be, and it would reassure me if I knew that you were carrying on to the UK.'

I think he may have been a little shaken by this, but he agreed. He didn't look very happy as he rejoined Mum. We said goodbye, and they made their way to the F28. I feel better knowing that they are out of it.

The rest of the day was quiet, and Rowan House [the family home] feels rather empty, with just Bagpuss the cat and I rattling around in it. I spent a few hours bringing the latest *PN* up to date. I can't decide when to publish it. Too soon, and we may miss something important. Deadlines, though, have never been very important, and readers always seem to be pleased to receive it, even if it's late.

The FIBS [Falkland Islands Broadcasting Station] news this evening revealed that the new Marines detachment have been picked up in Montevideo by the [British Antarctic Survey ship] *John Biscoe*. They should arrive in Stanley in four days' time.

BBC World Service crackled through well enough on 9.915 megahertz this evening. It was reported that the British Embassy in BA had formally 'expressed regret' to the Argentine Government for the 'tit-for-tat-you-buggers' incident in the LADE office. No one here feels any regret.

The Argentine press has inflated the story incredibly. Some papers are saying the LADE office was 'stormed' and the Argentine flag was 'torn down' and had slogans daubed on it. At least one paper has also claimed that LADE officials were assaulted. All nonsense, of course, but the Argentines are a bit too fond of their national symbols, so the reports will not help at all.

BAS in South Georgia is reporting that there is no sign that the remaining Argentines are being evacuated from Leith.

I was chatting to Tony Hunt [Rex Hunt's son] today, and he said that he understands *Endurance* has been instructed to remove the Argentines if necessary. That was probably chatter over the roast mutton at lunchtime. Interesting, though.

Thursday, 25 March

Government House released an update about the situation at Leith Harbour. Apparently, the weather has been appalling there over the last 24 hours, which dramatically reduced visibility for the BAS field party keeping an eye on the area. However, they were able to see about twelve Argentines, some of them working around the jetty with machines of some kind.

At 8.00 this evening [Councillor] Terry Peck chaired a public meeting at the Town Hall. I went along, of course, and have prepared a story for *PN*. There was much anger, directed fairly equally at the UK Government and the Argentine Government. But local outrage doesn't make any difference.

Friday, 26 March

WS [World Service] news reported that the Argentine polar ship *Bahia Paraiso* has been to Leith, but it's not clear what she was doing there. It seems she departed before dawn today.

RRS *Bransfield* is on her way from Punta Arenas to Stanley. No official statement, but BAS sources say that she was buzzed by an Argentine aircraft about 130 miles west of the Islands. This happened about 2.00pm. This seems to me to be aggressive behaviour, and it puts us all a little more on edge.

The Penguin News

THE FALKLAND NEWS MAGAZINE

26th MARCH 1982 — No 19

22 pence

SOUTH GEORGIA CRISIS PAGE 3

P.O. Box 178, PORT STANLEY, FALKLAND ISLANDS

talks to continue?

The latest round of Falklands negotiations took place in New York on the 26th and 27th February. Originally scheduled for late December 1981, they were postponed when General Galtierri assumed the Presidency in Argentina.

The two representatives of the Falklands Legislative Council, Tim Blake and John Cheek, returned to the Islands on 2nd March, but did not immediately inform Falklanders of what had been discussed at the meetings. Indeed, at the time of going to press, we still know very little about the subjects that were covered. Governor Hunt did say in a speech over Falkland Radio that Argentine proposals had been discussed, but ironically it was necessary to tune in to the English language service of Radio Argentina to find out something about the meaning of this. However Buenos Aires too was in a secretive mood, and said only that the Argentine delegation had suggested that talks take place at monthly intervals in order to speed up the process. Two days after their return to the Islands Messrs Monk and Blake did agree to answer questions at a press conference organised by Falkland Radio which was broadcast the same evening. However they were evasive in their answers, to say the least, and refused (cont'd p. 6

HOSTEL IS DECLARED UNSAFE

The controversial Stanley School Hostel, which the contractors claim is completed but which the Government refuse to accept, has now been officially declared a dangerous structure.

Director of Public Works, John Broderick, who is at present in London discussing the project with the Overseas Development Administration, contacted Stanley recently to say that calculations based on ODA figures indicate that the roof of the building is in places dangerously weak. As a consequence signs have now been posted outside the building advising the public of the danger. Authorised persons can now only enter the building wearing protective helmets.

The roof of the main dining and assembly area has already been given extra layers of concrete following the suggestion about a year ago that it may not be strong enough.

Construction of the Hostel began in 1979 when Trans-ocean Construction and Trading, a company formed specially for the project, began the digging of a huge pit which, when filled again, would provide the foundations for the structure. The "gunite" method employed on the hostel was still experimental, and it is believed that prior to this ...

IN THIS P.N.

A WORD FROM THE EDITOR:

Time again to humble myself and apologise for the lateness of this issue We had intended to bring out number 19 at a much earlier date, but considered it wiser to stall for a while until the results of the February talks were known. As it happens we still do not know very much about what was discussed; government secrecy knows no bounds. But we are now able to tell you what

Front page of the delayed *Penguin News*, the last edition before the invasion.

John Biscoe is reported to be 'hove-to' about 100 miles from Montevideo. What this means, I don't know. Weather in that area is unlikely to stop her, but I wonder if the Foreign Office – scared of its own shadow, as ever – is worried about how Argentina might react if they embark the new Marine detachment.

Saturday, 27 March

The latest (troubling) South Georgia news is that [Argentine Foreign Minister] Costa Mendez has said that his government has made a firm decision about their approach to the crisis (so it's a 'crisis' now). He said that Argentina will protect their men at Leith Harbour. He said the naval support ship *Bahia Paraiso* is in the area 'to provide protection'.

Bahia Paraiso is not armed, as far as I know, although she might have some marines on board. However, the point is that if even this relatively harmless ship were to get in the way of *Endurance*'s efforts to evict the men, the result would be unpredictable. Options for defusing the situation in any face-saving way seem to be slipping away.

Bransfield arrived in Stanley this afternoon. The ship's crew held a dance in the Town Hall this evening. Seems a bit remarkable given that everyone has a growing crisis on their minds, but the ship is heading north soon, so this was an end of season knees-up.

Sunday, 28 March

Eric, the purser on *Bransfield*, came by the shop to say hello today. Normally, Dad buys perfumes and watches etc [for resale] from Eric's onboard emporium of duty-free delights. As Dad's not here, I gave Eric a cup of tea and we had a chat. I couldn't buy anything but I did glean some good information. He confirmed that the ship had been buzzed repeatedly by an Argentine plane. He claimed to have heard on the BBC that Argentina has dispatched up to four ships to South Georgia, including two destroyers and a submarine. I have not heard this anywhere else, but it could be true. Given all of this, Eric seems to be looking forward to heading north to a UK summer. I can understand that.

Maybe London has nothing to say, but it would be good to have some indication that they are going to support *Endurance* by sending another warship or two to the region. I'm starting to think that this, combined with a strong diplomatic message of 'enough is enough' is the only way out. Otherwise their next move might be against the Falklands.

BBC WS news reported at 8.00pm that the British ambassador to BA has had a meeting at the Argentine Foreign Ministry, and both sides have said they wish to avoid a conflict. That is an obvious thing to say and it's meaningless.

Eric's story has been confirmed: the Argentines are sending two corvettes, two destroyers and a submarine to South Georgia. They are escalating things deliberately. The plan for *Endurance* to sort the situation out is not viable.

But life goes on almost as normal here. The *Bransfield*'s crew are still celebrating the end of their Antarctic season. I was invited aboard with about a hundred others this evening. Excellent food and plenty of duty-free gin and tonic from Eric's bottomless liquor cabinet. We were decanted from the ship at about 10.00pm, having pretty much forgotten about South Georgia and the Argentines, and anything else for that matter.

On [BBC World Service's] 'Calling the Falklands' this evening they played 'Don't Cry for Me, Argentina' for the BAS men on South Georgia. A bit of a lame joke.

No word from the parents, but they must be in BA, and possibly Uruguay, by now. I'm glad they are not here. I've decided that I can't wait any longer to publish the latest *PN* and I'll put the finishing touches to it, including the very latest South Georgia updates, if there are any. I'll be up all night tonight getting it out.

Monday, 29 March

Penguin News finally went on sale today. I opened the shop specially from 5.30 to 6.45pm, and sales were brisk. I'll get more copies to the Co-op and the West Store tomorrow. I updated the South Georgia crisis diary to the last minute, but as there is no outcome yet, obviously I haven't told the whole story. I think the editorial reflects the general feelings of anger and frustration here. I said that a line in the sand – or should that be snow? – needs to be drawn and the Argentines must know they have gone too far. I suggested that *Endurance* can at last show her worth by evicting the landing party at Leith Harbour, but I don't really know how practical that is. Anyway, we don't even know where *Endurance* is now.

RRS *John Biscoe* arrived in Stanley at about 4.30pm with the new Marines detachment on board. It's good to know they're here. The crew are telling some vivid stories about how earlier today they were buzzed repeatedly by Argentine Air Force C130 Hercules planes. There were two aircraft taking it in turns to harass the ship. One guy said that the aircraft came so close to *Biscoe* at some points that some members of the crew wanted to turn the ship's fire hoses on them. That's one way of getting your plane's windscreen washed.

I heard this evening that Argentina has three submarines, which sounds impressive, but two are undergoing repairs as they are unable to submerge. Or if they do submerge, I suppose they won't come up again.

We opened the Youth Club this evening from 7.00. The kids turned out in good numbers. The dart board was popular, though rather too many of the darts seemed to be going in entirely the wrong direction. The new clubhouse is excellent.

At about 8.00pm the fun was interrupted by loud aircraft engines. We went outside and saw an Argentine C130 low overhead. It didn't land. Perhaps this was one of the planes that had been harassing the *Biscoe* earlier today. Now they are harassing us.

This is not scary – yet. But I am starting to worry about where it's going. We started off with suggestions that diplomacy was fraying around the edges, and we are now seeing aggressive aerial manoeuvres and more warships heading towards South Georgia. What's the next act?

Chapter 3

Invasion

(30 March–2 April)

Tuesday, 30 March

World Service reports that [Foreign Secretary] Lord Carrington returned abruptly from Brussels to address the Commons. He is quoted as describing the situation as 'potentially dangerous', and security in the area is to be reviewed. I really don't know what that means, and I wonder if he does. If 'reviewing' means considering what ships and men might be deployed to sort the Argentines out, then it's not going to be a very long review.

I've got to know a visiting Argentine photographer, Rafael Wollman. He flew in a day or two ago. I don't think he knows any more about what's on the Argentine agenda than we do, and he seems to be here on the off chance of a good story. Anyway, he's a nice guy, about my age, and we've had a few coffees together at the house.

He tells me that the mood is ugly in Buenos Aires. The Anglo-Argentine community is being picked on, which is very unfair. I think they hold on to their British heritage only out of nostalgia. I've met some who were barely able to speak English and I once had the misfortune to witness an Anglo-Argentine bagpipe band.

I was reflecting a bit miserably about the way that normality is starting to slip away, when something happened to restore my spirits. We were not really expecting the LADE F28 to arrive as it should, but then this afternoon I heard the whine of jet engines from the north-west, and in swooped the aircraft. It was carrying a very welcome forty-eight bags of mail, which [Postmaster] Bill Etheridge and his team opened very quickly. I think Bill knew that we needed a morale boost.

Four reporters from British national newspapers were on the plane. Simon Winchester from the *Sunday Times* is one, and I think there are also a couple of guys from the *Observer*. I'm not sure who the fourth one is.

I had a phone call from a reporter on the *Star* this afternoon. Nice to be wanted. I gave him a précis of the situation and the mood here as best I could. I mentioned the overflights by C130 and the harassment of RRS *John Biscoe* and *Bransfield*.

I also told him something that I had just heard: that the Marines are guarding the airport around the clock now. About ten of them are at the airport at any time.

He asked about the whereabouts of *Endurance*, and I said this is being kept secret, but she must be in the vicinity of South Georgia. I assume that plans for her to round up the Argentines at Leith have been shelved, as she couldn't take on a 'real' warship.

Then the guy from the *Star* dropped a bombshell. He told me that his paper had heard that an invasion is imminent and local men are being drafted into the Defence Force. There has been no such mobilization, of course, and I told him that. But I was shaken. This was really the first time that I had heard anyone who might be in a position to know talk about a real risk of invasion. Perhaps the clues have been there for a while and we have been deliberately ignoring them. But the risk of conflict does seem to be moving from South Georgia to the Falklands.

Wednesday, 31 March

BBC Radio London called this morning. The interview was live. As we were waiting to go on air, the interviewer said that there was a real sense of crisis in London, and speculation that if Thatcher does not handle this well, then her government could fall. Then he said, 'OK, we're live' and he introduced me.

I said people here are not panicking all, but that there is a mood of anger and frustration about the Argentines' behaviour. He asked about local defences and I pointed out that our defences are very slim indeed but improved to some extent since *John Biscoe* came to our rescue with the new Marines detachment from Montevideo. That does not quite double the Marines' presence, as a number have gone to South Georgia on *Endurance*, but it has made a difference.

The reporter said there are rumours that a squadron of ships, perhaps including a nuclear submarine, is being assembled in the UK to sail south, and this may be confirmed later today. What did I think about this?

'Good,' I said. 'But whatever they are planning, it could be too little, too late. It's a shame that the government didn't turn their mind to the defence of the Islands months ago, rather than announcing the withdrawal of HMS *Endurance*. It takes several weeks for a ship to get to the Falklands from the UK, and right now we feel very lonely and vulnerable.'

He wished me luck and hung up.

About ten minutes later, World Service also referred to the nuclear submarine rumour. They said that it may already be on its way. WS also reported unsubstantiated but credible reports that the Argentine aircraft carrier *25 de Mayo* is on its way to South Georgia. Poor old *Endurance* had better make herself scarce.

Vice-Comodoro [Hector] Gilobert returned to Stanley on the F28 on Tuesday, supposedly 'to help calm the situation'. Gilobert is an affable guy and he has friends here, including Rex Hunt and [Chief Secretary] Dick Baker, not to mention our family. So his return may be a good thing.[1]

Thursday, 1 April

Today it really feels that the situation is slipping out of control, with neither of the two sides – three sides, if you include us – prepared to back down or compromise.

But life has continued more or less as normal. Offices and shops have all been open, and I haven't heard of anyone leaving Stanley for the safety of the camp. From talking to people, I know everyone is nervous. But there is also a feeling that after so many years in the shadow of the Argentine claim and with only half-hearted support from London, some sort of climax might not be a bad thing. I kind of support that if it is only a bad-tempered clash at South Georgia that puts the Argentines back in their box, but I think we have gone beyond that possibility.

According to rumour, the destroyer HMS *Exeter* could be in the area soon. She was in the Caribbean and is capable of about 30 knots, but I think she'd need to refuel en route and I doubt if there is a Navy tanker in the South Atlantic.

There are low-level signs that the Marines are stepping up activity. Fortunately, we now have about seventy Marines here. Uncle Jack [Sollis, captain of the government's small coastal steamer *Forrest*] was on patrol in Port William and Berkeley Sound last night with Marines on board. I understand that they are also on watch at the airport, presumably in case the Argentines try an Entebbe-style lightning raid. Marines are also on watch at Cape Pembroke Lighthouse. But the Defence Force has not been mobilized.

I was rattling around the house late this afternoon, not knowing quite what to do other than wait for the next BBC news, when someone knocked on the door. It was Roman, one of the Polish refugees. Somehow we seem to be able to communicate a bit. I sat him down and we cracked open a bottle of gin from Dad's liquor cabinet. Dad's a believer in the restorative power of gin and tonic, so this seems like a good time to give it a try. Roman put his hand over the glass when I tried to add some tonic to his gin. He went on to knock it back in one. His eyeballs protruded briefly, but I guess that's how they do it in Poland.

He brightened up considerably, and asked me (to quote him), 'What the fuck is happening, Graham?'

The Poles have picked up some good English very quickly.

'Well, you know the Argentines want the Falklands and South Georgia?'

'No. What for do they want Falklands and South Georgia?'

'Frankly, Roman, I have no idea, but they do, and you need to listen to the news and be careful, because it's getting nasty.'

Roman was thoughtful. 'Hmm. I thought it was only Poland that had problems with the military.'

I poured two more gins, and this time I knocked mine back like a Pole. After a while Roman left, wandering west to his lodgings at the east end of Fitzroy Road. I feel very sorry for him. He is thousands of miles from home, has no idea what his future holds and has found himself in the middle of a crisis. It is very worrying for us, but it must be worse for him.

I decided to go the Upland Goose to see if Rafael and the British journalists were there and had heard anything new. I took my little pocket short-wave radio so that I wouldn't miss the next news bulletin. I found them in the lounge by the main entrance, chatting quietly. They didn't seem to mind me joining them, especially as I had my radio with me. We huddled around it to hear the WS News.

The UK has called for an urgent meeting of the Security Council. The Foreign Office is saying they have put proposals forward to resolve the issue, presumably proposals that would enable BA to save face. But the Argentines have rejected every proposal. Why wouldn't they? They have the UK on the back foot now. Plus, Rafael says the Junta's aggression is proving very popular at home.

Simon Winchester and the other Brits are quite laid back about the whole thing. Someone went to the bar and brought back a few drinks. We sat there chatting about almost anything but the Falklands for a while, until someone came by and said we should tune into FIBS [local radio], as Rex Hunt was about to give an address.[2]

He came on the air at 8.15 with a cheery 'Good evening' and got straight to the point. The Argentines have said they will not continue diplomacy, and there are signs that an invasion is planned. Serving and reserve members of the Defence Force are to report to the HQ, as they will be on sentry duty at key points throughout the night. The Marines, he said, are on full alert. He asked everyone who did not have a reason to be out to stay indoors. The schools will be closed tomorrow, and FIBS will continue to broadcast through the night. He closed by saying that he may need to declare a state of emergency before dawn tomorrow.

I felt the blood draining from my face. Looking back, everything had been pointing towards this, but I had never really admitted that it was likely to happen. I had been refusing to address my fear of invasion. Now I couldn't escape it, and my simmering worries were replaced by full-blown fear.

No one said much. Everyone was clearly shocked. But the British reporters quickly pulled themselves together and headed off for the Cable and Wireless Office to file reports to London. I said goodbye to Rafael, who indicated he was going to defy the semi-curfew and go out with his camera. I wished him luck. I had no idea what I would do, except make notes in this diary for *Penguin News* – if I'm ever able to publish it again.

The family will be worried about me, so I walked to Cable and Wireless and tried to find the words to put into a telegram to Michael.[3] It was hard to find the right words. I couldn't reassure him that I was OK as I didn't know if I was.

I decided that whatever I said would be pointless, but I needed to send something. After several rewrites, I simply wrote this: 'Situation grave. Parents in Uruguay.' I then went home to the cat.

Author's note

From this point, the story develops rapidly, so rapidly and in so many dimensions within and beyond the Islands that it was often impossible to write down my observations and thoughts in detail. My diary notes over the next 48 hours or so, therefore, are often brief and they do not cover everything that occurred.

As I recall the crisis 39 years on, this does not surprise me. My brain was overloaded. I was stressed, and worry was transforming into fear. This did not help me to handle the situation well. Nevertheless, in all their brevity, these notes do convey what it was like for Islanders as we were invaded.

I phoned Patrick [Watts] at the radio station and said I'd join other part-time staff if he wanted help. He said thanks but the situation was under control. If I wanted to come in at some point, that would be fine. I may do that.[4]

The weather is calm and warm and the sky is clear. Where's a storm when you want one?

I understand that heads of government departments were called to GH at 4.30pm to be briefed about the situation. I drove past GH a little later and could see smoke rising from the garden. This, I'm told, was staff burning files. I was also told that they were smashing coding equipment with sledgehammers.

FIGAS Islander [aircraft] has been flown from the airport to the racecourse, I guess to keep it out of harm's way, or perhaps so it can carry out recce flights.

9.20pm: Harold Briley on WS says meetings are going on and [President] Galtieri is expected to make a public address soon. Briley says that many ordinary Argentines he's spoken to do not want to see violence.

WS reporter at the UN says Britain believes an invasion force is already on its way.

11.00pm: WS reports that UK has two unnamed ships in the area. Is one of them *Endurance*? More are on the way. Perhaps this is an attempt to deter Buenos Aires at the last minute?

Friday, 2 April

00.30am: Rex Hunt on radio (may not be perfect record but noted to the best of my ability): 'There's no indication that the Argentine Task Force has turned back. If things continue, we can expect them off Cape Pembroke by dawn. Do not be

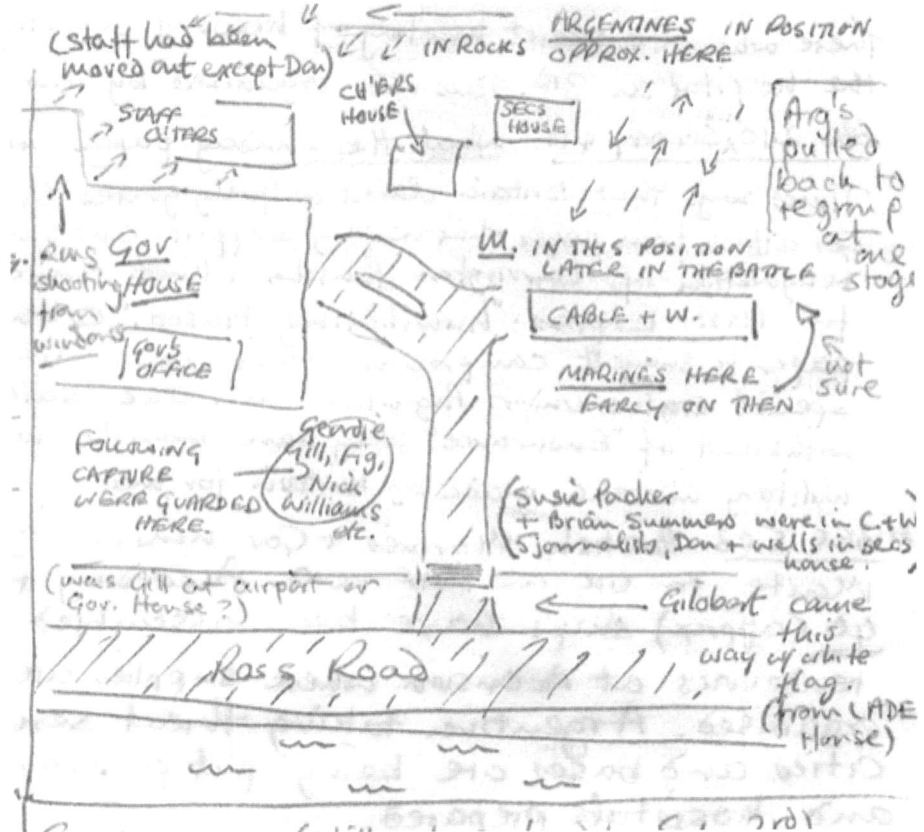

Sketch map of the attack on Government House drawn by the author on the day of the invasion.

inquisitive and go to see. You will only get in the way. Stay in your homes, and we will keep you informed by radio.'

BBC 1.05am: UN Security Council has called on both sides to 'exercise the utmost restraint'.

Argentine paratroops and marines are reportedly mobilized, and a military governor has been appointed.

KEM Hospital is preparing for casualties. All staff called in and beds being prepared etc.

Argentine fleet now expected around 4.00am. Light at Cape Pembroke lighthouse has been extinguished.

FIBS 4.25am: Governor says that Reagan has been on the phone to Galtieri appealing for peace and saying that VP Bush could come to BA to talk to him.

Galtieri said that he appreciated the President's concern, but the only solution now is for the UK to recognize Argentine sovereignty and hand over the Islands. Hunt added that as from now he has absolute powers and anyone on the streets will be arrested. Argentine nationals in Stanley are being rounded up from the Upland Goose and other places. Complimented Marines and Defence Force on their morale, ending, 'I am proud to be their Commander-in-Chief.'

5.55am: Governor back on radio saying that first ships have been sighted and a landing craft is coming through the Narrows. Latter quickly corrected: 'Landing craft' is actually *Forrest* returning from Port William.

6.05am: Explosions and shots heard from the direction of the Marines' barracks at Moody Brook.

6.08am: *Forrest* arrives back at Government Jetty.

From where I am at the Upland Goose it's not possible to see much of what is going on. Relying on what little we can see and hear and information broadcast by FIBS. The fighting appears to be concentrated around GH and the east of Stanley. It's at its heaviest from about 6.20 to 7.00am.

7.05am: Governor on FIBS says they are pinned down by about 200 Argentines [later proven to be a considerably smaller number], and the Argentines seem to be firing at the Marines' vehicles more than at the men. He does not know if there are any Argentine casualties. He will talk to them if they send a man in, but otherwise no.

More sporadic fire until about 7.20am. Governor now says it is 'only a matter of time'.

Reports phoned through to FIBS from east end of Stanley. There has been fighting in the area. Lots of smoke, and vegetation is on fire. It's possible to see three warships in Port William, one very large. Their aircraft carrier.

7.30am: Reports phoned in of very large, tracked troop carriers driving through east end of Stanley. Marines still fighting there. More troop carriers seen at Canopus, about three miles away. Obviously, they are driving up from Yorke Bay.

Dr Haines phones FIBS to say that all patients at the hospital are safe and no casualties have been admitted.

7.36am: They are pinned down at GH. Governor Hunt on FIBS: 'I'm not surrendering to the bloody Argies, I can tell you.' 'Every time someone moves, they open fire.'

We can see large helicopters around the airport.

7.47am: Garbled message from Argentine coming through on normal radio frequency: '. . . wish to avoid bloodshed and damage to property . . .' (Very hard to understand most of it.) '. . . Our concern is for welfare of the people of the island . . . A call to the British colonial government of the islands . . .'

7.55am: From the Upland Goose we can see Gilobert [of LADE, who returned to the Islands a few days earlier] carrying a white flag. Walking from east towards Government House. Trying to negotiate a ceasefire?

Another crackly Argentina broadcast: 'We are here with a naval Task Force . . . exercise Christian principles . . . we hope you will act prudently . . .'

8.05am: Gilobert has reached GH and perhaps a delegation will emerge soon.

8.08am: More firing heard around the Yorke Bay/airport area.

8.14am: Gilobert broadcasting in Spanish from GH through FIBS:[2] 'I am with Dick Baker [Rex Hunt's deputy] and we want to talk to the commander of the force. He can come to St Mary's Church near the Town Hall with a white flag. There is absolute guarantee of respect.'

Gilobert and Baker are now near the church with several policemen also there. We can see a large delegation of armed Argentines approaching along Ross Road carrying a white flag.

8.45am: A C130 Hercules is approaching the airport. Negotiating party now leaving church area and heading towards GH.

I took camera to front door of Upland Goose and snapped pictures of what seems to be regular troops marching up the road. Several very large armoured personnel carriers following them. Troops have weapons at the ready but not showing much aggression. There are even some smiles. I guess they know they have accomplished their mission.

I can see an Argentine flag being raised on the St Mary's flagpole 100 metres away. Largish concentration of soldiers by the gymnasium also 100 yards away. They are cheering.

9.00am: Tuned into Radio Newsreel from BBC WS. They have no idea what is going on. They say there are fears that an invasion is imminent. Atmosphere in Commons reported as 'very grave'. PM has just had long meeting with First Sea Lord and RAF chiefs.

No reports of local casualties, thank God. Both sides are helping the wounded, but there appear to be remarkably few. Three Argentines have been shot by the Marines and are in the hospital. One is very seriously injured and not expected to survive.

Second C130 lands at the airport. A truce has been agreed and the firing has stopped.

10.12am: John Fowler [Superintendent of Education] says that all children at the camp hostel are safe.

10.16am: FIBS has been renamed 'LRA Radio Islas Malvinas'. 'Communiqué Number One' commences with playing of the dirge-like Argentine national anthem and is followed in Spanish and English by a statement about the invasion being code-named 'Teatro Colon' and commander of the operation was General Osvaldo Jorge Garcia.

10.32am: In a final message broadcast by FIBS, Rex Hunt says he did not shake the hand of Admiral Busser, the Argentine officer who was given safe passage to GH by Baker and Gilbert. He said he does not shake hands with enemies. He paid tribute, though, to Gilobert. He told Busser that he and his forces are here illegally and he would not have agreed to a ceasefire had British forces not been severely outnumbered and outgunned. Hunt said there had been no time to communicate with London, but they will have guessed what has happened from the silence. Final message: 'Rest assured; the British will be back.'

Conflicting messages are emerging about casualties. The Marines say they killed three Argentines, wounded three and captured two. Earlier reports were that just one [Captain Pedro Giachino] died and two were seriously injured. [This proved to be correct.]

10.39am: A second invaders' tape, Communiqué Number Two: British officials will be sent back to UK today. Garcia is taking control over Falklands, South Georgia and South Sandwiches.

Immediately followed by Communiqué Number Three: All civilians must remain in their houses. Any found outside will be arrested. If it is necessary to communicate any issue to the occupiers, a white flag should be hung outside. All pubs, clubs etc must remain closed. All instructions to the community will be broadcast over 'Radio Islas Malvinas'.

Communiqué Number Four: Continuity of local way of life is guaranteed. Likewise freedom of worship, respect for private property, freedom of labour, freedom to remain or leave the Islands. Improvement of standard of living and healthcare promised, along with essential public services. 'Population is exhorted to continue their normal activities.'

Nothing heard or seen of Governor and other GH staff since about 10.00am.

At least two Argentine helicopters are very active over town. A LADE F28 has flown in, and another aircraft circling overhead.

Seems calm, so I left Upland Goose and walked home, to stoke the fire and feed the cat if anyone asks, but really to have a look around with my camera. Soldiers are everywhere, heavily armed but not looking particularly tense. They don't seem to take much interest in me, even when I take photos of them. Huge amphibious troop carriers, armed with heavy machine guns or cannon, are almost blocking roads. On Victory Green, beneath the Argentine flag, troops are taking photos of each other clutching weapons and looking smug.

At home, I tuned into the BBC News at 2.00pm and heard that the penny seems to have dropped in London. They have broken off diplomatic relations with BA. A nuclear submarine and other ships have been dispatched (but how long will it take them to get here?). House of Commons will sit in special session tomorrow. US Government has called on Argentina to withdraw immediately and NATO has expressed 'deep concern'. (Not clear to me if this is a NATO issue, but NATO is founded on the principle that an attack against one member country is an attack against them all.)

Telephone exchange is working, but badly, with Argentine soldiers at the exchange. I tried ringing Robert [King] to see how they had ridden out the invasion, and my usual request for Robert's number was greeted with a puzzled '*Que?*' from the operator. I suppose there is something funny in that.

3.20pm: I was amazed when the phone rang and I picked up the receiver to hear a voice say, 'This is BBC Radio London. Can you tell us what's going on in Stanley?' I told them everything I knew, including that there had been no casualties among our forces and that at least one Argentine had died, with others badly injured. I tried to sum up what I had seen on the streets an hour or two earlier and the content of the radio 'communiqués'. The reporter was speaking in very urgent and excited tones as if he feared we would soon be cut off. In fact, after just a couple of minutes we were cut off, presumably by someone listening at the exchange. I'm glad I got some news out, though.

I walked down to the Town Hall area, where hundreds of troops were thronging. I found Rafael Wollman there and we greeted each other with relief. There was no sign of the British reporters. As Rafael and I talked, an Argentine Hercules flew low up the harbour, flanked by two small propeller aircraft. We both assumed that the C130 was carrying Rex and Mavis Hunt and others from GH, along with the Marines.

Rafael had learned from the Argentines that some Marines had escaped to the camber [on the opposite side of Stanley Harbour] and (to quote him), 'None of them has been killed yet.' Good luck to those guys. Rafael said he had been told a major operation to find them will commence tomorrow.

Someone, an Argentine civilian in the crowd (no idea who he was or what he was doing there), came up to me and told me aggressively that four Argentines were killed at GH in circumstances that amounted to atrocities (I guess the Argentines know a bit about atrocities). One, he said (his nose in my face), had almost been 'cut in half' with a bayonet and another was a medic going to the aid of the first casualty. The civilian claimed that he was also bayoneted. I just don't believe it.[5]

I learned that the first group of invaders landed about midnight last night near Eliza Cove and points to the south-west and had a long hike to their target at GH and Moody Brook. This was clever, as everyone in Stanley was expecting just one force to land around Yorke Bay. By the time the main landing did commence at Yorke Bay, the Marines were fully engaged around Government House.

I went home via the Upland Goose to tell the Kings what I had been able to pick up. I checked out our 2-metre radio transceiver and charged it up. If the phones aren't going to work, then it might be useful.

7.00pm: Announcement over 'Radio Islas Malvinas' informed that we are now subject to a dawn-until-dusk curfew.

A bleak and depressing BBC News report: there is now some doubt about the practicality of a British response. Lord Carrington will not commit himself to saying that the Islands will 'definitely' be liberated. The best hope seems to be persuading the Americans to help.

'Radio Islas Malvinas' announced around 9.00pm – a report clearly written by an Argentine official but read by Dave Emsley – that there are still some Marines at liberty. 'If anyone knows of their whereabouts they should report this to the nearest authorities.' As if anyone would do that! I assume that the Marines are now taking on a guerrilla role, and this will certainly be worrying the Argentines. Good luck to them.

This 'advice' is also broadcast: 'People are not recommended to transit without identity cards and must not carry any weapons or guns.' Clearly, they don't know that much about the Falklands. We don't have ID cards.

I ran into the British journos heading toward the hotel. They had been doing their best to file their stories back to the UK, but Cable and Wireless is firmly under Argentine control, and while they had left telexes there to be transmitted, they were not convinced that they went. I doubt if they did.

Simon Winchester [of the *Sunday Times*] said they had been told they would be flown out today. As it turns out he lives in Iffley, just a short distance from where Michael [my brother] lives in Oxford. I jumped at the chance of getting Simon to carry a letter to Mike, so I ran home to type a letter that I hoped would reassure him and put him in the picture about what had happened over the last few days. This done, I headed back to the Goose, where Simon and the others were getting ready to leave, and he took the letter. I thanked him very much for this kindness. He said he was happy to help. He said I should contact him at the *Sunday Times* when the dust settles, with a view to writing reports as a 'stringer'. Whether this can be during the occupation is not clear.[6]

The phones are behaving bizarrely. At about 9.50pm I was trying to ring the Kings at the Goose, but the line seemed dead. Then I heard the voice of Connie Baker [wife of Dick Baker, the Governor's deputy]. She had, it seems, been trying to get through to the exchange. I explained who I was and asked if I could help? Connie blurted out, 'We are still here!' I said that was good to know.

'Can you get the word out that we are still here?' she said. I said I would do my best. I asked how they all are, and Connie said they are fine, though it had been a terrifying night, especially for Dick, who had first helped round up and imprison Argentine Gas del Estado civilians and later had helped negotiate a ceasefire.

I tried to call the radio station to see if they could slip a message into the Argentine official edicts and propaganda letting people know that at least one official representative of London is still here. However, I couldn't raise the operator. So, I used our 2-metre radio to call anyone who might be listening. Doreen Clarke came up immediately. I told her about the Bakers and asked her to try to call the radio station, as my phone was not working properly. She said she would do so and clearly she succeeded, because about an hour later, Dave Emsley let slip the news about the Bakers: 'It might reassure some people to know that a senior rep of HMG is still here,' he said.

I've been awake now for almost forty hours, but I don't feel tired at all. It's the adrenaline, I guess.

11.00pm: World Service reports that the UK is sending a 'substantial naval Task Force'. This will include at least one aircraft carrier. Marines have been placed at readiness to board ships. According to the BBC, Buenos Aires has said that the invasion involved approximately 2,000 troops, with more following soon afterwards. That tallies with what we see here.

They say that the only source of news from within the Islands has been a ham radio operator. I don't know who that is, but it may be an unhelpful revelation. The Argentines will, I'm sure, be rounding up all radio transmitters soon, and the names of those who possess them will be easy to find, as records of radio licences issued will be held at the Post Office. I wonder if Bill Etheridge and his staff will think to destroy them.

[The BBC's] Harold Briley in Buenos Aires reports that many thousands of Argentines have been on the streets celebrating the 'recovery' of the 'Malvinas'. He points out that President Galtieri is now being celebrated as a hero.

The House of Commons will meet for an emergency debate about the crisis in a few hours. This will be the first time that the Commons has convened on a Saturday since the Suez Crisis. It's so strange to be at the centre of world events.

No other news seems to matter in the UK. According to WS, some front pages have pictures of the Argentine flag being raised over Government House. Very silly of the Argentines to let that photo get out, as it'll create fury in the UK. Nearly all papers are very critical of the government for ignoring the Falklands and allowing this to happen. I'm very glad they are making that point, because the government deserves a hammering.

Chapter 4

Careful What You Say

(3 April)

Saturday, 3 April

Exhaustion finally hit me after midnight and I went to sleep on the sofa with the cat. That was comforting. He seems to be happy as long as he gets his raw mutton and fish. Not sure what I need. Probably a drink.

I woke up to the realization that we are living under occupation. It feels just as I expected it would: repressive, humiliating and worrying.

Our lack of freedom hit home last night while I was walking to collect my jeep which I had left on John Street (carrying a white tea cloth in lieu of a flag, as we have been instructed to do). I was challenged by troops, and when I explained in Spanish where I was going I was given an armed escort. It's a strange feeling, walking through my own town with a white flag and surrounded by armed troops.

While walking, I counted fifteen heavy tracked troop carriers, most armed with heavy machine guns or cannon. Most of them were parked and almost blocking the road near the FIDF Drill Hall.

Yesterday evening, I also attempted to get a telegram to Mum and Dad, who I assume are in Buenos Aires, although if they have any sense they will have crossed the River Plate to Montevideo and will be thinking about flying on to UK. The telegram office is closed. I'm massively relieved they are not here but I feel it's important to let them know that I'm OK. I also want to hammer home the point that they mustn't return. It isn't safe, of course, but I also want the freedom to act on my own.

Bill Etheridge announced on local radio that the Post Office remains closed. Bill [my uncle by marriage to my mother's sister Alice] has a dry sense of humour and it hasn't failed him. He said his staff couldn't open today 'because we are busy cleaning up after having some unwelcome visitors yesterday'. I'm guessing that the subtlety of this message got past the Argentine censors who are now running the radio station. It briefly put a smile on my face.

BBC World Service at 10.00am: Addressing Parliament, Mrs Thatcher sounds coldly determined to retake the Islands. She is receiving heavy criticism because this happened on her watch. She said a fleet is being assembled and it will include the aircraft carrier HMS *Invincible*. I wish she and other ministers had been so committed to our freedom before the invasion. They sent all the wrong signals to Argentina and miscalculated badly.

Portsmouth is reported to be a hive of activity as HMS *Invincible* is prepared for sea in double-quick time. The crew have been recalled from Easter leave, and Prince Andrew will be a helicopter pilot aboard her. Some ships that are at sea have been ordered to Gibraltar, where they will bunker and stock up with food and ammunition before heading for the South Atlantic.

WS's 'From Our Own Correspondent' programme is devoted to the crisis. Among the stories: Reagan and Galtieri have spoken on the phone for an hour. I suppose Reagan was trying to use his influence to convince Galtieri to withdraw, but I think BA has boxed itself into a corner, and any peace plan will need to ensure that they save face. Such is Argentine machismo.

The Governor and the captured Marines have arrived in Uruguay, courtesy of the Argentine Air Force. I expect BA was keen to get rid of them before they could be accused of holding them as hostages, which would only increase international outrage. Rex Hunt is said to have had a phone conversation with Thatcher.

No news of the Marines that remain at liberty somewhere in the camp. I don't believe they will have been able to get very far, as they will be on foot and carrying their equipment.

I went to the West Store [Stanley's only supermarket] and it was full of people stocking up for whatever might be coming. From chatting to a few people, I learned that the camp schoolchildren[1] are being returned to their families.

I walked towards Stanley's eastern exit and at 11.15 a convoy of Land Rovers began assembling there, packed with children and a few teachers. The kids looked excited and the teachers and drivers tense. At the head of the column was [Director of Education] John Fowler. After a few minutes of negotiations with the Argentine guards, the convoy headed off towards Bluff Cove, Fitzroy and Darwin. It was soon out of sight.

There is a palpable feeling of relief around town. Everyone had feared that there would be very high casualties, not least among our own Defence Force, who were ill-equipped and trained to stand up to an invasion. That the Defence Force and the Marines escaped without a single casualty seems remarkable.

The Defence Force guarded key points through the night, and at least one section was posted to the racecourse to defend the Islander [aircraft] and engage with any Argentine helicopter that tried to land there. Fortunately, the Defence Force was ordered to return to the Drill Hall shortly before the firing commenced at around 6.00am. However, the section defending the racecourse was one of the last to head back to the HQ, and they were rounded up and held by the Argentines. Turning out was very courageous, and withdrawal was also brave and wise.

I met [my cousin] Stuart [Wallace] on Fitzroy Road, and he had a warning about the telephone system. 'Be very careful what you say, especially if any journalists get through to you from the UK,' he said, 'They're listening.'[2]

Stuart was clearly tired and very down. He was guarding key points with the FIDF last night. Neither of us could summon up a smile. I think he knows better than most what the Argentines are capable of. Ignorance might not be a bad thing at the moment.

Stuart believes they are becoming aware of the 2-metre radio network and they'll start confiscating transceivers. This will be a doddle for them as all sets are licensed to individuals and the records are held in the Post Office.

I walked to the Town Hall, which has been taken over by the Argentines as their HQ. Dozens of people were milling around, including some who are obviously journalists flown in by the military to trumpet their success in the Buenos Aires newspapers.

Hector Gilobert[3] was in a crowd outside the main entrance. There did not seem to be much in the way of security, so I pushed my way through to him. Hector was wearing combat fatigues. Previously, he had always been seen around town in civilian clothes, so I wondered where he got his uniform from at such short notice. Did he, in fact, know about the imminent invasion and arrive in the Falklands a few days ago with his uniform in his suitcase?

Anyway, he was friendly. He was not exactly apologetic but he seemed genuinely sorry about what had happened. 'Is there anything I can do for you and your family?' he asked me.

'Yes, there is,' I said. 'My parents may be in Buenos Aires and I need to get a message to them telling them that I'm OK and insisting that they do not return.'

'Why do you not want them to return?' said Hector.

'Look around you,' I said. 'This is no longer the place they knew and loved.'

'It's not what I wanted,' he said.

He produced a notebook and pen from his fatigues and told me to write a note that he would try to get back to [his wife] Tessie, who's a friend of Mum's, so that she can pass it on. I explained that if she contacted Dad's friend Bernardo Mayer in BA, he would be able to find my parents, assuming they were still in BA. If not, Bernardo could probably pass it on to them in Montevideo.

I wrote a quick note giving them the essential information and making it quite clear that they should not return. Hector took it, tucked it into his breast pocket and shook my hand. He seemed a bit sad. I guess over the last 24 hours his sense of duty has collided with his personal feelings about our little community.

One or two of the journalists realized that I was a local and they wanted to talk to me. I answered a few questions in a way that they probably didn't like. One asked whether I believed 'The British would try to take back the Islands'.

'It's not so much whether they will try, but *when* they will take them back,' I replied. 'So Argentina might like to rethink what it's done.'

Actually, I'm not so sure that they will come to our rescue, and once the Argentines are dug in they may not be easy to remove. But there is no reason why I should share this with them.

A few other reporters shouted questions at me and shoved their microphones in my face. By this time, though, the press officers were getting nervous and stepped in to stop the conversation.

They moved on to talk to Monsignor [Daniel] Spraggon, who had appeared from the church across the road. I ran into a Gas del Estado man whom I met a few days ago. He had been friendly enough then and was still that way today. He had been arrested early on the night of the invasion and locked up in the Town Hall. I asked him if he and his colleagues had been a fifth column, ready to help the invaders, and he insisted this was not so. He said they were as shocked as we were.

Early this afternoon, people are starting to leave Stanley overland, but by late afternoon the roads out of town to the south-west and west are closed and policed by heavily armed soldiers.

Some people, mainly those outside Stanley, are chatting very cautiously and anonymously on the 2-metre radio network.[4] I've been using our set to listen in and glean some interesting news. Someone reported that Darwin and Goose Green have been taken by troops from their ship the *Isla de los Estados*. That this ship is such an unfriendly presence now is a bit ironic, as up until a matter of weeks ago she was visiting Stanley carrying gas bottles for domestic use and other sundry supplies. Now she's carrying troops. Brooke Hardcastle [the Falkland Islands Company's farming manager based at Darwin] apparently received the Argentines and then went with them the short distance to Goose Green, where the residents were required to surrender all their weapons.

I met Terry Peck on the road earlier today and we had a brief chat. He said he thought that the Argentines will probably try to jam the World Service. I'm not at all concerned that they've stopped FIBS relaying it, but if they decide to jam the short-wave broadcasts from London, then we'll feel really cut off.

Terry spent most of the night at the police station, having re-enrolled as a special constable.[5] He'd had some contact with the Marines following their surrender. Terry said the dead Argentine had been advancing towards Government House shouting that Rex Hunt should come out and surrender. Our Marines shouted back that if he continued he would be shot. He either did not understand this or ignored it, and they opened fire.

I went to the Goose this afternoon to check that the Kings are OK and let them know that I'm OK. Aunt Ning [King, my godmother] was pleased to see me and fed me tea and cake. I'm so glad the family is here, as I know I'm always welcome there.

I also hoped to catch up with Rafael Wollman at the Goose, but the Kings said he had checked out in a hurry and been taken to the airport by Argentine troops. This doesn't surprise me, as he will have wanted to get his films back to BA for the papers. It's a real scoop for him.

From our upstairs window at Rowan House I can see that the [Argentine naval support ship] *Cabo San Antonio* has berthed at the East Jetty. Through the binoculars I can see a large number of military vehicles, mainly light jeep-type vehicles and trucks being unloaded. No sign of armoured vehicles.

The radio station has been told it cannot relay BBC World Service News or 'Calling the Falklands'.[6] Instead, we are being subjected to national news from Argentina and a heavily rewritten version of the international news. That hardly matters, of course, as we have our short-wave receivers and can listen to the news directly from London. Quality of reception varies a lot, though.

WS is reporting that a second aircraft carrier is joining the Task Force. She is HMS *Hermes*. She was due to be pensioned off until this crisis came along. Both carriers will be equipped with Harriers, both land-based ground-attack and air-defence types. The main elements of the Task Force are to leave the UK tomorrow, but some elements are already on their way south.

I'm having trouble believing that this massive response is being organized to liberate us. We've gone from not mattering at all to the British Government to being the only thing that does matter.

The Security Council has managed to show a little backbone. None of the permanent members vetoed a resolution condemning the Argentine action, which means that Britain has the authority to go to war.

It was announced this evening that King Edward Point in South Georgia has been seized by Argentine troops. But after our invasion, South Georgia now seems like a sideshow.

World Service reported that there has been a day of intensive activity in Portsmouth as *Invincible* is prepared. Sea Kings were being tested overhead and, remarkably, Prince Andrew will pilot one of these helicopters.

The Ministry of Defence has said that the military challenges are difficult but 'not insurmountable'. That hardly sounds like a great vote of confidence, but is good enough, I suppose.

It's a bit lonely rattling around Rowan with just the cat for company. But actually he's pretty good company and takes my mind off our plight by demanding that life must continue as normal. It's not bad being a cat. I can, of course, visit the Kings at the Upland Goose at any time, and I will go there later.

The Argentines seem to have picked up on the fact that many people have 2-metre radio transceivers. Patrols have been visiting homes and confiscating them. I still have ours, but I don't know for how much longer. Paul [Howe] and I have agreed on code names so can use our sets to keep in touch if necessary.

Late tonight, I was trying to get some sleep but couldn't resist tuning into BBC WS one more time. To my surprise, Simon Winchester is back at work in Argentina. Winchester told WS that as he was being deported from the Falklands by air he saw the Argentines unloading airport defence equipment (by which I suppose he means anti-aircraft weapons) and a large radar. I hope for his sake that the Argentines don't realize he's reporting such valuable information.

Chapter 5

To Fitzroy with a Friend

(4–6 April)

Sunday, 4 April

According to BBC WS at 2.00am today (my normal sleep patterns are shot) the Sunday papers are full of opinion columns about the Falklands. The *Sunday Times* says that the Government 'almost wilfully ignored' the threats from Argentina. (I suspect Simon Winchester may have contributed to this story.)

The Government has also been roundly attacked by papers like the *Telegraph* and the *Mail*, which normally support it slavishly. One demands the resignations of Thatcher, Carrington and Nott [Defence Secretary]. The *Express* call the crisis a 'humiliating fiasco'. Another paper says that the plan to withdraw of HMS *Endurance* was a 'crass military mistake'. Indeed, you could say that.

The *Observer* is the only paper to suggest that a peaceful compromise with Argentina might be possible. They say Islanders might be given special status under Argentine rule. That idea would get short shrift here and, given the current mood, in the UK too. But oddly, it's the kind of idea that Foreign Office officials might have proposed themselves just a few months ago.

I took a quick spin around town with my camera this morning. I have to be careful taking photos, but I grabbed a few. The Radio and Space Research Station [near the point where the Stanley Airport road enters the town] has taken a hit, with a huge hole in the east end of the building. Houses in the area are also shot up, but no locals were injured.

WS reports that any demonstration of disrespect for the Argentine military or the Argentine flag will result in three months' imprisonment. Neither I nor anyone I've managed to speak to here have heard this, but it's believable.

The Argentines I see around the streets look less tense today. Perhaps they haven't heard the news about the Task Force that's being assembled.

'Radio Islas Malvinas' reports, somewhat gleefully, that the seven Marines who managed to escape Stanley after the invasion have been rounded up and are in custody. That's a pity, and it won't do much for morale here, but on the other hand, they could not have expected to achieve a great deal while on the run. There's precious little shelter in the camp, and while we've had fine autumn weather recently, it could become very wintry very quickly. The Marines were interrogated, and with the Argentine Government's preferred interrogation methods being brutal, to say the least, that would not have been much fun.

I visited the Kings at the Upland Goose in the late morning and was reassured to find life going on there more or less as normal. Aunt Ning fed me fresh coffee and biscuits, while Des seemed to be fretting about how he will handle the situation if the military try to take over the hotel, which seems very likely.

Des and Barbara arrived back from the morning service at the Cathedral while I was there. Barbara was tearful. 'We will leave, won't we, Dad?' she said to Des. I think Barbara's desperate unhappiness and thoughts of leaving will be echoed in many homes today.

Later today, I learned that Des's fears had been well founded. About twenty-five military officers have arrived to form the Argentine government administration. The girls said that an Argentine major, who appears to run the police and/or intelligence unit, arrived at the Goose and demanded that most of these officers be accommodated there. If the Kings refuse to accommodate them, the hotel will simply be taken over. So they are moving into the east end of the hotel.

Among the new arrivals is Vice-Comodoro Carlos Bloomer-Reeve, who I understand will be 'Chief of Secretariat', which is probably something like Chief of Staff to the new Governor. Actually, I'm glad to see him, because I know he has many friends among us and I believe he'll do what he can to protect us.[1]

Word is that the manned barriers at the exits from Stanley have been removed and people are free to leave the town. There does not seem to have been an exodus, but some people have left for the farms, especially Fitzroy and Goose Green, where they will be safer. I can't say I blame them.

I understand that there was a secret meeting of FIG [Falkland Islands Government] heads of departments yesterday at the hospital. This was organized by word of mouth, and the only item on the agenda was whether civil servants should continue to do their jobs under occupation. My source said the general feeling was that, all going well, British rule will be re-established soon, and there was therefore a need to keep the government resources and systems in reasonable shape until that time. Also, many Islanders would find it reassuring to see familiar faces at offices like the Treasury, hospital and the Post Office.

But of course such signs of normality are exactly what the Argentines want, so it's a moral issue. The heads of department decided that any civil servant who does not want to work will not be required to do so. Furthermore, the departments will only do what is necessary to maintain the system and that which is in Islanders' interests. Teachers are apparently refusing to work, so schools will be closed.

Later in the day, World Service reported that the Governor and the captured Marines are now on their way back to the UK from Montevideo aboard an RAF

VC10 aircraft. Approximately forty ships are being assembled and will rendezvous at Ascension Island, which is being set up as a forward supply depot.

Carrington has described the Task Force's mission oddly: 'To free the islands from alien occupation'. To my knowledge, there's no sign that the invaders came from somewhere else in the solar system.

From BA, Harold Briley is reporting that the Argentines are taking the threat seriously and cities and military bases in the south of the country are being put on a war footing, with hospitals being prepared for casualties.

The new Argentine Governor has been named as General Mario Benjamin Menendez. As far as he is concerned, we are now under a military government, just like the rest of Argentina.

We hear the Marines at South Georgia were forced to surrender, but not before putting up stiff resistance. I've heard rumours around town that three Argentines were killed there and, incredibly, the Marines shot down a helicopter and put a hole in a corvette with an anti-tank weapon.

I wonder if all of this is starting to give the Argentines cold feet. Foreign Minister Nicanor Costa Mendez says he is willing to discuss the whole issue with the UK and even with us. I'm not sure if that is a genuine sign that they will compromise or just more empty talk the like of which we have heard before. But I suspect that no compromise would be acceptable to us or to the British public that did not involve humiliation for the Argentines, and they will not accept that. But I hope I'm wrong. I'd like a good night's sleep without worrying about what the future holds. I'd like to wake in the morning to find that everyone had regained their senses.

Monday, 5 April

This morning Cable and Wireless announced over local radio (I can't get used to 'Radio Islas Malvinas') that they are accepting telegrams to be sent overseas 'that are not of an explicit nature'. I guess that means telegrams of the 'We are fine, how are you' type, rather than the 'We've just been invaded by thousands of troops from a country that likes to torture and kill its own citizens' variety.

I was at the Upland Goose this morning scrounging tea and biscuits and seeing what news I could pick up. Des [King] said he had heard that the Argentines are building a basic air strip on the West, near Chartres. I guess this makes sense if they are going to garrison the West in any meaningful way. But building a strip capable of taking even a modest aircraft like a [Fokker] F27 would be a major job.

Since its takeover, the radio station can only be relied on for propaganda. So news of importance is being put around by word-of-mouth. Someone told the Kings that there was to be a meeting of those interested in looking after the older folk and people who are living alone. This seemed to me to be a good idea, so I went along to the meeting. In my mind I dubbed the group 'the Care Committee'.

Among those there were Mike Bleaney [husband of Dr Alison Bleaney], John Leonard, Duffy Sheridan, Chris McCullum and Les Biggs. Terry chaired the meeting and between us we built up a list of about fifty people who should be visited regularly and given whatever help they need. I've been allocated Uncle John [Bound] and Venie Summers. My guess is that Venie will welcome visits and help. But I'm not so sure about Uncle John. In fact, I argued (unsuccessfully) that he's only in his early sixties and is far more capable of looking after himself than most of us. On top of that, he's probably armed to the teeth, as the Argentines haven't collected all the guns from around town, and even when they do, Uncle John will probably have half his armoury under the floorboards. I'll try to drop by and check on him later today.

The view from the top floor of Rowan House with a pair of binoculars was interesting today. I can see what looks like a frigate near the entrance to Port William. And there is a big radar dish on Canopus Hill, just south of the airport. I can also see several anti-aircraft guns poking into the sky near the airport.

Talking of aircraft, several small turbo-prop fighter or ground-attack aircraft flew low over Stanley this morning.[2] I think they landed at the airport, but I don't know if they are now a permanent installation there. I think that is very likely, as they would not need much in the way of runway length. Jet fighters, on the other hand, would need more tarmac than Stanley airport can offer.

I grasped the nettle of visiting Uncle John. Best to get it over with. I knocked cautiously on his front door. No answer. Perhaps he was having a snooze in the sitting room, which I hadn't been in since my grandmother died about twenty years ago. I tried the door and it was open, so I entered, calling out, 'Uncle John! It's Graham. Are you home?'

I looked in the kitchen and the sitting room, but he clearly was not at home. I was attracted by the amazing collection of cups and other trophies from his rifle-shooting. He's still one of Stanley's best shots. I was reading the inscriptions when I heard the door open. I knew immediately that I was in trouble.

'Hello, Uncle John,' I said, before he had a chance to say anything. 'The Care Committee – well, that's what I'm calling them – thought I should check you're OK and see if we can help you with anything.'

Uncle John is a very private man. And he looks like the actor James Robertson Justice, especially when angry. Which he was now. *Very* angry.

'Well, I do not need your attention, and neither does the silverware. So hop it! Now! I'm perfectly capable of looking after myself.'

He scowled at me from beneath his beard and I moved quickly to the door. I stopped and looked back over my shoulder. 'Well, if you do need anything . . .'

'I won't. AND YOU CAN TELL THAT TO YOUR BLOODY COMMITTEE TOO!'

God, he's scarier than a fully-armed Argentine. For light relief, I decided to take the Daihatsu [the small jeep I owned at that time] and my camera down the road towards the airport for a look around. But I only got as far as the Common Gate [the eastern entrance to Stanley]. Several young soldiers manning a roadblock wanted to know where I was going and why. I didn't have a good answer, so they searched the jeep and found my camera pretty quickly. They wanted to know what I was doing with a camera. This seemed to have the potential to take a nasty turn, but I explained that I ran the local paper and hardly ever went anywhere without the camera. This seemed to satisfy them, but they turned me back.

There seem to be fewer troops in Stanley today than there were immediately after the invasion. On my way back from the Airport Road, I stopped at Simon's [Simon Goss] to have a chat and see how they were. He thinks, probably rightly, that many of their troops will have been moved outside Stanley and perhaps the crack invasion troops have been withdrawn.

Simon is taking Elizabeth and the children [Roger and Corina] to Port Harriet House tomorrow. It belongs to his uncle, Dick Hills, of course. The Hills themselves and the Keenleysides may also be going out there. I didn't say it, but I wonder if it will be safer in the camp if a real shooting war starts. Apart from being a bit lonely out there, there might be more danger of troops running amok. Anyway, I'll be sorry to see them go.

A rare announcement of interest came from the radio station. Apparently, unexploded weaponry is posing a danger around Stanley. I will keep that in mind if I am tempted to kick a grenade.

WS is reporting that Lord Carrington has resigned. That seems about right to me. Basically, we are in it up to our eyeballs because the Foreign Office cocked everything up. Carrington has been replaced by Francis Pym. Richard Luce and Humphrey Atkins [junior minister and Commons spokesman for Carrington respectively] have also fallen on their swords. They'll all have a bit more time to consider the consequences of their actions – or inaction.

Thousands of people have gathered in Portsmouth to cheer off the two biggest ships in the Task Force, HMS *Invincible* and *Hermes*. I find it amazing that this is happening just a few days after the invasion. I suspect that generals in BA are experiencing a different emotion, like gut-clenching fear. If they are not, they should be.

Costa Mendez has gone to meet other members of the Organization of American States to plead for their support. He'll probably get bucketloads of verbal support, but I can't see any of the other South American countries being stupid enough to get involved on the ground. Apparently, he's also hoping to see

Al Haig [US Secretary of State]. If he's looking for mediation, then Haig may be in a good position to do this.

Thatcher is reported to have said the Task Force will consist of around thirty-six ships and it includes at least one large container ship. It'll be the biggest UK fleet assembled in peacetime. I suppose it still seems like 'peacetime' in the UK, but it feels like far from that here. The cruise ship *Canberra* is being taken over as a troop ship, and there's also talk of a hospital ship being mobilized. The scale of this is staggering.

We've caused the pound to lose value against the US dollar by two cents. Sorry about that. And Tesco has said it will no longer sell Argentine corned beef. Not sorry about that.

At the Goose this afternoon for a tea, biscuits and gossip catch-up, I met an Argentine military police officer in the lobby who was surprisingly chatty. He wanted to know about me, and in turn I asked him why we're seeing slightly fewer troops on the streets. He said the black-capped commandos and others involved in the invasion have not been sent back to 'the mainland' (as he put it) but have been embarked on the ships again and are standing by in case they are needed. He asked me what news I had from the BBC, and I told him that there was still speculation that a lot more men were killed during the invasion than was being claimed by BA. He insisted this was wrong. Just one, he said, and a few wounded. '*Te lo juro*', he said when I looked doubtful, 'I swear it's true.' He admitted, though, that the Argentine troops had a lot of respect for the Marines.

At 7.20 this evening WS broadcast a sober-sounding message specifically for British citizens in Argentina. They are advised by the FCO to leave the country by normal commercial means. As the FCO contributed to this mess, they might have the decency to arrange some special flights.

The men who will become the administrators for the military government in the Falklands arrived yesterday afternoon aboard a LADE F28, General Menendez among them. I was told by someone who would know that there are military officers installed to head each government department and they are meeting with our heads of departments, presumably to learn how the government is run, and probably to try to persuade the local civil servants to stay on.

This and the secret meeting of heads of departments have led to a degree of normality returning to the government. The Treasury reopened today and there was an immediate rush to withdraw savings. As a result, withdrawals have been limited to £500 for each account holder until further notice. I took my place in the queue to get as much money as possible out. £500 will keep me and the cat fed for quite a while.

The new administration got straight to work telling us what to do. From now on we must drive on the right side of the road. That could lead to some interesting situations. Checkpoints will remain in place at various unspecified points around Stanley, and army patrols will continue to circulate. Both are 'to be respected'. The radio station is now officially renamed 'LRL 60 Radio Nacional Islas Malvinas'. New programmes will include 'popular Argentine music'. Policy over news coverage is still to be decided. Well, I hate tango music and the news will be propaganda, so not much there for me. Thank goodness for BBC World Service.

Patrick Watts, who is still at the radio station, managed to get a brief interview with Carlos Bloomer-Reeve, and he was asked about rumours that the Argentines are monitoring telephone conversations and opening mail. Bloomer-Reeve denied this. That, of course, doesn't mean they are *not* monitoring the phones.

The Post Office will be open tomorrow, more or less as normal, but the staff will only accept postcards and letters; no packets or parcels. I wonder if the government of occupation will accept our stamps with 'Falkland Islands' and the Queen's head on them. They might eventually become interesting collectors' items.[3]

Four Argentine jet fighters roared low over Stanley yesterday afternoon, and then continued to circle for about ten minutes. It was hard to tell, but they may have been Mirages. They were clearly not able to land but they were fitted with big drop tanks so had plenty of fuel to get back to the continent. I think it was a show mainly for our benefit.

The jet fighters appeared again today at about the same time and performed pretty much the same act. I suppose it's possible that they may be flying off the Argentine aircraft carrier, which might be in the area. In that case, they can't be Mirages. I must find my I-Spy Book of (not so) Modern Military Aircraft.

Tuesday, 6 April

Today, my responsibility for Venie Summers resulted in a call from her family at Fitzroy. They wanted to know if I would be able to drive the old lady out to the farm, where they believe she'll be safer. Mrs Summers is an old friend of Dad, who's a contemporary of her sons. The boys spent their youth together fishing and shooting. Venie is lovely and once gave me an old and beautifully crafted ship-in-a-bottle, which I treasure. So of course I'm going to help her in any way I can. Keith and Teddy Summers [family members who live in Stanley] have said they'll come along in their Land Rover.

Venie finds it hard to walk, so getting her into the passenger seat of the little jeep was not easy. Once she was comfortable, though, I strapped her in tightly with the safety belt. That way she will not bounce around too badly when we run out of road. She was a bit emotional and very grateful. I said that she had always been very kind to our family and this was my way of returning the kindness.

We had to drive slowly, so it took about three hours to get to Fitzroy. Keith and Teddy disappeared ahead. Venie and I chatted about the old days in the camp and even though driving across the camp was rough, she never complained. I'm not sure how old she is, but well into her eighties, I think.

We did not run into any Argentine roadblocks while leaving Stanley, but just after we left the end of the road, near Ponies' Pass, I saw an Argentine Army Mercedes four-wheel-drive hopelessly bogged. They had plunged straight into a swamp within minutes of leaving the road. They have a lot to learn if they wish to be mobile around the Falklands. Pat Whitney had already reached them and, rather oddly, was helping to extract the Mercedes from the mud. My guess is that the men in the vehicles had stopped him and made it clear that he had better help – or else. We waved cheerily at the glum-looking Argentines and carried on.

Near Bluff Cove we saw four jet fighters screaming towards Darwin at low level. I guess the pilots had been performing over Stanley again and were either going to reprise the show over Goose Green or head home. A little later, we stopped for a breather near the top of Fitzroy Ridge. Although I had been driving quite slowly, the track was rough and Venie must have found it difficult. It was a lovely day, with the sun streaming down through a thin layer of high clouds. We sat there in silence for a few minutes, both admiring the view. Then Venie became nostalgic and began reminiscing about the years she lived at Fitzroy. She spoke about her boys, Dad and Uncle John roaming the camp for long days before returning to her with fish, geese and duck for her to cook.

Several of the same small propeller fighters I saw yesterday appeared as dots in the distance and flew directly at us and over us. They proceeded to dance around the sky above Fitzroy as if it was theirs to play with. This both angered me and upset me. I felt tears coming into my eyes and I had to hide this from Venie.

I had this overwhelming conviction that this place belonged to her, not to the Argentines who were arrogantly showing off in the sky and the idiots who had got bogged to their axles the moment they left the road. They might think that some event took place 150 years ago which entitles them to be here today, but I knew, and at that moment felt intensely, that it was only Venie, her family and people like her who have the right to call this place home.

I pretended there was some dust in my eyes, discreetly wiped them, and we carried on, across Fitzroy Bridge and into the settlement. Teddy and Keith were already there and everyone came out to greet Venie. She was grateful and a little emotional. 'Give my love to your dad,' she said, as I was leaving. I said I would, of course.[4]

I stopped off at Bluff Cove on the way back and bummed a cup of coffee off the Kilmartins. Diane offered me a place in their house if I had to get out of Stanley quickly, which was very kind of her. However, Bluff Cove might fill up very quickly. There are already fourteen people in one of the two houses, including three of the defectors from the Polish fishing fleet.

The return journey was quick and relatively easy, and I did not see another Argentine until I drove across the cattle grid and through the gate into Stanley.

I was called by Cable and Wireless soon after I got back to Rowan House. They had a telegram for me. I quickly drove up to the C&W office to get it. The telegram was actually from McLean and Stapleton in Montevideo, passing on a message from Dad: 'Your message received. We will act as suggested.' This is a great relief, as it can only mean that they have reached Montevideo and are now planning to continue to the UK. This leaves me free to do whatever I need to do to get through the coming weeks, and that might mean leaving Stanley for the camp.

As the situation becomes graver, quite a number of people are clearly planning to leave the Islands. Some are locals, but mainly they are government contract staff, including teachers. There is a faint feeling that we are being abandoned, but to some extent at least, I sympathize with these expat Brits. They signed up for fairly comfy and well-paid positions which came with some social status, not to be invaded, live under a military regime and be subjected to tango music on the radio.

But leaving the Falklands may not be that easy. LADE has announced that their regular passenger flights will not take place, at least for the time being. I ran into one of the staff on the road early today and asked him if this was only temporary. The guy, who is usually friendly, just clammed up.

'Don't ask me,' he snapped. 'I have no idea. These are not normal times, you know.'

I asked him if many residents are booked to leave.

'Yes,' he said. 'But don't ask me anything else. I work for the Argentine Air Force, remember.'

I dropped by Church House this evening to see Pete [King] and Rosemary [Allan]. Pete said he had been into work [at the Government Secretariat]. He's responsible for issuing passports and he said that there had been a rush for them. He has issued about fifty new ones to people wanting to get out.

WS reports that according to a UK opinion poll, most Brits are in favour of military action if necessary. There seems to be widespread regret that Lord Carrington was forced to resign, as he had been a well-respected Foreign Secretary until his big Falklands mistake. I think that the dispute with Argentina would not have been high on his list of priorities, but it probably should have been.

A frigate and the *Isla de los Estados* are anchored at the east end of the harbour. The radar dish on Canopus Hill is revolving, and that must mean that they have an air defence system working.

Chatter at the Goose was that a LADE F27 had landed twice on an improvised airstrip on the West. I think this may be an Argentine porkie, planted among us to suggest that they have a far better command of the Islands than they actually do.

F27s are tough and don't need a long strip to land on, but preparing an airstrip in less than a week is ridiculous.

More ominous and dictatorial stuff from 'Radio Islas Malvinas' this evening. Radio transmissions, both in the ham amateur bands and on the local 2-metre network, are forbidden. A penalty of between three months and two years in jail will be levied by courts martial for this offence, the severity depending on the extent or potential extent of damage to Argentine forces. Of course, military courts can have no legal jurisdiction over civilians. But they are the occupying government, so they can do what they like.

There are no signs of reinforcements in Stanley, which they will certainly need if the Task Force is not withdrawn. No sign of artillery or armoured vehicles yet, either.

The maximum withdrawal from the Treasury [savings bank] is now reduced to just £50 per person.

Chapter 6

Bunker Building

(7–10 April)

Wednesday, 7 April

Yesterday, Pete King heard that red crosses must be painted on the roofs and walls of the hospital and the nurses' accommodation. Both of us have more nervous energy than we can use up at the moment, so we went along to the KEMH [King Edward Memorial Hospital] and offered our services. We were presented with paint brushes, a couple of ladders and pots of paint, and we set to work on the nurses' building.

Pete is better at heights than I am and didn't seem to mind clambering over the roof, but I find it hard. However, it was a bright and fairly calm day, so we had a surprisingly enjoyable afternoon. From the ridge of the roof we could get a good view of land to the west, and it is clear that the Argentines are operating helicopters from the higher ground above Government House, near the racecourse. Their main helicopter type seems to be the Bell Huey, of Vietnam fame. Pete was as funny as ever, and I came back home to Rowan feeling cheerful and a lot better for having done something useful.

LADE air services seem to be resuming, at least after a fashion. An F28 flight is planned for later today, and I understand that eight or nine local people will be aboard it. Most of them will be contract officers getting out while they still can, but I think a few locals are heading out too.

Al Haig [US Secretary of State] has embarked on shuttle diplomacy, according to WS. He's met separately with [Argentine Foreign Minister Nicanor] Costa Mendez and he's going on to see the Brits. Good luck to him.

There may be a slight softening of the Argentine position. Sounding desperate, BA has appealed to the non-aligned countries to help find a solution. And they have told the UN that compensation will be offered to any Islanders who cannot accept Argentine nationality and wish to leave.

We have not heard that offer expressed here. I don't think many locals would accept what amounts to a bribe, anyway, but most of us don't have British passports that allow us to live anywhere other than the Falklands. Most passports issued in the Falklands specifically state that the holder has no right to live and work in the UK.

Preparations for war in the UK sound like organized chaos. WS reports – with a bit of a snigger – that the Task Force does not have enough maps, so MoD office boys have been sent off to clear all maps of the Falklands from the shelves of Hatchards, London's main seller of maps.

Parliament has authorized the government to spend almost whatever it wants to take back the Falklands. That'll be helpful as the cruise ship *Canberra* has been taken over, and I bet she doesn't come cheap. Men are working around the clock to adapt her for troop-carrying.

Another warship, HMS *Fearless*, carrying 500 marines, has set sail. Apparently, she is a dedicated assault ship with landing craft.

I settled in to listen to 'Calling the Falklands' with the Kings at the Upland Goose. It was a special edition containing mostly messages from people in the UK with families here. It was quite poignant. Some people presented their messages in person over the phone, and more than one was on the verge of tears. The situation is bad here, but it must look even worse from thousands of miles away. Then there was a summary of the day's Falklands news, much of it delivered in grave terms.

Nott also spoke on the programme but not revealing anything new. He signed off with 'We are constantly thinking of you.' I bet he is. The Falklands has become his worst nightmare.

It's now being presented by a veteran WS news reader and journalist, Peter King. I remember him reading the news back in the early 1960s. He's got a great voice and he tries to inject humour and warmth into the programme when he can. And he has introduced a new signing-off catch phrase: 'Heads down, hearts high'. Seems like good advice.

We are not seeing a huge number of soldiers in the streets of Stanley, but those we do see tend to look miserable. They are not very well clothed for the winter and some of them look like they may have come from the north of Argentina. They often look hungry, too. I spoke to one soldier outside the West Store who asked me for food or some money for food. I went in and bought him a few bars of chocolate. I can't stand by and watch people suffer and I'm not going to make any apologies for that. This young guy told me that the rations are poor: one small tin of meat, three boiled sweets and enough coffee or cocoa for a couple of mugs a day. We are only a week or so into this situation and the troops are looking neglected. That doesn't bode well for them.

Some good, though slightly odd, news was broadcast over local radio today. The 'law' covering use of radios has been amended, allowing those in the camp to use the 2-metre network, although not short-wave equipment. I guess they have realized that the people on the farms need to be able to contact others in case they have a medical crisis. The 2-metre network is short-range, so it can't be used to send information out of the Islands.

[My cousin] Leatrice managed to get through to me on the phone from the Channel Islands this morning. She is very worried about her parents. I was able to tell her that Aunt Beat and Des are fine and her brother Bernard has taken them to camp. I'm not sure about this, actually. I went by their house a day or two ago, but there was no sign of life, so I assume that Bernard has taken them to North Arm. No point in worrying Leatrice more than necessary.

Jill Harris told me that she has also seen some pathetic-looking soldiers. She saw one who was dragging his rifle along the ground and crying. I think she gave him some food. It's tragic.

I was asked today if I would be able to get a family to Douglas Station. I had to think about this. I only have the little jeep, which barely has room for three in comfort, plus Stanley to Douglas and back would be a two-day trip. We would certainly get bogged, and without another vehicle to help, the trip could take a lot longer than two days. Eventually, I said that I would help if they could find a second vehicle. They will give it some thought and call me back if necessary.

News from other parts of the Islands has started trickling through on the 2-metre network now that it's operating again. The population of Fox Bay East has packed up and moved elsewhere en masse. I don't know where they have gone. Port Howard or Port Stephens seem likely.

I went back to Rowan House at about 8.00pm and settled in for the evening. The cat Bagpuss doesn't care about the great drama that is unfolding and was almost mugging me for food. We've plenty of mutton and fish in the deep freeze, so he has nothing to worry about. Stomach full, he then curled up on the sofa. I opened a can of beans and tuned into the radio, both local and World Service.

Local radio – propaganda only now, along with some supposed public service announcements – reported that General Menendez was sworn in as the military governor today in the Court and Council Chamber at the Town Hall. Depressing. The BBC had the dramatic news that the UK is imposing a 200-mile maritime exclusion zone around the Islands: 'Any ship entering the zone after 12 April will be liable to attack.' I think they would only be able to carry out this threat if they have a nuclear submarine in the area, and it still seems a bit soon for that. However, there could, I suppose be a sub in the region by the 12th.

I don't quite know how I feel about this news. I suppose I should be pleased that the UK is showing such determination. But it's a major step closer to war, and that frightens me. I drank coffee and kept the 2-metre set and the BBC on quietly until I fell asleep in the armchair.

Thursday, 8 April

Atmospheric conditions made it very hard to hear the World Service this afternoon, but that's normal, as the BBC doesn't beam transmissions towards our part of the world until later in the day. Apparently, in reply to London's declaration of an exclusion zone, BA has said that Argentina will not be responsible for the safety of British ships in its territorial waters, including Falklands waters, of course.

Representatives of the British community in Argentina have apparently asked Mrs Thatcher to find a peaceful solution. They would be better off asking their own government for this, but I suppose they might not feel very safe approaching the military Junta with such a suggestion. People have gone missing in BA for less.

Work continues apace preparing the cruise ship *Canberra* for use as a troop ship. A helicopter landing pad is being fitted, and some 2,000 men will board the ship. I suppose if you are going to war you might as well go on a cruise ship.

I went to the West Store today, supposedly to buy some food but also to see what gossip I can pick up. People are, of course, talking about nothing other than the crisis. Rumours still circulate about what happened during the invasion. Someone heard from someone else (who probably heard from someone else) that Argentine bodies have drifted up on the shore of Port William. If true, that might add substance to suggestions that one of their landing craft was hit.

I was struck again by soldiers on the streets looking miserable, poorly clothed and sometimes asking for help.

I spent a while trying to figure out what I will do about *Penguin News*. I could go on trying to produce it, but there are practical problems. I've been relying on the [Government] Secretariat to scan stencils for me, and lately I've run low on ink so I've been buying that from the Secretariat too. I doubt if that cooperation would continue under the new regime. It would be good to produce the paper, but only if it is something I can be proud of, and for how long would the Argentines tolerate a publication that tells the truth? The choice then would then probably be to censor it or close down. The latter would be preferable.

There is another issue too: the population of Stanley is rapidly declining as so many people head for the relative safety of camp. I would be able to distribute a paper to a declining number of people in Stanley, but getting it out to camp would be impossible.

I've decided I will start working on the next edition and hope that I can go on to print it. I'll try to ask Carlos Bloomer-Reeve to set up interviews with Menendez and other senior Argentines here. Let's see how I get on with that.

Costa Mendez has expressed optimism about the possible outcome of negotiations. Wish fulfilment or realism? Time will tell, I suppose. He had better be ready to make a major concession if he wants to secure peace.

Italy, France and Belgium have joined other EEC [now European Union] nations in banning arms sales to Argentina. Australia has shut off all credit facilities for Argentina. Nice gesture, but it won't make anyone's eyes water in BA.

Peter King ended the message section of 'Calling the Falklands' this evening by playing 'We'll Meet Again'. Jesus, things must really be bad if they've got Vera

Lynn out of retirement. The old song still does it, though. I felt some prickling around the eyes and reached for the cat.

I dropped by the Upland Goose in the evening and Aunt Ning kindly gave me supper. They didn't have any news, but the Argentines have consolidated themselves in the east end of the hotel. Mostly it's the handful of propaganda merchants they call reporters, plus some of the military officers who are now running the government. The guy who now runs what was the local radio, a Sr Mora, is also lodged in the hotel. He seems to be bustling up and down all the time, commandeering the phone in the hall and shouting into it.

I'm feeling depressed and worried about the outlook. I've started planning a bunker or shelter of sorts at Rowan House. I think the best place is in the corner of the garage. The garage's concrete foundations and lower wall are cut into a slope, so the south side is just below ground level. I have a stack of pallets that I can form into a low shelter, using the concrete walls on two sides. I can disguise it and fortify the pallets with bags of coal. It won't be comfortable, but Rowan itself won't give any protection at all.

Friday, 9 April

One week ago we were invaded, and in that time life has changed utterly here. We are front and centre of the world stage, which at any other time might be a privilege but right now feels very uncomfortable.

The more I think about it, the less I feel that all of this is actually about us. The Argentines would rather we were not here at all, and while London goes on about restoring our freedom, that rings more than a bit hollow. We didn't have the right to determine our own future or (in most cases) even live in the UK before the invasion, and that didn't seem to worry London then. Why should they care about our rights and freedom now? We really are pawns.

I tuned in to RAI [Radio Argentina International] today. It seems an international book fair is underway in BA and people are being invited to buy a book that will then be donated to the people of the Falklands. Nice thought, but not likely to be well received, even if they turn up. Not that many people read books in Spanish here.

I was in the Goose bar earlier today and a military police officer came in. He was looking for some officer billeted at the hotel but having trouble communicating, so I thought I would step in and help with my Spanish. What I really wanted to do was start a conversation and see if I could learn anything. I'm guessing that for his part he saw the chance to plant a bit of propaganda which might be passed on. He told me that the Argentine Air Force has several old Lockheed Electra four-engined transport planes that they planned to pack with explosive and then fly at the Task Force ships in suicide attacks. Full marks to him for his inventiveness.

I've got no doubt that Argentine pilots are good, and they are patriotic, but they're not that stupid.

Pending use in their main role as kamikaze aircraft, I think the Electras were shuttling in and out of Stanley last night and today. During the morning they were quite visible with binoculars at the airport. Apparently, they are very good aircraft for use on short or poorly surfaced runways. Stanley's runway is certainly short.

'Calling the Falklands' ['CTF' from here on] this evening announced that a formal request for the evacuation of civilians has been received in London from a group of 'leading citizens' in Stanley. There have been whispers of this here. It seems that a group of people who might consider themselves to be important members of the community met at the hospital and drafted a request for mass evacuation before a shooting war starts. The only name that I have heard is that of the Senior Medical Officer Dr [Daniel] Haines. There was certainly no consultation with rank-and-file Islanders. The letter may have been smuggled out with one of the departing expats a few days ago.[1]

Rex Hunt responded to this on CTF, saying that this 'does not amount to an official request'. He thinks that 90 per cent of Islanders would rather suffer casualties than live under Argentine rule. That would seem to be a major assumption. I suspect that quite a few Islanders might prefer not to die in the crossfire.

London seems increasingly determined to restore its damaged pride come what may, so they won't see the message from our 'leading citizens' as very helpful. One can't go in with all guns blazing to 'restore the freedom of Islanders' if we've all decamped back to the mother country. So I assume no one in London is planning our evacuation.

This afternoon, I spent a few hours heaving the pallets into place in the garage and nailing them together. I've found some 4x4 timbers that are helpful too. It's shaping up as a very fine bunker, and I should finish it tomorrow. It'll be small but almost perfectly formed and a good hideout for one man and a cat. Des and Paul at the Goose have also been working on a shelter in one of the hotel sheds.

Saturday, 10 April

Huge disappointment today when Mum and Dad arrived back. I had every reason to assume that they were heading on to the UK, but they apparently made their way to Comodoro Rivadavia, where they convinced someone they knew at the LADE office to let them on one of their planes. They ended up flying into Stanley on an F27 with fifty or more troops.

It was mid-morning when they knocked on the door at Rowan. I'd been keeping it locked even when I was at home. I was completely dumbfounded when I saw them through the window, and I'm afraid I let them know it.

I'm still furious and not at all sorry for telling them that what they'd done was completely ridiculous. They were both sheepish like I've never seen them before. It was role reversal really; normally it's me who gets the telling off, not them.

Mum tried to explain, but I don't think she was even convincing herself.

'We were so worried about you, and the house and the shop, dear. We know it doesn't make sense to you, but we *had* to come back.'

She said that they had scrounged a lift to town from Stanley airport (which they said was thronged with troops and littered with equipment and anti-aircraft weapons) off 'a very helpful Argentine officer'.

She looked at Dad. 'What was his name, Nap?'

Dad, who had not said anything and just looked dejected, said, 'Menendez, I think he was called. He had a driver and a fancy jeep.'

This was getting ridiculous.

'Menendez? He's their military governor! You scrounged a flight on a troop carrier, then you got a lift with their head honcho?'

I suppose I started feeling a bit sorry for them, so I went to the kitchen and made them some tea, before leaving them to unpack and consider how in the name of God returning to occupied Stanley with a war brewing could help any of us.

I stormed off and avoided the house for the rest of the day. I'm still furious that the parents have voluntarily complicated their own lives and mine. I know how they will behave now. Nothing will persuade them to budge out of Stanley, and my conscience won't allow me to leave them, even though I would like to be flexible enough to leave Stanley if necessary, and maybe even do something of use. My options are now closed down and I'm stuck here come what may.

I came home later and did some more work on the bunker, which is, of course, now too small. Anyway, right now I can't think of anything much worse than being crammed into that funk hole with Mum and Dad.

The Argentines have obviously discovered that licences for all radio equipment are held at the Post Office, and that means they know precisely who has short-wave transmitters and 2-metre sets. Obviously, they fear that we will try to get messages out of the Falklands, either to London or to the Task Force when it gets closer. Accordingly, Radio Islas Malvinas has announced that all owners of radio transmitters are to bring their equipment to the Post Office today, where it will be taken off their hands and receipts will be issued.

Strangely, according to the edict, the radio sets will be returned to their owners next Monday with new licences. I don't believe this for a minute. They'll keep them and probably put them to use among their own forces. Many radio transmitters were confiscated during the first few days of occupation, and I'm sure they were never returned.

A later change to the edict indicated that more remote settlements on the West and on the small islands can keep their radios in case they have to summon help in emergencies. But these transceivers are to be disassembled, 'with the valves kept at least a mile from the sets'. It's nutty stuff, really.

Later in the day, I went along to the Post Office and handed over our 2-metre set. It was ticked off against the list of people who own equipment. There are times when I wish our bureaucrats were not so damned efficient. It also niggles that the list of licence-holders was not destroyed before the Argentines could get hold of it.

Late this afternoon, WS is reporting that it has been suggested in the UN that a peace-keeping force could be deployed to the islands, led by Peru, which is trusted by Argentina.

The cruise ship *Canberra*, which is now southbound packed with troops, has been shadowed for much of the day by what is described as a Soviet spy ship. I wonder if they are passing information to BA? The Russians must like having so many NATO assets deployed 8,000 miles away from Europe.

The aircraft carriers are said to be conducting helicopter and other exercises while also steaming steadily south, towards us and who knows what.

Chapter 7

No Chocolate Eggs

(11–14 April)

Sunday, 11 April

Isla de los Estados sailed from the East Jetty at about 8.30 this morning. She was high in the water so could not have been carrying much, if anything. With the blockade of Falklands waters starting tomorrow, the crew will be hoping to be out of the 150-mile exclusion zone within the next 18 hours or so. I guess that is possible, but only just.

I drove out to Bluff Cove early this morning and got back mid-afternoon. I was thinking of carrying on to Fitzroy to check on Venie Summers and her family, but the days are getting shorter now and I was a bit concerned about the possibility of getting stuck after dark. So I didn't get any further than Bluff Cove. The track was wet, but the little Daihatsu often seems to float over the softer camp in a way that those Argentine Mercedes vehicles certainly can't.

I was interested in what I might see on the way in and out and I wanted to check whether they are controlling the exit from Stanley. The answer to that is yes, they are, although they didn't turn me back. I was stopped at a checkpoint near the power station and told to get out of the vehicle. They then kept me under guard while they searched it. I don't know what they were looking for, but perhaps radio kit. After a few minutes I was told I could carry on.

Before the end of the road, near Ponies Pass, I was flagged down by a small group of soldiers attempting to get three of the FIG [Falkland Islands Government] road-building trucks into Stanley. One had broken down, and they wanted me to lend them some tools. I couldn't help and didn't want to anyway. I understood from the soldier that the tipper trucks are needed to enlarge the apron at the airport. That makes sense. Judging by the number of large planes flying in and out, that must be causing them a real problem.

Seeing Stanley recede in the rear-view mirror was a good feeling. Life has changed totally, and I feel a bit nervous there most of the time. But they don't seem to be in control out in the camp. I hardly saw any sign of the Argentines, and the small planes that were dancing around the sky when I took Venie to Fitzroy last week were nowhere to be seen.

I visited the Kilmartins and the Dobbyns. There are about twenty refugees at Bluff Cove, including most of the Polish guys. Everyone seems to be fine, and Diane [Kilmartin] repeated her invitation to shelter at Bluff Cove if I want to get out of Stanley. I said that the parents have just returned so there was not much chance of that now, but it is a kind offer.

Late this afternoon, back in Stanley, I tuned into the BBC. Tension is increasing. The MoD says that Argentina has now withdrawn nearly all its ships from the area, apart from one destroyer and a frigate. I wonder if they are aware of the *Isla de los Estados*, which by now must be near the edge of the exclusion zone.

Al Haig has left BA and is on his way to London. I hope he has some serious concession to offer. He claimed there is a 'mood of cautious optimism'. There's not much of that here. Almost everyone I speak to is assuming the worst and they are making plans to get enough food in, build a shelter and hunker down in Stanley, or get out of town.

This evening, Menendez broadcast an Easter message on 'Radio Islas Malvinas'. It was the usual religious and patriotic crap, with hopes for peace. I hadn't even noticed it was Easter. No chocolate eggs for us, that's for sure.

Canal 7, the Falklands' first TV station, appears to be almost ready to broadcast. It's based at the radio station, and according to the radio, arrangements are being made to get TV sets for Stanley residents. The new station has apparently been carrying out test broadcasts. I guess you've got to hand it to them: setting up a TV station in less than ten days is not bad going. Pity that hardly anyone has a TV set. It doesn't interest me much anyway. It'll just be another source of propaganda.

Around dusk there was a lot of activity near the cemetery. I have no idea what was going on, but there are lots of soldiers in the area and Harold Rowlands, who lives very near the cemetery, told me that he felt very uneasy and moved to a friend's house. I don't know if he's planning to stay there.

Mum whipped up some dinner tonight. I must admit, it's good to have some real food again.

Monday, 12 April

I found it hard to sleep last night. I was still awake at 1.00am and tuned into WS. Harold Briley, reporting from BA, said that the government there had let it be known that there could be a withdrawal if British forces turn back. So it seems they are still in a mood to talk so long as they don't feel their 'honour' is at stake.

Briley has become a great source of information lately. He doesn't seem to be intimidated by the government in BA. They don't like journalists who question their wisdom and authority, and they have a nasty way of letting that be known.

I set the alarm for 4.00am so I could tune into WS again before reception becomes poor. I feel that with the blockade commencing today we are getting closer to the point of no return. WS confirmed that the blockade has begun.

Francis Pym [the Foreign Secretary] says that the Argentines may have anti-shipping mines around the Islands. That includes Pt William and Berkeley Sound.

Pym is also saying that there must be a complete Argentine withdrawal from the Falklands before any compromise solution can be agreed. I think Haig is going to get fed up with his shuttling soon, but full credit to him for trying.

And yet, according to WS, some of the newspapers are editorializing positively about the outlook for peace. They see Haig chasing his tail and assume that the frantic diplomatic activity means the outlook for peace must be high. I wish I shared that view. Haig is due to arrive in UK very soon and will have a lengthy meeting with Thatcher this morning.

Argentine planes started shuttling in and out of Stanley soon after dawn, arriving and departing at roughly the rate of one every half-hour. The airport has never seen use like this, and some of the planes are much larger than anything that has used the runway in the past. From upstairs at Rowan I saw several Aerolineas Argentinas Boeing 737s arriving and departing. There must be little or no margin for error.

I have a feeling that London will have figured out that the airport is essential. As soon as they get within range they'll bomb it. That should be quite a show.

I've been reflecting a bit more on what I saw during the drive to Bluff Cove yesterday. I noticed about 100 soldiers using spades and shovels to dig around the south side of Sapper Hill. I assumed then that they were digging foxholes and fortifications, because Sapper Hill commands the southern approach to Stanley. But I wonder now if they were planting mines.

There are fortifications visible in the rocks around the summit of Sapper Hill. They were also digging on the rifle range slightly to the north. They could be mining that area too, or installing anti-aircraft guns or missile batteries.

This afternoon, I was in the Goose and heard that Bill Luxton has been arrested by the Argentines. Apparently, they took a helicopter out to Chartres and picked him up with his wife and son.[1] It is being said that they will be deported later today. They would be very silly to treat him roughly, as everyone is watching. It wouldn't do their cause any good at all.

My source also said that Dick [Chief Secretary] and Connie Baker are to be shipped out very soon. It seems remarkable that he has been allowed to stay for this long. I can only think that they've overlooked him for some reason. Dick is a good guy, and we really need him to stay.

'Argentina is turning the islands into a fortress,' said BBC WS this evening. From what I've seen, that's the truth. They added that key towns in Patagonia are also being reinforced, particularly Comodoro Rivadavia.

BA is saying that its 200-mile territorial zone will be patrolled by ships and aircraft. Everyone with shipping in the area must be feeling nervous. Spain has ordered all its ships in the South Atlantic to fly Spanish flags very prominently.

The *Bahia Buen Suceso*, which we know was involved in the South Georgia situation, arrived in Stanley yesterday afternoon. She's moored at the FIC (Falkland Islands Company) jetty, and we speculate that she is carrying the Marines and civilians captured at South Georgia. They've put heavy security (including some nasty-looking dogs) in place around the jetty, which supports this theory. Local people are being ordered away from the area.

On the religious front, the Archbishop of Canterbury has been praying for peace. He says we Falkland Islanders are a 'peace-loving and God-fearing people'. We are? Good to know about the prayers. Every little bit helps.

Bishop Cutts, the Anglican Bishop of South America, based in BA, has also been pitching in. He's cabled Mrs Thatcher, saying, 'War would cause the Islanders great suffering.' No kidding.

I took a spin around the FIC jetty area this afternoon. Their security is still very tight. Also, they appear to be digging trenches and other fortifications to the south and north of the cemetery. They've put a couple of large artillery pieces in place a little to the south of the graveyard. I don't know if that is a holding position for them or if they are there to cover the Narrows [the entrance to Stanley Harbour]. That might make sense.

Several dummy artillery guns have been placed on the grass between the beach and the south side of the cemetery. Gas cylinders have been placed between sets of wheels. They might look like artillery pieces to an aircraft several thousand feet up.

I also spotted a couple of armoured cars sporting heavy calibre guns. They have wheels rather than tracks, so I don't think they can be called tanks. Judging by the size of their tyres, they might be able to travel cross country.

I also managed to drive to the west, almost as far as the old Beaver Hangar,[2] where I could see hundreds of troops. So I turned back rather than risk being stopped. I think they are probably using the old hangar for something.

I have seen a lot of troops today, but nothing like the 10,000 or so that the Argentines say they have here. Could they be bluffing? I expect most of their troops are in the hills around Stanley and at other key points around the Islands.

Bill Etheridge told me that he is managing to get some mail out of the Islands. In fact, the military aircraft take small amounts most days. That surprised me. Bill remains in the post office with some of his staff, but he now answers to an Argentine civilian postmaster. He says that the Argentine is not unreasonable, and they are able to work together.

John Leonard tells me that the Americans living in the Islands have been invited to leave on a specially arranged flight. Most, if not all, are Bahais. They had a meeting and agreed that they will all stay here for as long as the Islanders do. Just one American couple has left on a military flight, but they had been planning to leave before the invasion. John and the other Americans here have nothing to do with the politics of this situation. They're good people.

Much as I suspected, the promise to return the radio equipment handed in last week has come to nought. Dad and I went to the Post Office today clutching the receipt they gave us and asking for the return of our 2-metre set. We received nothing but blank looks. To be fair, the officials have probably not been given any guidance. We don't expect to see the transceiver again.

Tuesday, 13 April

I tuned into the BBC at midnight last night for more news of deadlocked negotiations. After about twelve hours of talks in London, Haig was asked if there had been any progress.

'None at all,' he replied.

The Argentines have said that they will accept the Peruvians' proposal for a 72-hour truce. Well, they would, wouldn't they? They've achieved what they want and could do with more time to reinforce, so why not have a truce? London won't accept it.

I just missed Padre Bagnall [the Anglican chaplain of Christ Church Cathedral] when I dropped by the Goose this morning. That's normally a good thing, but apparently he was up in arms about Bishop Cutts' recent remarks from BA. The padre had been telling Des, who is a member of the Church Council, that Cutts 'has gone native and wants Islanders to accept Argentine rule.' I've never heard him being quoted as saying that, but maybe I missed it. Cutts has, however, always been seen as too pro-Argentine here.

Later in the day, Padre Bagnall and the Church Council officially let it be known that they have formally disassociated themselves from their bishop. This is powerful stuff for the ladies and gents of the Church Council. Usually, they spend their time nattering about nothing more serious than the annual bazaar. I always thought that one day the indomitable Peggy Halliday would strut the world stage. Al Haig, be afraid.

There is to be a special meeting of both Houses of Parliament tomorrow, and they will want to know exactly what has been discussed with Haig. We'd like to know too.

The Falklands continue to make big headlines in the papers, according to WS, but perhaps we are slipping a little. Israel's possible military activities around Lebanon are stealing some thunder, and I wonder if they are manoeuvring while much of the world's attention is directed at the South Atlantic.

It's subtle, but I wonder if I'm picking up shades of the old British ambivalence to Islanders in current government statements. Our views are being described as 'important, paramount and dominant', but there are rarely, if ever, references to our 'wishes' being sacrosanct.

Rosemary [King] shared a rumour with me. She heard yesterday that another Argentine body had washed up somewhere in Stanley Harbour. She didn't see it and it's not clear who did. Could be true, though, and if so, the poor guy might be another casualty of the invasion.

Two small Argentine fast gunboats arrived in Stanley today. They are about 50ft long and painted white, which makes me think that they are coastguard vessels in normal life. Seen through the binoculars from the Rowan House crow's nest, each seems to be armed with a single heavy machine gun or cannon. They must have run the blockade.

WS reports that Haig has broken off his negotiations and returned to Washington, supposedly to consult with Reagan. Before boarding his plane he said the situation is increasingly grave and time is running out. He has apparently left both BA and London with some suggestions to mull over. Buenos Aires issues a petulant-sounding statement, describing the UK as 'inflexible'. That's a pot-kettle statement if ever I heard one.

LADE operated an almost normal passenger flight out of Stanley this morning. Dick Baker and his family were on the flight. A few Islanders also seized what might be the last chance to get out. I don't blame them for leaving. It's becoming frightening here, to say the least. Bill Luxton and his family were shipped out on the same flight. Their deportation is chilling. The Argentines claim to respect Islanders but they'll get rid of us if they want to. If I was Bill Luxton, I would be very worried for my safety.

I heard from my source at the Goose that the seven Marines who evaded capture on 2 April were eventually captured at Long Island and were flown out today or yesterday. They are now in Comodoro Rivadavia and will be flown on to Montevideo, where they'll be handed over to neutral diplomats. The whereabouts of the twenty-two Marines who inflicted a bloody nose on the Argentine Navy in South Georgia is, however, still unknown. I still think they're on the *Bahia Buen Suceso* at the jetty.

Wednesday, 14 April

I spent a while with Pete, Rosemary and Robert last evening at Church House. We listened to the radio, chatted and drank a bit too much. Great company. Pete and I discussed what to do with our darkroom in the loft of Church House. We decided to leave it for the time being and I'll develop some of the photos that

I took on 2 April soon. But we had probably better dismantle it if the situation gets worse.

Earlier today, Robert saw one of the troops in the school next door, which they seem to be using as an HQ, set fire to a tent. He was running around waving his hands and shouting for a fire extinguisher. That doesn't sound particularly funny here, but as Robert acted it out, it was hilarious.

More seriously, we spoke about rumours of Argentine conscripts being treated very roughly, perhaps even shot, for trivial offences, including asking for food from locals. I know that the Argentine government doesn't put much value on the lives of its own people, but I really don't want to believe they would be treated so badly.

Leaving Church House in the dark, I felt a bit vulnerable. There is no real threat from British action yet, but Argentine soldiers might well have itchy trigger fingers. Walking up the drive to John Street I noticed a fully manned machine gun that I had not spotted earlier by the west entrance to the school. It may only be manned at night. I should have turned right towards Rowan House, but instead I turned left and walked along to the other entrance to the school with Robert. Lo and behold, there was another manned machine-gun nest.

Robert and I then headed up Philomel Hill and passed an eight-man foot patrol, heavily armed and looking nervous. We passed each other silently and I turned right along Fitzroy Road. Robert peeled off to his house, and a few minutes later I was closing the door of Rowan House and glad to be doing so.

I missed a thrilling Falklands milestone last night. TV was broadcast here for the first time. The propaganda-riddled news was broadcast simultaneously on radio and TV. I'm told that, according to that first transmission, there will be programmes every night now between 7.00 and 9.00pm. It has also been announced that a shipment of TV sets has been received from BA and these are now available to buy on hire-purchase. I can't see them being particularly popular as the news broadcasts will not be reliable. I expect the service is designed mainly for the troops.

The *Isla de los Estados* berthed alongside the *Bahia Buen Suceso* late yesterday evening. She can't have got to the mainland and retuned in such a short time, so I think she must be shuttling men, ammunition and supplies around the Islands. If there are British submarines now enforcing the exclusion zone, she'd be a big, slow target for them.

Troops broke into the Youth Club today but left quickly, after we complained to the military police. I really don't know how we got away with it. I think that will change if the situation gets more serious.

One of the girls at the Goose overheard a couple of Argentine officers indicating that they have 15,000 troops here. That's more than I thought. The officers commented favourably on their troops' behaviour.

'Imagine the damage that 15,000 American or British troops would cause,' he said. Yeah, but they are generally not worried about being shot by their own officers.

The third emergency debate of this crisis took place in the Commons today, and Thatcher addressed it.

'The eyes of the world are now on the Falklands,' she said. 'Whenever blatant aggression occurs, it must be overcome.'

The BBC described the PM as 'fairly restrained', but the precondition for an Argentine withdrawal of forces is not 'restrained' at all. In fact, I'd say it is a clear threat.

Michael Foot [Leader of the Opposition] said that he supports sending the Task Force. In fact, there seems to be solidarity among the parties, although some seem more enthusiastic than others about military action.

Another sixteen Harrier jet fighters are to join the Task Force, and another assault ship, HMS *Intrepid*, is also sailing south. She is carrying Marines and landing craft and has a large helicopter deck. Perfect for the job, if it comes to it.

Dick Baker evidently made it safely to Montevideo. He's been talking to the press by phone from there. He says, rightly, that local civil servants have been able to keep vital services going. He also described the behaviour of the Argentines here as 'correct', which is, I think, a reasonably restrained description, although the arrest and deportation of Bill Luxton and his family almost certainly goes against the Geneva Convention regarding the treatment of people in occupied territories. But it could be a lot worse.

Perhaps Bloomer-Reeve's senior position enables him to moderate behaviour, but how long will that restraint last? There is an ominous and threatening atmosphere here, and that became obvious to me last night on the way home from Pete and Rosemary's.

This afternoon, I went to the Secretariat and asked to see Bloomer-Reeve. I wanted to talk to him about resuming publication of *Penguin News*. He was welcoming enough. He said he'd heard that Mum and Dad had come back. They'd been friends, of course, back in what I guess what we must now call the 'good old days'. He looked a bit puzzled that they had come back from the safety of Uruguay, as well he might.

Regarding *PN*, he told me straight that publishing would be 'a bad idea'. He did not seem to want to be more specific than that, but he looked me very seriously straight in the eye when he said it. I must assume he meant they would want to censor it, and if I stepped out of line I could expect trouble.

I'm still used to the affable old Bloomer-Reeve of a few years ago, rather than this man in green combats. So I pushed back a bit, saying that if they want life to return to normal here, then allowing my little newspaper to be published would be a good start. I asked if he could arrange interviews for me with some of the senior Argentine military representatives, including General Menendez. He sighed and agreed, though clearly reluctantly. He said he'd try to set up an interview with Menendez for 12.30pm next Monday at Government House, five days from now.

BBC WS early this evening is reporting a government spokesman saying that if the Argentines violate the 200-mile blockade it will be a clear sign that they have given up on negotiations.

'They will know what to expect,' he added.

Torpedoes, I assume.

Chapter 8

Fuel Runs Low

(15–19 April)

Thursday, 15 April

The two small patrol boats spent yesterday patrolling the harbour, continuing after dark, when they often swept the water and coast with their searchlights. They must be looking for covert landings by the SAS or the SBS. It seems too early for that to be a real possibility, though.

Lewis Clifton told me he has it on good authority (though he didn't want to reveal his source) that soldiers searching houses a few days ago were ordered to shoot civilians and the (few remaining) local police officers if they tried to escape. We agreed that this must refer specifically to a raid on the home of Peter and Emily Short, who are ham radio operators. I heard separately that they were given a very hard time by the officer in charge of intelligence based at the police station. He is a Major Patricio Dowling, and he is clearly trying to instil fear into us. The Shorts have now left town.

I tuned into the BBC at lunchtime today. Reception was very bad but just about intelligible. Haig is not yet giving up his diplomacy, although he described the situation as 'exceptionally dangerous'. He is on his way back to BA now. Galtieri has said Argentina will not renounce its claim to sovereignty. That's OK; no one would expect them to, and if that is his only requirement for saving face, then this might be a glimmer of hope.

There are reports that the Argentine Navy may be preparing to put to sea. However, it is unlikely that they would enter the 200-mile exclusion zone, knowing that Royal Navy submarines may be lurking. They may not be in the area yet, but who would take the chance?

Latin American solidarity seems to be holding, even though most South Americans believe the Argentines are too big for their boots. Venezuela has condemned British plans to recover the Islands.

The Russians are not coming out in full political support of the Argentines although it's clear that they favour them. They seem content to feed intelligence to BA and watch a major NATO member divert its assets to the other side of the world.

The papers report a gung-ho attitude in Parliament. However, gung-honess is getting a bit thin on the ground in Stanley. I think most people here are getting very worried. At home, Mum seems to be able to keep herself busy with domestic things, but Dad is brooding. A lot of people have packed their bags and left for the farms, where they think they will be safer (will they?).

Many of those I've spoken to who are remaining in Stanley would like there to be an evacuation of civilians. This was, of course, requested by those senior civil servants who met in secret at the hospital and smuggled the message to London. But it's clear that this is not being considered in London.

Last night, I spent a few hours at Church House, drinking and chatting with Pete, Rosemary and Dave Colville. Dave, Pete and I decided to walk up the drive to John Street and try to talk to the young troops manning the machine-gun nest there. We offered them some cigarettes and chocolate, partly because it was damned cold, with a brisk south-easterly blowing, and we genuinely felt a bit sorry for them, but also because they might share some interesting information with us. No chance. They were extremely nervous, although they took the fags and chocolates. They told us to keep on moving and not to talk to them, explaining very quickly that they could be punished for talking to locals.

There are persistent rumours that Argentine officers are applying extreme discipline to ordinary troops, many of whom are very young conscripts. It's rumoured those two soldiers were shot for breaking some relatively minor regulation. They may have been looting. I can see that morale is already bad among the conscripts, and there are reports of rampant diarrhoea and foot problems from the constant damp. If the rumours are true, then the Argentine high command is as stupid as it is cruel.

Comparing notes with Pete, Rosie and Dave, it seems that the Marines and BAS [British Antarctic Survey] civilians captured at South Georgia were flown out from Stanley around midnight the day before yesterday. Trucks were seen around the East Jetty at that time, and since then there have been no soldiers and dogs in the area.

Remarkably, some more mail arrived from the UK today. It was just a few bags but good for morale. Nothing much of interest arrived for us. The parents were hoping to hear from [my brother] Michael, but it could well be that any letter from him is still sitting in some Argentine post office.

The *Isla de los Estados* left the East Jetty some time last night or in the very early hours of today. Destination unknown, but almost certainly delivering military supplies around the Islands. The crew will be nervous, knowing that they are blockade-busting.

There was an accident at Stanley Airport yesterday. I suppose it was inevitable that a plane would bite the dust eventually. A LADE F28 (I've probably travelled on that plane several times) overshot the runway when landing and its undercarriage collapsed. No talk of casualties.

The King girls and I checked on the Youth Club today and found that all the sweets, drinks, the dartboard and a number of other things had been stolen. We walked over to the police station in high dudgeon and an MP spoke to us. He was tetchy, and I think we may have to watch how we behave regarding the Youth Club from now on. However, he took notes of what had been stolen. I suspect he screwed up the paper and binned it the moment we left. We shouldn't push our luck for a few boxes of Mars Bars and some cans of Coke.

This afternoon, I notice several groups of troops putting new telephone cables up around town. These look like they will link positions around the perimeter of town with their HQs in the gym, the Town Hall and the schools.

Harold Briley is reporting on WS this evening that General Menendez has acknowledged difficulties in integrating Islanders into the Argentine system. In other words, we are not cooperating. I'm delighted that he noticed. He particularly mentioned the difficulties caused by teachers in Stanley refusing to work. This is odd, as even if they had agreed to work, both schools have been taken over by troops, and all the children from the camp have returned to their farms. The senior school even has machine guns at both entrances. If that isn't a disincentive to go to school, I don't know what is.

Most of the teachers on contract from the UK have now returned to the UK. I understand, though, that Phil Middleton is continuing quietly with classes at his house for some of the children working towards O-levels.

Just before I hit the sack at midnight, WS reported that some Argentine warships have put to sea, and the Navy in BA has issued a communiqué warning shipping in the area that they may take 'defensive action'.

An opinion poll in the UK suggests that 80 per cent of Brits approve of the government's action since the invasion, 50 per cent believe that Argentine ships should be sunk if necessary and 66 per cent believe that British troops should stage a counter-invasion if necessary. It seems that the government has solid support and has recovered from the humiliation of the invasion. Thatcher is sleeping more easily in her bed, I would think.

Friday, 16 April

I couldn't sleep, so tuned into WS again about 2.00am. Ted Needham, the chief executive of the FIC [Falkland Islands Company] in London, says that he is maintaining contact with his staff here (how?). The company will, he said, 'continue to support the Islanders'. That's more than a bit rich. The FIC has never 'supported the Islanders'. Their whole reason in being is to suck money from the Islands for the shareholders in London, while spending as little as possible here.

Ronnie Lamb [the police chief who was deported with Rex Hunt on the day of the invasion] has appeared in one or two of today's papers wearing a kilt and holding up a Union Jack. I hope that's his fifteen minutes done.

The papers are also reporting disappointment that Washington has not come out in total support of Britain. That might be counter-productive, though, while Haig is still flying up and down the Atlantic like a man possessed. I think any time now he'll have a total breakdown and say, 'To hell with the lot of you. Take lumps out of each other if you want. Don't call me.'

According to some newspapers, there is a rumour that British diplomats may have been warned about the risk of invasion by Argentine delegates to the New York talks. There may also have been an offer to buy the Islands outright. I wouldn't rule any of this out.

I heard this morning that both MV *Monsunen* [the inter-island ship operated by the Falkland Islands Company] and [the small government ship] *Forrest* have been requisitioned by the Argentine Navy.

Mum and Dad opened the shop for just a few hours. I can't see the point, but it's their decision. Stanley's population, and therefore the pool of customers, gets smaller every day. But I suppose there is some logic in checking out the building every day and letting the Argentines think it is occupied. Furthermore, I think Mum needs to keep active.

I was with them at the shop for a little while, and the interpreter from Government House came in. He is a harmless young guy doing his military service who comes from the Welsh community in Patagonia. He was gloomy and said that (to use his phrase), 'There are many long faces among the military here.' He said he is worried and just wants to go home. He said that a crowd of Anglo-Argentines are being flown in soon, led by the much-despised Bishop Cutts. They will, he said, be trying to convince us to accept Argentine rule.

'By the way,' he said. 'It's not so bad. We Welsh settled there, and no one bothers us.'

I heard today that the two FIGAS [Government Air Service] mechanics, both seconded from the RAF, conveyed useful intelligence to London when they were thrown out. They gave the MoD details of Stanley Airport and confirmed the Argentines are not trying to enlarge the runway to accommodate fast attack aircraft.

At about 2.30 this afternoon, two Canberra bombers (British made and sold to the Argentines) flew low over Stanley. They were surprisingly quiet. They didn't land; too big for our airport, I'm sure. Two Mirage jets flew over very noisily later in the afternoon.

I thought earlier that these flyovers were demonstrations for our benefit, and originally they may have been. But now, as the likelihood of a shooting war increases, I think the pilots are familiarizing themselves with the terrain over the Islands.

A few days ago, it was announced over 'Radio Islas Malvinas' that petrol, diesel and kerosene are being rationed. Drivers can only buy 10 litres of petrol a week, which is hardly anything, and a little more diesel. Dad is hardly using his Land Rover, but we will take it to the YPF station once a week and top up its tanks, just in case we need to do a runner from Stanley.[1]

This afternoon, I drove the Daihatsu down to the station for my petrol ration. There are machine-gun nests (real, not simulated) within the YPF tank farm and on the north side of the front road, opposite the cemetery. The weapons seem to be mainly trained out over the harbour. Trenches have also been dug around the YPF plant, and there is at least one real anti-aircraft gun and a couple of dummy guns. They must assume the YPF plant will be a prime target if it all kicks off.

On the way back from the petrol station, I headed up Snake Street and, pretty much on a whim, I turned left through the Common Gate instead of right, back into town. This took me on to the Airport Road. I thought I'd waste a bit of my precious petrol driving to the east, just to see how far I could get. No camera today, so I wasn't too worried about getting into trouble. I managed to get about two miles down the road, almost to Rookery Bay. Then I was stopped at a roadblock, questioned and told to get back to Stanley, pronto. The troops were not at all friendly and their weapons were at the ready.

There was a lot of Argentine traffic on the Airport Road, all driving on the right, of course, so I had to do the same. There's a large concentration of troops by the Common Gate, and, on the west side of the gate, are some defensive trenches and a well-concealed anti-aircraft gun.

Tonight, the BBC reported that Simon Winchester of the *Sunday Times* has been arrested for alleged spying in Ushuaia. The two guys from the *Observer* were also arrested. I'm afraid the Argentines may be very rough on them. I wonder if Michael will ever get the letter I gave Simon on the day he left Stanley, which seems an age ago now.

Isla de los Estados steamed back into Stanley late today. She's a big target, so if I was the skipper I'd being staying as close to the coast as possible and only steaming at night.

Saturday, 17 April

A quiet morning following a decent sleep, which is rare these days. The 'news' from Radio Islas Malvinas revealed that an Argentine soldier lost his foot yesterday when he stood on an anti-personnel mine. They claim that this was planted by the Royal Marines, but I am sure beyond any doubt that the Marines did not have mines in their armoury. However, I do believe that the Argentines themselves will be planting minefields, as they are a cheap and easy way of defending their positions.

The radio news warned civilians that they should stay away from 'areas where there may be mines'. And these areas are where exactly? Aren't minefields supposed to be clearly marked?

People at the hospital are saying that about fifty soldiers were flown back to Argentina the day before yesterday suffering from dysentery and similar problems. Some were said to be 'touch and go'.

Patrick [Watts] called me this morning from the radio station. He asked me if I would resume presenting 'Saturday Choice' [a pop music programme]. I think he wants to keep a local influence over it as much as possible, and there is some sense to that. I thought about it for a minute and then said yes. It won't be supporting their propaganda work; I enjoy it, and the programme might cheer people up a little. Also, the exposure to what's going on among the Argentines at the station will be interesting.

I duly went to the station this evening. The programme was a doddle, as ever. No new records to introduce, of course, but that didn't matter. I did pick up some interesting information from the Argentines who were in and out, drinking coffee and smoking their bloody awful Jockey Club cigarettes. It's clear that they are very concerned that a resistance movement is being formed. I've not heard anyone on our side suggest that this is happening, but we are only two weeks into the occupation. If they continue to believe this, however, I think we can expect military rule to get harsher.

I also picked up that one soldier has certainly died and the mine incident in which a soldier lost a foot is true.

It's been a comparatively quiet day. Planes still going in and out of the airport, but less frequently than they were.

Sunday, 18 April

Anti-aircraft guns in and around Stanley were tested early this afternoon. There was no warning, and the cacophony was deafening and terrifying. They've located a double-barrelled AA gun just 75 yards or so from our house, in the large garden of a house that LADE was renting before the invasion. It's now packed with Air Force personnel.

After this drama, and still a little shaken, I walked down to see Peter and Rosemary at Church House. They gave me their usual welcome with a cup of coffee. But when we sat down, Pete told me that a squad of soldiers had visited Church House yesterday, led by Major Dowling, who is now becoming feared around Stanley. This is worrying. Peter saw them coming, dashed upstairs to the loft, where we have our darkroom, and hid some of the more dangerous negatives and prints that we had left lying around. Dowling insisted on going up to the loft and asked a lot of questions. Pete said he knows that the equipment is mine. Safe to say, I think, that we are now both noted in Dowling's files.

We discussed this and agreed that as they now know we have a darkroom, it might be best if I approach Bloomer-Reeve and point out that we are keen amateurs and would like to have the green light to take photos for use at some point in *Penguin News*. We don't think they'll grant that, and we will look naive, but if we are open about it, they may be less inclined to think we are spying.[2]

I felt a bit down this evening, and the mood at home was bleak. I'm still convinced that the parents made the wrong decision when they returned, and I am starting wonder if they realize this. We are not discussing it, though. Things are still a bit icy.

I don't know how I feel about the outlook for the next few weeks. I am worried, sometimes scared, often depressed and occasionally strangely excited by what is going on and what may be about to happen. There is even a small part of me which would be disappointed if Haig pulls a rabbit out of his hat and secures an agreement whereby the Argentines withdraw and we return to colonial life. There may be some logic to that: if there is a diplomatic agreement, it is unlikely to be one that gives us more rights than we had before.

Monday, 19 April

I made an early morning visit to the Post Office in the hope that there might be mail. No joy, but I did meet a few people for a chat. Word is trickling in from the West that Fox Bay East is chock-a-block with Argentines. This may well be their major base on West Falkland, as there is a reasonable harbour there. But contrary to earlier rumours, there is no sign that an airstrip capable of accepting medium-sized planes is being built there or anywhere on the West. Most of the locals have left the settlement, except for Richard and Grizelda Cockwell.

I forgot to mention last night that, according to 'Calling the Falklands', a special service was held at St Paul's Cathedral yesterday. I must not, *really I must not*, be cynical, but in a special message to us, the Archbishop of Canterbury, whose voice sounds unfortunately like that of Lord Haw Haw, reassured us that he is thinking of us and is in touch with Padre Harry Bagnall in Stanley. Firstly, I can't imagine how he's remaining in any kind of regular contact with Harry Bagnall, unless he's got a divine telex machine; and secondly, does the Bish really think that we gather around a priest who is lucky to have twenty people sitting in the pews each Sunday?

This kind of thing just doesn't wash with me. For years no one in the UK knew anything about Falkland Islanders and cared about us even less. Now they are scrambling to be our best friends.

This snippet from CTF is interesting, though. Some of the RAF's Vulcan bombers, which were designed to carry nuclear weapons, are being fitted with conventional bombs. I wonder what they are going to do with them if it comes to it. They are being tested in Scotland and it has not been ruled out that they will be used 'outside the NATO area'. That means they will soon be flying south.

A few people are actually returning to Stanley from the camp. Not many, but the Goss, Keenleyside and Harris families have returned after a week or so at Port Harriet House. I spoke to Chris Harris, who said that on the way back to town they saw a lot of bodies stacked alongside the road between Ponies Pass and Stanley. If this is true, it's not clear what they might have died from, but exposure is quite possible. So far, the autumn weather has not been as bad as it might be, but still the nights are very cold. I certainly wouldn't want to be manning foxholes or bunkers in these conditions.

The Clarke family [there were several Clarke families in the Falklands, and I don't recall exactly who I spoke to] have returned from Goose Green, and they told me that there are a huge number of troops there. They appear to be digging in around the settlement and are using the airstrip. Anti-aircraft guns have been flown in by helicopter.

It seems to me that the family was lucky to get out, as the Argentines have introduced a curfew for locals. Everyone must be in their houses by sundown and lights must be out by 11.00pm, which is presumably when the generators are turned off. They are not allowed to get together in the club. This all sounds very grim. Never mind; the Archbishop of Canterbury will be thinking of them.

Coincidently, local radio reported that Menendez visited Goose Green and Fox Bay East yesterday. He is reported to have met with the locals at both places (there are hardly any at Fox Bay East, of course). He described the visits as 'fruitful'.

It was also announced today that Stanley's water supply will be rationed. This will be done by the simple expedient of turning it off to some parts of town at night. I don't know if we will be warned when our part of town will be affected. I suppose that means we will now have to keep buckets and baths full of water.

I spoke today to Charlie Coutts, one of the guys working at the water filtration plant, and he said that the situation is this serious because they are supplying water to over 3,000 troops as well as locals. Pre-invasion, the system supplied only about 1,400 people, so demand is about three times what it was. This situation can only get worse.

Anna at the Goose [who continued to go to work at the Treasury] said that she, Tracy [Peck] and Robert [King] had a quiet day at the Treasury and filled in their time by going through the [Savings Bank] ledgers trying to work out how many people have left Stanley. They reckon that between 470 and 480 people are still in town. A fairly small number flew out of Stanley and the rest have scattered around the farms. The majority will be on East Falkland.

Some remaining teachers are leaving by LADE tomorrow. One told me that he and his wife will request financial assistance from the embassy in Montevideo to get back to the UK and repay it later.

Galtieri is on the move, too. Local radio news this evening reported that he left for Washington this afternoon, where he will put a peace proposal to the US and Britain. He could surely have done this through Haig, but perhaps he wants to top up on duty-free Scotch.

Chapter 9

A Stormy Meeting

(20–24 April)

Tuesday, 20 April

WS News very early hours of this morning: the naval Task Force is now said to number sixty ships. This is just incredible. They have virtually every available warship heading south, including two carriers, then ships commandeered from the merchant navy. Defence analysts are saying that the first of the ships should be in the area of the Falklands and South Georgia by Thursday or Friday, just two or three days from now.

London is saying that at first sight the proposals from BA, via Haig, 'do not satisfy requirements'. The plan is said to involve dual British and Argentine government, with both flags flying. The Islanders would have a role in government. There would be a joint police force, and long-term resolution of the sovereignty issue would be discussed under UN auspices. What intolerable political porridge that would be.

This morning, I went to the Secretariat to meet Bloomer-Reeve. This was pre-arranged, and he knew I wanted to see if they can guarantee my freedom to publish *Penguin News* in some form without censorship. If so, I want interviews with General Menendez and other senior military men. Bloomer-Reeve wasn't there, so no meeting. I'm not going to produce a paper that is controlled by them. Better to have nothing at all.

As well as the teachers, several local people left on the LADE plane this morning. I think they are smarter than we are. Anyway, the population of Stanley has just dropped by another thirty or so. Today's flight will be the last to take civilians out of the Islands. When the Royal Navy is in the area, which must be soon, flights in and out of Stanley will be very dangerous. I wouldn't fancy looking out of the window of an F28 and seeing a Harrier pilot tipping his hat to me.

I hear that as many as four Argentine doctors may now be working at the hospital, presumably cooperating with Drs Bleaney, Elphenstone and Haynes.

Tomorrow is the Queen's birthday, and Robert told me that most of the civil servants still going into their offices intended to take the day off as a protest against Argentine rule. That's clever.

David Phillips is supposed to be the source of a rumour that three soldiers died of exposure last night on Mount William. It sounds completely feasible.

Troops are now digging trenches at the west end of Victory Green, right up by the Youth Club. In fact, it looks like they are even tunnelling under the foundations, which makes sense, as the concrete wall will give them shelter. Our feeling is that protesting against this would be more serious than complaining about stolen tins of Coke and Mars Bars. The military police and intelligence unit at the police station is starting to get a nasty reputation, mainly thanks to Major Patricio Dowling. We'll have to let it go.

Mum prepared a nice dinner tonight. Conversation is still difficult. They opened the shop for an hour or two, and a few customers came by. I suppose trying to create a sense of normality is good for Mum and Dad and the customers. We listened to 'Calling the Falklands', with its increasingly anguished messages from families in the UK, its news summaries and interviews. WS is looking after us well.

One of those interviewed tonight was the commander of the Marines garrison on South Georgia when the Argentines attacked. He's 22-year-old Lieutenant Keith Mills. He said the Argentines fired first, but after that the Marines peppered an incoming helicopter with small arms. It seemed to carry on flying with smoke pouring from it, but then crash-landed. A corvette then approached, and the Marines stuck an anti-tank rocket into it, forcing it to turn around. The ship then started shelling the Marines from a safe distance.

The officer estimated that they fought for about two hours before surrendering. He didn't know how many men might have been killed or injured in the helicopter or on the ship.

Clearly concerned about sounding balanced, WS said the Argentines' claim the Marines had said there would be no resistance, and both the helicopter and the ship were therefore ambushed. That, I would say, is complete rubbish. Anyway, if you play with fire you are going to get burned.

Thatcher has now had time to consider Haig's ideas. She says the proposals are deficient in several ways, not least because 'there is no provision for Islanders to determine their own destiny'. What a turnaround! Is this really the same government that before 2 April showed absolutely no regard for our self-determination?

Clocks would normally go back one hour at midnight tonight, but it's been decreed that this will not happen. They obviously want the Islands and the mainland to be on the same time.

Wednesday, 21 April

I couldn't sleep so at about 4.00am I tuned into the BBC to see what the papers are saying. The *Daily Mirror* claims that ships could be in a position for an assault on South Georgia by tomorrow.

The Task Force had its first contact with the Argentine Air Force today. A long-range Boeing 707, apparently on a reconnaissance mission, approached to within 12 miles of some ships. A Harrier was sent up to intercept the 707 but had orders not to shoot it down. The 707 flew away again after a while, but it does mean BA now has a clear idea of where the lead ships are.

The Russians continue to tinker in the margins. They have apparently sent up two special satellites which will fly over the Falklands area every 24 hours or so. I heard yesterday that a Russian ship called in at Port William. What was that all about?

Late this morning, I saw smoke billowing from Port William. Through binoculars from the top floor of Rowan House I saw Argentine planes bombing the two tussac islands in Port William.[1] The planes appeared to be their small prop-driven ground-attack planes called Pucaras. The smoke is blacker than one would expect from burning vegetation. I assume they are testing their weapons or giving their pilots some bombing practice. Whatever the reason, it's a stupid bloody thing to do. The islands are home to thousands of birds and seals. I hope most managed to escape.

Having had a look to the east of Stanley earlier this week, today I took the Daihatsu up towards the west. There was little military activity until I reached the Beaver Hangar. Lots of troops were milling around there. I continued a bit further to the west, but by Felton Stream I was running into more troops than felt comfortable and I was getting some unfriendly looks. So I turned around rather than risk meeting a hostile group. However, from that point I could see clearly as far as Moody Brook and the old Marines' barracks. I counted ten helicopters at Moody Brook. Another flew low over me. So that means that there are at least eleven choppers based there. They look like Bell Hueys.

'Calling the Falklands' this evening reported that [Foreign Secretary] Francis Pym is maintaining the diplomatic pressure by saying that the UK will not exclude the possibility of military action at any stage. This stance is not necessarily reflected in Parliament, where there seems to be growing recognition that a shooting war would be a tragedy.

Depressing news via local radio this evening. They have decreed that Port Stanley is now renamed 'Puerto Argentino'. Well, if that gives them a nice warm feeling, fine. But our colourful little capital will always be Stanley to us.

In the absence of trustworthy local news, rumours are getting a grip. This afternoon I heard a disturbing one. 'Someone' (it's nearly always 'someone', who heard from 'someone') saw one or more soldiers being executed by firing squad near Sapper Hill recently. I think it's unlikely to be true. I can accept that the Argentine officers treat their conscripts badly, in fact we *know* they do. However, it's hard to see them behaving as appallingly as that. But it was a nasty lingering thought in my mind as I tried to get some sleep.

Thursday, 22 April

General Galtieri is to visit Stanley today. As well he might. He's got his country, the UK and us into this mess, so perhaps he should inspect his handiwork.

We have been nudged out of the BBC headlines by Israel's aggressive behaviour against Lebanon. The Israelis must think that with attention directed towards us, it's a good time for them to even scores in their part of the world. Sorry, Lebanon.

According to the WS correspondent on HMS *Hermes*, the carrier should be in a position to launch air attacks by Friday. That's tomorrow. Oh dear. What's the betting Stanley Airport is going to get it first? The reporter said *Hermes* and the ships with her will soon be on 'permanent defensive alert'. But it's unlikely that they will get within range of Argentine fighters and bombers operating from the coast. They'll be looking out for submarines, though, as the Argentines have a couple of good conventional subs.

Dave Colville[2] is leaving by air today. I thought there would be no more flights available for civilians. I saw him briefly this morning, intending to ask him what he thought about resuming publication of the *Times* and *Penguin News*. He cut me short and he said that, as he's not a local, the Argentines are shipping him out. He'll get a free passage (very nice of them) to BA, and then he has to make his own way to Uruguay and on to UK. I assume the embassy in Montevideo will help him. I wished Dave luck. I'll miss him.

Then I tried to see Bloomer-Reeve again. I told the guard on the door of the Secretariat why I was there and surprisingly, he let me in. I went up to Bloomer-Reeves' office, where Dick Baker had been until not that long ago. BR still looks quite smart in his pressed uniform, but he is by no means as affable as he was a week or so ago. Frankly I'm surprised he met me. I again asked for the interviews with Menendez and others, and again he said he would arrange them. So I'm now supposed to see Menendez at Government House next Monday at 11.00am.

'But don't be foolish enough to take any more photos,' Bloomer-Reeve added quickly. 'It's been noticed.'

I asked him if this is because of 'military secrets', and he said, 'No, we have no secrets.' Rather, he claimed, seeing a camera may undermine the morale of troops, and they might not take kindly to it.

He told me that tomorrow he'll be meeting with a representative group of local people, at his invitation. He said he wants to find out about the issues that most concern them and to see how he may be able to help them. I think Bloomer-Reeve is genuine in this. He lived here in happier times and still has friends here, which helps. I think it's very fortunate for us that he is Menendez's right-hand man.

Later in the day: absolutely no sign of Galtieri, although I believe he did visit. But why would he want to see us anyway? We're hardly going to be throwing rose petals in front of his car. Presumably, he met with Menendez and other senior commanders to give them last orders and check on their preparedness for British attack. I hope he spoke with some of the ordinary soldiers. If he did, then I think he'll know they are not ready, and never will be.

Late this evening, US radio said that during his visit Galtieri told soldiers to 'fight to the last man if the British attack'. You'd better get them some good food and warmer clothing, then, Sr Presidente.

The large freighter that's clearly visible in Port William from our upstairs front windows must be Argentine, and she must have run the blockade. The smaller *Isla de los Estados* is shuttling containers between the big ship and the East Jetty. *Bahia Buen Suceso* is still tied up there and looks like she's in the way. I wonder why they don't move her. Broken down?

There's been an increase in flights in and out of the airport today. When I woke up this morning and trained the binoculars on the airport I could see a Boeing 737 parked up. That type is definitely too big for the runway. I wonder if it brought Galtieri in?

This evening, local radio announced that LADE hopes to operate the Air Service's [Britten Norman] Islander aircraft around the islands, carrying mail, freight and passengers. They also hope to have the two [De Havilland] Beavers [both float planes] in the air again soon. At times like this they do seem to have a genuine wish to return life here to something like normality again.

About a hundred Sony colour TVs have been delivered to Stanley, presumably by the big ship in Port William. They are being sold for just £110 and are available from the Post Office. I wonder how many locals will want them. Again, though, it's a sign that they are trying to normalize the situation.

Mum and Dad are still making supreme efforts to go on with life as normal, spending at least a few hours most days opening the shop, even though there are fewer customers than ever in Stanley, no orders are coming through from the farms and there would be no way of getting goods to camp customers anyway.

I really don't feel that Mum fully appreciates the gravity of all this. Dad does, and he's now helping me by scribbling notes on bits of paper or in the margin of this journal. I think it's important that he's busy and doesn't just sit around dwelling on things.

I spent some time this evening reinforcing the bunker in the garage. From the outside it now resembles nothing more than an untidy heap of bags of coal, pallets and bits of timber. There is a little entrance to crawl in, and I'm quietly proud of it. But I hope to God we don't have to use it.

Friday, 23 April

Last night, local radio broadcast details of civil defence plans for Stanley. British air raids are considered to be a real possibility, and if possible, the public will be warned of impending raids over the radio. At the same time, hospital and Fire Service staff will be told to report for duty. A group of civilians has drawn up a list of buildings which can be used as shelters, and members of this group will be going from house to house with this information.

I had the usual trouble sleeping last night. Perhaps I was upset by the talk of air raids. I tuned into WS and it seems that at about midday today the Task Force will go to an advanced state of alert. I don't know exactly what that means, but presumably they may shoot first and ask questions later. I would think this also means that the potential for mistakes is increased, meaning we could fall into all-out war before diplomacy is given every chance.

Analysts in BA and London are suggesting that the Task Force may almost be ready to have a bash at South Georgia. Ships have apparently been seen (not sure by whom) only 50 miles or so from the island. Recapturing it would be relatively easy and a feather in the UK's cap. It would also show BA that the Task Force can hit hard.

Galtieri has responded to this speculation by saying that South Georgia will be defended in the same way as the Falklands. But what really matters is the military balance, and there can't be many troops on South Georgia. It is way out of range of the Argentine Air Force, and their ships don't seem to be on the high seas – except, perhaps, their submarines. So I think it would be relatively easy to retake South Georgia, although that familiar Falklands phrase 'weather permitting' might be very relevant here.

Saturday, 24 April

Listened to WS news over breakfast. The MoD is denying that troops have already landed on South Georgia, but they are not denying that their ships are very near the island. Francis Pym is on his way back to London from Washington and few details are being released about his talks there. I suspect he was concentrating less on trying to secure a diplomatic deal with BA and more on persuading the Americans to come down clearly on the side of the UK.

At 1.00pm today we received bad news. A helicopter from HMS *Hermes* has crashed in the sea. The pilot has been rescued, but others who were on board are missing.

Word is going around town that local radio will make an important announcement at 3.00pm today. This could be anything; more Argentine propaganda perhaps, or an edict about tightened security measures that apply to civilians. My money is on the latter.

Barbara, Alison and I opened the Youth Club today for the first time since the invasion. It was open for just one and a half hours in the early afternoon. The evenings are drawing in and no one really wants to be out after dark, but during daylight hours it is probably safe enough. Nevertheless, this is pushing our luck about as far as we can. Of course, there are not as many kids in town as there used to be, but those who came to the club seemed to enjoy it.

To be on the safe side, we told the military police in advance that we were opening the club. They were not happy but eventually agreed, providing we gave them a list of everyone who was in the club, kids and adults alike. And no one was allowed to look out of the windows. That was a hard one to enforce, of course.

I think opening the club was a good idea. It put some smiles on faces, including ours, and reminded everyone of better times.

The 3.00pm radio announcement was a bit of an anti-climax. It was regarding the use of air raid sirens. A fluctuating tone means that a raid is likely soon and 'preparations should therefore be made' (like what? Dive under the bed?). A second siren means that a raid is imminent. A later oscillating tone will mean it's safe to emerge.

Early this evening Alison and Mike Bleaney[3] visited the house with some sheets of information prepared by the civil defence group. The group (I should have asked who else is on the committee) has put together a short list of heavily constructed buildings that are safer than the average tin and timber Stanley house and can therefore offer a degree of safety. The various owners have agreed they can be used by anyone who does not want to stay in their own home if (when?) it really hits the fan.

The most significant 'safe' building is the [Falkland Islands Company] West Store. It's built of concrete blocks a foot or so thick. There's no shortage of chocolate, alcohol and fags there, so people might be queuing up to get into it. There would be worse places to meet your maker.

Afterwards I walked to Sparrowhawk House to visit the Smiths. John, Wrecker [Jeremy] and Martin, with help, I think, from Rag [Robert] McCaskill, have built a terrific air raid shelter. It's perfect. They've built it under the floor of their front porch. It's dry, there are concrete walls on all sides, and it even has a few inches of concrete on the ceiling. They can get into it through a hatch in the floor of the porch and they've got a small door on the side that they could escape through if necessary. It'll be pretty cosy, to say the least, but there's room for John and Eileen, Anya (who is looking as cute, cheeky and funny as ever), the three boys and perhaps anyone else who happens to be around. Absolutely amazing!

The Smiths are great. Laughter is never more than a few minutes away. Eileen fed me tea and buns and we all compared notes about what's going on. They seem to have no intention of leaving town, which I'm pleased about. Visiting Sparrowhawk House always cheers me up.

David and Col Barton at Teal Inlet sent a message through to Mum and Dad today inviting us to go to Teal Inlet, where they would put us up. I think it would be safer at TI, but there is no guarantee of that. It's a very kind offer, though.

We talked it through, and both Mum and Dad felt that at this stage they don't want to go to the camp. I pretty much agree with that. But if we leave it too long, it'll probably be impossible to leave town.

Patrick asked me to present 'Saturday Choice' again tonight. Again, I thought about it for a bit but said yes. Anna came to the studio with me and helped me to select the records. I was surprised to find that we had more than enough requests, messages and dedications, which had been phoned in or popped through the studio letterbox.

A bit silly really, but we played [Rod Stewart's] 'Sailing' and said it was specially for all our new friends 'on the oggin'. We figured no Argentine would understand that. I suppose it was also unlikely that anyone in the Task Force would hear it, but it amused us.

I went back to the Upland Goose with Anna for a bit. Someone there said that the comedy show screened on Argentine TV earlier this evening was from Rex Hunt's collection of video cassettes. I think it was *Fawlty Towers*. We listened to the BBC news. A diplomatic note from the British (actually not a very diplomatic note), delivered to BA via the Swiss embassy there, advised the Argentine Government that if any of their aircraft overfly or approach the British Task Force ships, they will be considered hostile and treated appropriately; in other words, they'll be shot down.

There is speculation that an operation to retake South Georgia may already have commenced.

Word among the Argentines lodging at the Goose is that eight Anglo-Argentines have arrived in Stanley, supposedly on a 'peace mission'. Perhaps we'll hear more about that tomorrow. It's not at all clear to me what they might reasonably hope to achieve.

I made my way back to Rowan House quite late, through the streets which were dark and almost deserted. Stanley can be a quite sinister place these days.

Chapter 10

The Gloves Come Off

(25–28 April)

Sunday, 25 April

I stayed awake to catch WS news at 1.00am. They had the news that we'd been expecting: operations to retake South Georgia have commenced. The Navy attacked an Argentine submarine which was on the surface in Grytviken harbour, using rockets and machine guns from helicopters.

BA's propaganda merchants are on the defensive. They are saying that although two helicopters did attack Grytviken, they were repulsed by Argentine forces. They did not mention the submarine.

I can imagine that lots of people around the Islands are sitting quietly in the dark listening to the BBC. It seems that a team of about twelve Special Boat Service Marines landed on South Georgia to prepare for the main attack.

Despite the drama of South Georgia, it's actually fairly quiet around Stanley today. Word is being put around mouth-to-mouth and via local radio that the team of Anglo-Argentines will be in the Post Office at 5.00pm and they want to talk to local people. I'll be there for sure, and Dad has said he wants to go. I don't think we are terribly interested in their message, which will surely be that life under Argentine rule isn't so bad; look at us – we drink Earl Grey tea and eat fruit cake. Still, it'll be interesting.

More news about South Georgia crackled through on a very bad signal. Nothing is being said on the local station, of course. But the island has been recovered. London says the Argentines offered 'only limited resistance', although there was about two hours of fighting. That doesn't sound particularly 'limited' to me. There were no casualties on the British side, and Argentine casualties are not known.

All BAS [British Antarctic Survey] scientists, who had been lying low in remote points as far as possible from the Argentines, are reported to be safe. Cindy Buxton and Annie Price[1] were with the BAS men and were also rescued. I'm glad to hear that.

A signal went back to London saying, 'The White Ensign is now flying alongside the Union Jack in South Georgia. God save the Queen.' I'm not much of a one for jingoism, but I must admit that this even sent a shiver down my spine.

I suppose this demonstration of British force will either make the Argentines realize that they are up against a very capable enemy and should therefore accept a peaceful solution, or enrage them so much that they stop talking.

Terrific theatricals at the meeting with the Anglo-Argentines in the Post Office today. I counted forty-three local people there. I just stood back and watched the pent-up emotions explode. Five of the Anglo-Argentines (who I must admit showed some courage in coming here) were lined up in front of the Post Office counter, with no sign of an Argentine military presence.

They took it in turns to say why life as a person of British descent in Argentina is perfectly fine. They have private schools with British teachers, they have their country clubs and they even have a branch of Harrods (although I've seen it and it's a pretty scruffy little place). Then one of them came up with their big idea, which I had not anticipated. They suggested that Islanders agree to let Argentina develop its own town and community somewhere else on the islands, completely separate from us. We would be left to live as we always have in Stanley and on the farms. They said this would probably be acceptable to BA, and after that we could all look forwards to peace.

There was a moment or two of silence. But then the crowd pretty much erupted, with everyone clamouring to tell the visitors what they thought. This was the first chance that any Islander has had to say what they think since the invasion, and it was a mass release of emotion. The common denominator of what people said – including Dad, who managed to get a word or two in – was that they could stuff their idea of a permanent Argentine presence of any sort.

Quite a few people said that they badly wanted peace but they had absolutely no sympathy with the Argentine position. A few pointed out that the ancestors of the Anglo-Argentines had *chosen* to live under Argentine rule. But we were being forced to do so.

I felt slightly sorry for the Argentines, as they were outnumbered and the gathering was getting very unpleasant. They were backing up against the Post Office counter. The meeting reached its climax when Bill Curtis began spitting vitriol at them.

'I came here with my family to get away from militarism,' he said. 'And then you turkeys turn up with the same shit. Now piss off!'[2]

Some of the younger women in the Argentine party began to cry, and at this point a couple of Argentine officers, who must have been listening just out of sight, entered and ushered them out on to Ross Road and away. I guess they are now flying back to Buenos Aires.

I felt a little sorry for one or two of the women who were obviously scared and in tears, but apart from that, I thoroughly enjoyed the meeting. And I think all those who spoke out did, too. I feel that a very strong message was sent to the Argentines.

Dad and I went home, to find that Aub and Sonia Summers had invited us all to their place for a bite to eat. As always, the old chap rustled up something tasty. We had a surprisingly enjoyable evening. It felt strange to be socializing again, but it had been a good day. We were all cheered by the news from South Georgia, and there were a few laughs at the expense of the Anglo-Argentines in the Post Office. Everyone left early, though. Night-time does not feel safe.

Monday, 26 April

'Treacherous!' exclaimed Nicanor Costa Mendez, describing the attack on South Georgia (according to the BBC this morning). I don't seem to recall him applying the same adjective to the Argentine invasion on 2 April. He was supposed to meet Haig late yesterday but instead they spoke on the phone.

WS went on to report that the Argentines are 'suspending' negotiations in the wake of South Georgia. It's notable, perhaps, that they do not say 'ending' negotations.

Apparently, just one Argentine was wounded during the operation at South Georgia. That's good. The Argentine submarine *Santa Fe* was attacked on the surface while trying to escape and is reported to be listing, leaking oil and smoking.

Later in the day, WS reports that the Queen had just finished discussing the crisis with the PM when news about South Georgia came through. [Labour Party leader] Michael Foot has called a meeting of his shadow cabinet for tomorrow. I'd expect them to be very much against military action. Yesterday, [Liberal Party leader] David Steele called for an all-party conference on the Falklands crisis. However, none of this hand-wringing by party leaders may matter at all. The government is obviously doing the right thing by most Brits.

The Argentines are at last saying they have 'lost contact' with their forces on SG. Some authorities in BA have admitted that there was an 'apparent' British victory on SG, but they claim that Argentine troops continue to resist in the interior of the island. That's more bullshit from BA. The interior of South Georgia is one of the most hostile places in the world, and if there are any Argentines 'holding out' there, then I expect the Brits, now comfortably installed at King Edward Point, will be happy to let them stay there.

I heard this afternoon that the five Anglo-Argentines who attempted to talk to us at the Post Office yesterday did not feel safe enough to make their way to their lodgings after the meeting. They called Bloomer-Reeve for help, and he arranged a full military escort.

All of today's UK papers lead with the victory on South Georgia. Some even have photos of the attacked and disabled submarine. The *Express* was almost alone in expressing caution. Their editorial said the UK needs to consider the possibility of long-term failure in the Falklands: 'They cannot expect to protect them for the next fifteen years.'

It's reported that 150 Argentine soldiers were captured at SG, and the British troops who landed numbered fewer than this. Thatcher says they will be returned forthwith to Argentina. She said that minimal force had been used during the attack, and she is maintaining contact with Al Haig. The message from the UK to BA seems to be 'We have shown what we can do; now talk seriously, or else.'

Bill Luxton and John Cheek[3] have been speaking on our behalf at the UN. The Argentines may come to regret deporting Luxton.

The Organization of American States has again exhibited no enthusiasm for war. Good, obviously. Instead of committing full support to BA, it is calling for peace to be maintained.

The question being asked both in London and among people here is, 'Are we at war?' Everyone I speak to hopes that negotiations can continue, as the alternative is so awful. But fighting has started, while talks are clearly going nowhere.

I'm experiencing a strange mix of feelings. Sometimes, since 2 April, I've been frightened, especially on the actual invasion. And I worry most of the time. But I must admit that I find this exciting. I know I shouldn't, because so many lives are at stake. Occasionally, I even find myself hoping that negotiations will fail and the Task Force will continue south, with the obvious result. Really, there seem to be two sides to me. Sometimes the gung-ho side prevails, and at other times it's my more sensible and sensitive self that prevails. I don't like it.

BBC is reporting that a further 900 troops have left the UK aboard a requisitioned ship. They won't be in this area for another two weeks or so. WS analysts are pointing out that it is unlikely that the Task Force will attack the Falklands until after the current two-day meeting of the OAS, as that might push the member states into sympathy for Argentina. So perhaps we are all safe for the time being and there will not be any need to use that damned bunker, which I am starting to regret having built. I wonder if the Smiths have any room in their luxury shelter.

Out on my rounds today, I met Pat Whitney, who had just been out around the North Camp and said that the Argentines are at Douglas Station and in the vicinity of Teal Inlet. They are not yet occupying it.

Tension is much more obvious among the Argentines now. They look more serious and nervous. This morning, a bunch of officers in particular were in a flap and running around near the Goose, shouting a lot. I have no idea what it was about, but chaotic is the word that comes to mind.

I took a quick spin around the east end this afternoon and noticed that a lot more troops are digging in around the cemetery. The dummy artillery pieces are still on the green just above the beach.

I think quite a number of troops are being flown out to camp. They have some very large twin-rotor helicopters [Boeing Chinooks] operating from the football pitch and other flat green areas around town. They are heavily loaded with supplies and men, and they sometimes have vehicles and artillery in slings underneath the choppers. They invariably fly off to the west and come back from the same direction. I'm pretty sure they will be developing their defences at Goose Green in particular, because that area is conveniently situated in the centre of the Falklands and has a very good grass runway.

An alarming change of tone today on Radio Islas Malvinas (it's really not our old local radio station any more). The station has been broadcasting martial music for much of the day, along with the stern message that 'The time to fight has arrived.' The troops are being told to shoot with accuracy and 'defend this Argentine territory'.

In happy times, not so long ago, radio announcements would be more mundane, informing us that Micky Clarke had fish for sale at the public jetty, or that so-and-so had won £100 in the Working Men's Social Club sweepstake. Will we ever go back to that?

Dad, Aunt Ning [King], Billy Morrison and one or two others were invited to meet with Bloomer-Reeve this morning at his office in the Secretariat. They were invited to raise issues that concerned the community, which are mainly to do with safety and food supplies as the situation deteriorates.

Dad returned looking quite down, even deflated. I asked him what had come out of the meeting.

'Not much,' he answered. 'It was the usual propaganda. The problems are being caused by the British threats but Argentina wants us to resume and carry on with our normal lives. I don't think it was worth it.'

But I think he still has enough respect for Bloomer-Reeve to believe that he will pass the group's concerns further up the line.

I was comparing notes with Simon [Goss] earlier today and he said that nine light tanks or armoured cars – probably the latter as they have wheels rather than tracks – are parked up at the ESRO [European Space Research Organization] building [near Moody Brook]. Another two are well dug in near his house in the grounds of the Appleton Laboratory [near the eastern entrance to Stanley]. These vehicles are so well protected that only their turrets and main guns are showing. Their guns (I would say about 80mm calibre) are large for the size of the vehicles and they must pack a punch.[4]

As usual, this evening at Rowan House we tuned into 'Calling the Falklands' and were cheered to hear the smooth voice of presenter Peter King. He has just the right mix of gravity and good humour. The big news is about the programme itself: as from this evening, CTF will be broadcast daily.

Excerpts from tonight's programme: We are still dominating Parliament. Michael Foot has criticized the government's efforts to find a peaceful solution and said they should try much harder. He said that the majority of Britons would not support the government if a real war commences.

My ears pricked up when I heard the MP Eric Ogdon, who has visited the Falklands and is a prominent supporter, say that more help should be given to Islanders who are in the UK and are unable to get home. He suggested a special office to assist Falkland Islanders.

Reception was bad so I did not fully understand the PM's response, but I think she said that any Islanders stuck in the UK will be helped if necessary. And I think she went on to say that the same offer would apply to any Islander who can get out of the Falklands and travel to the UK.

Rex Hunt said that if people can leave the Islands by normal means they will be helped along the way to the UK by British embassies and then by the Home Office when they get to the UK. This sounds reasonable but is meaningless, as there is now no way of leaving the Falklands. If the offer had been made much earlier, more Islanders might have left. I have a nasty suspicion, though, that having us here reinforces the UK's justification for military action. Fighting for some empty islands would look ridiculous.

Thatcher has stressed that speed is important if the Islands are to be retaken, as the winter weather will deteriorate and make operations far more difficult. Indeed, some British papers are said to be speculating that special forces have already landed on the Falklands. That fear is almost certainly shared by the Argentines here and would account for the nervousness we see.

Admiral Sandy Woodward, who is in command of the Task Force from the carrier *Hermes*, said, 'South Georgia was the run-up to the big match', which he expects to be a 'push-over'. Argentine troops should, he said, 'leave now, or they will do so courtesy of the Royal Navy'. That's strong stuff and good for our morale if nothing else.

Peter King ended CTF with what has become his catch-phrase: 'Heads down, hearts high!' Not bad advice.

We all have an ominous feeling that 'something' is about to happen, perhaps not tonight or tomorrow, but within the next few days. I think the Task Force will go for the airport first, breaking the supply link with Argentina. In contrast with last night, when our little party lifted spirits, our mood is now low. Bed was the best option, but sleep was slow to follow.

Tuesday, 27 April

I set the alarm for the early hours to scan the radio bands. Reception is always better at night. According to the Chilean radio station I picked up at 1.50am, the Argentines are describing as 'totally false' the reports of even limited British landings. Scheduled flights in the south of Argentina have been suspended. Peruvian dockers have refused to work on British ships.

The morning passed quietly enough. But this afternoon, Brian Paul came by the house and asked if I would help him to black out the windows at the hospital. I was more than happy to help with this, so we worked away throughout the hospital for the rest of the day. If and when we are ordered not to show any lights, the medical staff will now be able to black the hospital out very quickly, while continuing their work. It felt very good to be doing something useful.

The mood around the hospital was cheerful enough, but at about 4.00pm the situation suddenly became worse. A civilian came into the hospital saying that Argentine troops were arbitrarily arresting men and boys on the streets and taking them to the police station. They included [my friends] Martin and Jeremy Smith. I found out later that they were all released after about an hour, almost certainly following intervention by Bloomer-Reeve.

More disturbingly, though, at about the same time a group of Argentines went through town arresting prominent locals. They came to the hospital to arrest the Chief Medical Officer, Daniel Haines, although I didn't see this.

In the same swoop they arrested Stuart [Wallace], Velma Malcolm, Gerald Cheek, Brian Summers and Owen Summers.[5] Our initial assumption was that they were being deported, or worse, but they were told that they were being taken to a place of 'safety' within the Islands. I heard later in the day that they were taken to the airport and loaded into a helicopter, which took them to Fox Bay East, where they were placed under house arrest. The Argentines have a strong garrison there.

Stuart was able to take Lillian and their kids. It's fairly obvious why they arrested most of the group, but it's less clear why they picked up Dr Haines. I heard around the hospital, though, that he has been very 'difficult' with the Argentines, and it's likely that they did not trust him running the hospital. His wife and kids also went with him. Apparently, Haines has been replaced by an Argentine doctor. I didn't get his surname, but he seems to be known around the hospital as 'Dr Mario'.

It was becoming obvious that there was a wider flap of some kind going on. There was a hell of a lot of running around and panicky shouting. At first we thought it was an attack on Stanley or nearby, but that wasn't so.

I think the panic followed the arrival of a group of harder professional troops, perhaps carrying instructions to General Menendez to get tougher on us. In any case, the gloves are definitely coming off.

Brian and I listened to local radio in the hospital kitchen as the Argentine announcer said in English, 'Extra precautions are being taken concerning the Islanders.' He went on to present a chilling message: 'Argentine law will now be fully enforced, and anyone collaborating with Argentina's enemies will be dealt with appropriately.' He didn't explain exactly what that means, but I'm pretty sure it wouldn't be pleasant.

Following this, there was another stern edict. All houses are to be blacked out at night, and a curfew will apply from 6.00pm to 6.30am. Civil defence groups will be allowed to operate should an attack occur during hours of darkness.

One of the Argentine soldiers who is supposedly defending the hospital let slip to me that 120 British soldiers had landed, but he didn't say where or when. I don't think he knew. It could be a rumour, but it makes some sense, as 120 is more or less a company, a basic army unit.

Local radio did not broadcast but remained on rediffusion [cable and speaker system to all homes in Stanley] all night. The medium wave transmitter was switched off. This is not normal, so we speculated that some attack or incursion is underway somewhere.

As Brian, I and a few others had not finished blacking out the hospital by 6.00pm when the curfew kicked in, we decided to carry on, and we spent the night at the hospital. Quite a few other people were also trapped there.

At about 10.30 there was a phone call from John Smith at Sparrowhawk House. He asked if someone could deliver some tablets to Eileen [John's wife]. I volunteered, and one of the young soldiers guarding the hospital said he'd come with me to provide some security. I was pleased to have him there. I didn't fancy being stopped by nervous Argentine soldiers.

The streets were completely deserted. Obviously, no locals were out and about, but the Argentines were also lying very low. It was spooky, to say the least. There was a loud burst of what sounded like anti-aircraft fire to the south of town, and some bursts of small arms fire in the distance. The soldier said that the shooting was probably men firing at shadows.

At the Smiths' I knocked on the door and John opened up, being careful not to reveal any light. He was very grateful indeed, and I was happy to help Eileen. The soldier and I headed back as quickly as we could, and it was a relief to get back into the warmth and light of the hospital. We sat around drinking coffee and listening to the radio for the rest of the night.

Wednesday, 28 April

Today the screws are being tightened further on us. It's been decreed that government offices can only open in the mornings, and shops must close by 4.00pm. Not that many of the shops are open anyway.

A large container ship arrived in Stanley Harbour yesterday afternoon. The Argentines gleefully proclaimed she had successfully run the British blockade, which she obviously had. You can hardly blame them for feeling chuffed about that, but they won't have liked what they heard next.

Shortly before midday, London announced that the blockade will become a full air as well as sea blockade. And the surface blockade is to be enforced by submarines. As from 8.00am (Falklands time) on Friday the 30th, two days from now, all military and civilian ships and aircraft carrying supplies to the Falklands will be considered targets.

All of this ups the ante greatly, I think. *Voice of America* has said that the Argentine fleet is manoeuvring about 450 miles from the Falklands, and they may be preparing to attack the Task Force. The thinking may be that they need to do this soon, since once the landing begins, it will be too late.

The Argentine Navy is relatively old, but they do have one aircraft carrier, the ARA *25 de Mayo*, and a heavily armed cruiser, the ARA *General Belgrano*, plus sundry other relatively modern destroyers and smaller ships. And they have one big unknown: their submarines. Some of them are thought to be pretty good, although one is now lying beached in South Georgia.

We are now in a much tenser and more dangerous phase compared to this time last week, when diplomacy seemed to be keeping everyone at arm's length and the Argentines seemed to be intent on treating us correctly.

The Government in BA must be hopping mad that the Organization of American States is not giving them any more than nominal support, refusing to invoke the Rio Treaty, which would commit all American forces to war. They are saying that the British should pull back but that Argentina should also avoid 'complicating' the situation. How delightfully galling for Galtieri, Costa Mendez et al.

Early this morning, it was reported that Haig – that man's determination and energy are incredible – has produced a package of proposals that amounts to a peace plan, but it's already looking frayed around the edges. I think that both sides would have a hard job selling a climb-down to their people. I wouldn't put a fiver on it.

For the last 24 hours or so, the weather around Stanley and towards the west has been terrible. I think that's causing many flights between the mainland and Stanley to be cancelled. But I have seen a few large planes, mainly Hercules C130s, coming in and out at low level.

Argentina has started a propaganda station aimed at demoralizing British soldiers, sailors and airmen. After a lot of dial-spinning on the short-wave bands I picked up what I think may be the station. It seems to be pretending it's the BBC, but I don't think it will fool anyone. It's not exactly Lord Haw-Haw-type stuff, but they falsely – well, I hope it was false – reported that twitchy British pilots have accidentally bombed a whale, thinking it was an Argentine submarine. And the station passed on messages and played records from supposed girlfriends and wives who said that a few barren rocks are not worth dying over.

CTF, on the other hand, boomed through this evening on 9.915 megahertz. I am worried that the Argentines may try to jam it soon. The main item was an interview with Rex Hunt, who I think has a somewhat inflated idea of his right to speak for us. If anyone in the UK is going to reflect the views, fears and thoughts of people here, it should probably be John Cheek, who's an elected councillor.

Anyway, Rex Hunt spoke about the imminent ratcheting-up of the sea and air blockade, saying that while he knew it would probably make life more difficult for us he was sure we wouldn't mind, as he knew we would put up with almost anything to see this through. Well, that may be so, but it's a fairly rash statement to make without any consultation.

Today, troops are still obviously twitchy, and the atmosphere around Stanley is still very tense. We have certainly entered a new phase. We speculate that they are particularly worried about infiltration by British special forces, who could be masquerading as locals in Stanley. I haven't seen any strange faces, though.

I went to the Secretariat to see if I could get some of the signs that Bloomer-Reeve has required Joe King to make in the Printing Office. They forbid Argentine troops from entering houses that have been abandoned by owners who have gone to camp or are sheltering in the so-called 'safe' houses around Stanley. I think we may need one of these signs ourselves soon. I got four of them, which will cover Rowan and the Woodbine too [the home of our friends Aub and Sonia Summers].

Late today, I dropped by Church House to see Pete and Rosemary. They told me that I'd missed a party of Argentine troops searching the building and our darkroom for the second time. They said they would 'shoot' anyone found in Church House's empty flats. So Pete and Rosie have decided to move out of Church House. This evening they moved to Pete's parents, Joe and Gladys. Robert is there, too, of course. The Kings' house is small but heavily built of stone and it will be much safer. Church House seems to be under suspicion now. I'm sure they are doing the right thing.

Chapter 11

Interrogation

(29–30 April)

Thursday, 29 April

It's foggy, cold and damp today, which pretty much suits the mood in our house and among everyone I've been seeing. Visibility is so bad that most of the Argentine helicopters have stayed firmly on the ground. There will be a lot of crews at the main chopper base at Moody Brook with too much time to think about what might be just around the corner.

The huge container ship which was moored in the harbour has been unloaded and is now moored alongside the east jetty. I was able to read her name through the binoculars: *Formosa*. The big question is, will she now take her chances and try to run the blockade back to Argentine territorial waters, or stay around here? She is much too big for inter-island work.

About fifteen people moved into the West Store last night. The FIC has said people can shelter there if they wish. It is relatively safe, as it's built of concrete blocks. They are unlikely to run out of food and drink there, too.

People have also moved out of their houses to go to other safer locations. The Kings have made it clear that we can move to the [Upland] Goose [Hotel] at any point. I think that time is rapidly approaching. Rowan House is just timber and tin.

Two Argentine fighter planes roared low and loud over Stanley early this afternoon. Even the Argentine Air Force seems jumpy. I decided to take a walk around town to see what's going on. Troops on the street are even more nervous today, and near the Post Office I was thinking about doing a U-turn and heading home, when I was stopped, quite aggressively, by a pair of soldiers. There wasn't a roadblock or checkpoint, and I don't know if they were just troops from the intelligence team at the police station randomly arresting people, or whether I had been targeted.

They wanted to know my name, what I was doing and where I was going. I said I was going to the Post Office to see if there was any mail for my family. This did not satisfy them. I was marched the 50 yards or so to the police station, then told to stand against the wall of the building, under the guard of a short, fat NCO, who waved his rifle around a bit too liberally.

Mike Luxton was also standing against the wall, looking worried. Probably sounding a bit more upbeat that I felt, I said, 'Hello Mike, I see they got you too.'

This prompted the fat soldier with the rifle to start yelling at me. '*Callate la boca, hijo de puta! No se hablan a nadie* [Shut your mouth, son of a whore! Don't speak to anyone].'

That shook me up more than a bit, and I did as I was told.

A few minutes later, Mike was escorted into the police station and I didn't see him leave. Perhaps he was interrogated and sent out by the back entrance. But about ten minutes later, I was also told to enter. A sergeant was seated at a table in the centre of the room, and on the table was a heap of files and a pistol. I was ordered to sit down and told not to say anything unless I was asked a question.

I sat there for a while, then the door opened and an officer came into the room carrying a file. I didn't recognize either of the soldiers, and I wonder if these were some new hard-liners who had replaced the MPs with whom we had liaised occasionally about Youth Club matters.

The officer looked at the papers in the file for a few minutes, then started asking questions. It was immediately clear that the file was dedicated to me. They asked me to confirm who I was, and as they clearly knew I spoke Spanish, the interrogation began in that language.

'Why were you seen taking photos of our troops and vehicles on the day of the invasion?'

I explained that I ran a small newspaper. Although we are not publishing at this time, I still need to record what is happening. He seemed to know this anyway, and did not react badly.

But then he homed in on the Church House darkroom. What exactly had I been photographing? He said they had inspected the darkroom and found negatives that showed Argentine soldiers and their equipment. I knew Pete had got rid of most or even all of the negs, so I wasn't sure if they were bluffing. But it felt very uncomfortable. I assume this guy was one of the soldiers who visited Church House.

'We found photos of our helicopters. I don't think you needed these for your newspaper.'

I thought on my feet a bit and told a lie. 'Those photos were taken by a man called Ian Jones, not me.'

In fact, I have taken pictures of their helicopters, and Ian may have done so too. But he did develop a few films there, and as he'd flown out of the Islands a few weeks ago and is now safely in the UK, there was no harm in my using him as an explanation. But they didn't want to accept this, or if they did they were going to test it by giving me a hard time.

Things got heated, and I can't remember all that was said. I do know I was nervous. Voices were raised and questions were being fired at me so rapidly that I didn't understand everything they said. I suspect the main purpose was to scare me and let me know that they knew me and can arrest me whenever they want. In that they succeeded.

It seems another officer heard the shouting, and he entered the room. He was a military police captain called Romano, whom I recognized from our Youth Club dealings. I knew he was reasonable and I was glad to see him. I don't *think* it was a 'good-cop-bad-cop' set-up, but it might have been.

The captain said, '*Tranquilo, tranquilo*!' [Calm down, calm down!'] He received some dirty looks from the other two but a grateful one from me. He offered me and them cigarettes, and I took one. It was one of their dreadful Jockey Club fags. I took a deep drag and immediately exploded in a fit of coughing. That successfully de-escalated the situation.

The intelligence officer eventually told me I could go, but I have to return with copies of *Penguin News* so that my story can be confirmed. I said I would do that. I headed off back home feeling very relieved. I think the whole episode took about an hour and a half.

On the way home I ran into Charlie Coutts, who it emerged had had a much worse experience with the intelligence people. Charlie was arrested yesterday and held for fourteen hours, which included a night in a cell. They had gone to his house looking for his Defence Force uniform, but he'd buried it, on the orders of an Argentine (probably Bloomer-Reeve) soon after the invasion. The trouble was that the Argentines did not believe this. They interrogated him several times before letting him go.

Early this afternoon, BBC WS reported that Washington is still waiting for London and BA to respond formally to Haig's peace plan. There will be a debate in the Commons today and Labour is expected to suggest that the UN play a much bigger role in the Falklands, both in solving the crisis and remaining to supervise whatever agreement is reached. That would not be acceptable here, although I'm not sure that anyone really cares what we think, not even London.

Nicola Colbert told me a disturbing story today. She believes that at least one soldier has been executed for desertion. She saw a young soldier moving around her sheds and garden at the back of her house on Davis Street. A short time later, two other soldiers arrived and told her they were looking for a missing man. She said she had not seen anyone who fitted the description, but they looked through her sheds with guns drawn. She later heard a shot nearby, and someone later told her there had been an execution. Nicola said she had also heard that executions were carried out at Moody Brook. It is hard to believe such stories. But it's obvious that the conscripts are a sad and neglected lot of boys. They are undoubtedly scared of their officers. And the Argentine military is well used to murdering its own people at home. But would they go so far as shooting their own men? Perhaps one day we'll know the truth.

I also met Eileen Vidal, who said she had been speaking to a civilian steward off the *Formosa*. This girl told Eileen that she and the rest of the crew had been evacuated from the ship at 6.00am today because an air raid was expected. She said that the crew feels particularly vulnerable because they still have ammunition and drums of petrol on board. So do we have a floating bomb in the centre of Stanley? The raid didn't happen, fortunately.

The water supply to most of Stanley was cut off at about 2.00pm yesterday and I don't think it has been restored to the entire town today. At Rowan we were not affected, but I expect our time will come. We have filled all the containers we can find with water, just in case.

A couple of jet fighters flew low over Stanley again around 11.00am. I assume these are training missions for the pilots, but they may have a morale-boosting purpose for the troops, too.

A significant local development this afternoon: the radio station has gone off the air. The medium-wave transmitter, which has considerable range, has been closed down, although the rediffusion cable system connected to 'boxes' in all houses in Stanley is supposed to continue working. But even that is intermittent.

The shut-down was announced before it happened, but no explanation was given. This is bad news for people living in the camp. Hundreds of refugees from Stanley are now on the farms, of course, and they will feel even more isolated. Then again, Radio Islas Malvinas broadcasts little real news these days.

I suspect they have cut off the MW transmitter because British aircraft could use it as a navigation beacon. I suppose it is also possible that the Brits were picking up some intelligence from the station. Anyway, it's gone.

Voice of America is reporting that Washington is not hopeful about diplomacy. Haig is reminding both London and BA that they need to formally respond to his peace plan. If I was Al Haig, I wouldn't hold my breath.

The complete blockade starts at 8.00am tomorrow. It's a fair bet, I think, that around then, if not before, the Task Force will attack the airport.

As I write this evening, the weather is chilly, grey and dark with drizzle. It's calm, though.

Earlier today, I saw a truck laden with soldiers in full combat gear moving out from the gymnasium, which appears to be the HQ of one of their professional regiments. These guys looked much tougher than the conscripts. They were wearing better fatigues and dripping with grenades and automatic weapons.

Bloomer-Reeve and Phil Summers [the Defence Force's commanding officer], have been visiting the homes of FIDF men who are still in town. Perhaps this odd couple are doing this following the regular troops' aggressive approach when trying to collect Charlie Coutts' FIDF uniform yesterday.

This evening, people are again moving into the West Store and other 'safe' buildings. There is a feeling around town that things are about to get very dangerous. Mum, Dad and I will stay home tonight, but we've arranged with Joe King to move quickly to their house, just 400 yards or so along the road, if the siren sounds.

At 8.00pm WS reported that it seems Argentina has not approved the Haig plan 'but has not entirely rejected it'. BA has requested clarification of some points. I suspect they are just playing for time.

Thatcher has said that 'gentle persuasion' may not be enough to convince the Argentines that they must withdraw. More aggressive talk is coming out of BA via the WS news at 8.00pm. They have declared a 200-mile 'war zone' around the Falklands and South Georgia, presumably measured from the centre of the Islands. The South Georgia threat is empty, but the threat relating to the Falklands is not. We are well within range from their mainland bases, although they won't be able to linger long over the Islands.

WS is shedding some light on why local radio (which I still want to call FIBS) closed down. They say this is because transmissions were being monitored in Chile and passed on to London. Sounds like Chilean intelligence people are helping the Brits.

The Swedish Government is asking London for permission to interrogate the officer who was in command of Argentine troops on South Georgia. Captain Alfredo Astiz is in British custody.[1] The Swedish legal authorities want to question him about the fate of a Swedish woman who disappeared in Argentina in 1977. Astiz is alleged to have shot her and then taken her to a military hospital, from which she never emerged.

Weather prospects for the weekend are bad and likely to get worse. The Argentines have been lucky so far, as the autumn weather has been generally quite mild. However, winter now seems to be knocking on the door. The Task Force would probably find helicopter and landing craft operations difficult this weekend.

Voice of America is speculating that the assault on the Falklands will begin with a major attack on Stanley Airport and the 'alternative airstrip' that they say has been created on the other side of Stanley. There is no other airstrip, of course, but their reconnaissance may have mistaken the racecourse for a runway.

Sleep does not seem to be an option tonight, although Mum and Dad have retired. I'm glued to the radio, trying to make sense of the distant voices fading in and out through the static. At midnight BBC WS reports signs that Washington is preparing a statement of support for the UK. That would be very good, and there might still just be a chance that the Argentines will see sense if they know that Washington has cut them off. Fingers crossed.

I looked out the upstairs front window at around midnight and the town is completely blacked out. No houses are showing lights and the streetlights are all off. There are only occasional beams of lights from their fancy Mercedes jeeps as they patrol the town. The *Formosa*, still moored at the East Jetty, is another story, however. She's lit up like a Christmas tree, making herself a fat target.

I'm lying on bed with a comforting cat purring alongside me and dozing a bit. But real sleep doesn't seem likely.

Friday, 30 April

Contrary to expectations, there was no dawn attack today. So the waiting and the speculation continues.

A summary of the UK papers' headlines came through in the early hours. They are mostly Churchillian in tone. The *Daily Mail* has 'The Final Challenge' splashed across its front page. The *Express* goes for 'Now is the Hour'. Most of the papers say that hopes for peace are fading. Ha! No kidding. They pretty much vanished weeks ago here.

The *Guardian* is speaking out for our welfare and arguing against jingoism. Their editorial suggests that Haig has one more task before he heads back to Washington for the final time: he should approach the Argentines requesting that they evacuate all Islanders from the war zone.

The *Guardian* (rightly) says that London has shown very little concern for Islanders so far, but they now have a chance to put that right. Their writers have done their homework. They quote Islanders who managed to get to the UK saying there is a very high level of anxiety here. The paper points out that a blockade could lead to starvation, and there'd be even greater suffering if a shooting war breaks out.

But they're wasting their ink. I honestly do not believe that anyone at a senior level, either in London or BA, genuinely cares about us. In fact, our presence here is useful, as it justifies all that has been committed and whatever is about to unfold.

At midday BBC WS reports an MoD claim that all Argentine warships are within 200 miles of their own coast. So the declaration of the blockade and the threat of attack seem to have worked.

Not so for air traffic, though. This morning I spent a while with the binoculars trained on the airport and I could see a fair number of aircraft, both jets and prop-planes, coming in and out; mainly Hercules but also Fokker F27s and F28s, the same LADE planes that we used to enjoy flying in better times. The crews and stewardesses were always very friendly then. I wonder how they feel about their changed role.

The box [rediffusion system] is back on, although MW transmission remains off.

Haig announced at 1.00pm that his peace mission has failed, and he warns that large scale military activity in the area of the Falklands and Argentina is now likely. It's chilling to hear this admission of failure and warning of imminent war.

Dad is quiet and sober, a little depressed, I think. Mum is busy in the kitchen, having taken in the news and decided that the best thing she can do is keep busy and prepare food. That is a good thing to do. Neither is thinking of opening the shop, even for an hour or two.

I suppose the good thing about this is that having admitted that diplomacy is dead, the US Government is able to come out clearly in support of the UK.

This they have done. Washington says that economic and military sanctions are being placed on Argentina with immediate effect, and they will give material support to the British effort, should they need it. The US will not actually intervene militarily, though. This must all be music to Mrs Thatcher's ears.

I wandered out for a little while and, of all people, encountered the young Welsh-Argentine translator who works at Government House. He has absolutely no interest in being here and now he's desperate to go back to Gaiman, where the Welsh colony is. He had a gloomy story about poor Argentine organization. A young conscript was shot dead the night before last, and two others were injured. They'd been challenged by soldiers manning a roadblock near Stanley, and when they didn't answer correctly they were shot.

This afternoon, I had a look at my little bunker and put some water, a few tins of beans, a rug or two and a camping stove in it. None of this made much of a difference. It still looks like it would be a miserable place to spend more than a few hours. But we may not have to use it. Des King has phoned from the Upland Goose and strongly suggested that we move down to the hotel today and stay for as long as necessary.

The Goose is a heavily built stone building and it will certainly be safer than Rowan House. Mum and Dad took little convincing and, frankly, neither did I. So we loaded bedding, clothes and the food Mum had been cooking into Dad's Land Rover and my Daihatsu and drove the short distance down the hill before the curfew started. We parked around the back of the Goose, out of sight of the road, in the hope that the vehicles will be safer there. It was a great relief to open the kitchen door of the Goose and be greeted by Aunt Ning, Des, Anna, Barbara and Alison. Their old percolator coffee pot was bubbling away on the Rayburn as usual, and the feeling of relative safety was wonderful.

The rooms in the east end of the hotel are taken up by Argentine and Uruguayan press and members of the military government who are running the various government departments. We local civilians are occupying the west end of the hotel. Aub and Sonia Summers joined us a little later, also clearly feeling relieved to have the warmth of company and a degree of safety.

We chatted about the situation and the grim outlook for a few hours, and we pecked at some food. Then people drifted off to bed. I've pitched my sleeping bag on sofa cushions behind a brick chimney in the lounge. It is surprisingly comfortable and cosy. I brought my tiny Panasonic short-wave receiver with me and I lay there for a while trying to tune into the BBC, *Voice of America* and Chilean stations. None are saying anything we don't know. All are of the opinion that diplomacy is dead and the Falklands, most probably Stanley itself, will come under heavy attack very soon, probably within hours.

It just seems like yesterday that we were living a peaceful and rather boring life, completely unknown to the rest of the world. And we were quite happy about that.

I would give almost anything to have that life back. Instead, our situation is about to get immeasurably more dangerous.

I just remembered that I was supposed to take some copies of *Penguin News* by the police station to prove my interrogation story of the day before yesterday. I might do it tomorrow, but unless I'm very much mistaken, they'll then have bigger things on their minds.

PART II

GOOD NIGHT, GOD BLESS

Chapter 12

Shock and Horror

(1–3 May)

Saturday, 1 May

My little bivouac in the Goose lounge is surprisingly comfortable and it feels relatively safe. I must have drifted off to sleep around midnight. Then, at 4.40 this morning, I awoke with a hell of a start. The first British plane (or planes?) to attack the Falklands was bombing Stanley airport. We'd anticipated it, but still, the shock was immense.

At first, I thought someone was pushing my (non-existent) bed back and forth, but then I heard another four or five huge explosions in quick succession and I knew pretty much what was happening.

Within a minute or so, the Argentines were unleashing streams of anti-aircraft shells and small arms fire into the sky. I feel pretty sure they were firing wild, as it was so dark. But the racket was dreadful and it went on for about five minutes, at which point I guess they realized that whatever aircraft had attacked would be well out of the way.

Everyone congregated in the kitchen, looking bleary-eyed and in various degrees of alarm. Aunt Ning put the coffee pot on the stove, turned up the heating and we started to feel a bit better. Almost exactly a month after the Argentines invaded, the counter-attack has begun. Like everyone else, I'm nervous, but this has also set my adrenaline running and I must confess that it's exciting. But I know now there is a narrow line between that and fear.

A large number of vehicles began racing around town. The journalists and Argentine staff officers who are lodged up the other end of the hotel also came down, looking dishevelled and confused. The journalists wanted me to tune into the BBC World Service, which I did, but no news came through until 8.00am, when London announced that the attack had been carried out by a single Vulcan bomber, which had flown from Ascension Island, refuelled in the air and then been guided on to the target by naval radar. These planes are huge and they are normally part of the nuclear deterrent. But we had heard they were being adapted for conventional bombing. Now we know why.

We were still digesting this news when there was a terrific roar followed by several bomb blasts. We rushed to the front of the hotel to see what was going on (perhaps not very wisely). Just as I got to the roadside I saw a small aircraft (obviously a Harrier, although I couldn't see it in detail) rocketing through the narrows [the entrance to Stanley Harbour] at just 50ft or so. The pilot flung the plane to the left and headed straight for the airport, where it dropped a couple more bombs. I counted about ten very heavy blasts and, oddly, they seemed more powerful than those dropped by the Vulcan.

It was broad daylight by this time, and the Argentine gunners were now wide awake and had targets. They opened up with all they had, including at least one missile. I couldn't see where it had been fired from, but certainly to the west of Stanley. The missile came rocketing down the harbour at a low level, flew past the Upland Goose and then suddenly turned upward and disappeared into the clouds, where it exploded. I don't think it hit a Harrier, as I think they'd all made good their escape to the east, a long way from where the missile detonated.

Fortunately, I brought my binoculars with me last night. I ran upstairs to the bathroom at the east end of the Goose and trained them on the airport. Flames are shooting 100ft into the air and there are clouds of oily black smoke. This must be coming from a fuel dump. The terminal is in one piece, but I think the green-tinted windows of the control tower are blown out.

Despite promises that we would be warned of air attack with a siren, there was no such warning before either air raid. Then again, the RAF would have done everything possible to keep the element of surprise.

I had another look at the airport at about 9.00am, and parts of it are still burning, but much less. I couldn't see if any aircraft had been hit, but there are at least two planes on the tarmac, their tail fins clearly visible, so they could be in flying condition. The big question is, have they managed to put this end of the Argentine airbridge out of action?

Argentine radio has confirmed the attack took place (as if we needed that) but they say that they drove the British aircraft off. Lies, of course.

Later this morning, WS is reporting that Galtieri held an emergency meeting with his senior advisors immediately after this morning's attacks. They've had a double blow: Reagan declares support for London and there is an overwhelming air attack. It should concentrate their minds.

Vehicles seem to be whizzing around with more purpose, and patrols and sentries around town are looking much more nervous and threatening. It doesn't feel good.

I've been going around with my little Panasonic almost stuck to my ear, manipulating the aerial every few minutes to improve reception. I picked up that analysts in the UK are saying the Task Force has split into several groups and precautions are being taken to protect the *Canberra*, which has 2,500 troops on board, from submarines.

Someone came by the Goose and whispered the news (I don't know how they got it) that the grass airstrip at Goose Green was knocked out by Harriers at about the same time that the airport was hit. Apparently there had been ten Pucara ground-attack aircraft on the strip yesterday, and these, along with any ammunition and fuel dumps, would have been the target. Apparently, there was heavy defensive fire, but no idea whether any of the Harriers were hit. The airstrip at Goose Green is close to the settlement, so I hope everyone there is safe.

A little later, one of the girls overheard two of the Argentines in the hotel talking about a Harrier being shot down at Goose Green. I don't think the Argentine officers and journalists lodged at the Goose realize how many of us speak Spanish, so listening in on their conversations can be very interesting.

I had a word with Joe Booth this afternoon as he came past the Goose. He saw a Mirage fighter fly low on the south side of Stanley at about 10.30am, and he thinks this plane was attacking the ships that launched the attacks on Stanley and Goose Green.

The clouds lifted this afternoon, and at 4.20pm a few of us were standing out in front of the Goose when explosions and large puffs of smoke began erupting around the airport. This did not seem to make any sense, as there were no aircraft involved. It suddenly dawned on me that the airport was being shelled by ships offshore. This continued for about fifteen minutes.

Just a few minutes after the shelling ceased, a jet came screaming in over Stanley from the east. We assumed it was another air raid. This seemed to be confirmed by what sounded like every weapon in Stanley opening up. I didn't see the fate of the aircraft, but soon word started to go around that the jet was an Argentine Mirage that had been attacking the ships which were pounding the airport with shellfire.

We can't be sure, but it seems that the unfortunate pilot had already been hit and was hoping to land or at least eject over Stanley. But the Argentines thought he was a Harrier and they shot him down.

Any excitement I may have felt is now being replaced by low-level fear. I've decided to keep a reasonable distance from the road and satisfy my curiosity about what is going on from inside the Goose porch.

At about 5.15pm five local men were marched past the hotel under armed guard. I ducked out of sight but I saw that among them were Robert Rozee, Glynn Jones and Paul McKay. I'm pretty sure that two of them were Polish refugees. They were all marched to the police station. I know how they must be feeling, but clearly the Argentines are more dangerous now.

Ten minutes later, another band of grim-looking soldiers marched two more Poles past the hotel, going in the direction of the police station. Later, I heard that the Poles were lined up in the police station yard for a while and then subjected to a load of shouted abuse. Presumably this was for not looking happy about occupation by a foreign army, and exercising their right to be on the streets in daylight.

A few hours later, I was again scanning the harbour with my binos, when one of the two white patrol boats came in and moored at the Government Jetty. The crew unloaded a body into a Land Rover. A small orange survival-type dinghy was also unloaded. This must have been the unfortunate Mirage pilot.

I don't feel any pleasure at the Argentines' own goal. All I could see was a dead man. It's obvious that we've crossed a line and there is going to be a lot more killing.

From what I've been able to understand from WS, it seems that while we were watching the airport being shelled, the ships were coming under air attack. The BBC's Brian Hanrahan on *Hermes* reported that two Mirages may have been shot down. I guess it was the body of one of these pilots that I saw being brought ashore at the jetty.

The Kings have made it clear that we are welcome to stay at the Goose for as long as necessary. I spoke to Dad about this, and we both felt that we should spend nights here, while continuing to visit Rowan House as much as possible. The cat is still there, and it will be good to let the Argentines think it is occupied. We have the little bunker there for a real emergency. So that's the plan.

We had dinner in the hotel and listened to CTF. A Foreign Office junior minister was interviewed and said he hopes that BA will appreciate that Britain is 'in deadly earnest'. What a shame these ministers and their diplomat buddies weren't 'deadly earnest' before this crisis began, instead of deadly bored.

CTF also reported that there had been a single Vulcan involved in this morning's raid and it dropped twenty 1,000lb bombs. Those sound like pretty damned big bombs to me. The Harriers that zoomed in a short time later were each carrying three 1,000lb bombs. The pilots of the Harriers that raided Stanley were quoted as saying that they met a heavy but ineffective barrage over the airport. Brian Hanrahan had obviously been told that he could not reveal how many Harriers were involved in the Stanley raid, but he said he 'counted them all out and he counted them all back'. So none were lost. I don't think we can be so sure about what happened at Goose Green, though.

Pym has arrived in the US (again) on what I think must now be a pointless mission. London has said that no further talks can take place while Argentina is still occupying British territory.

This evening, WS is confirming that the Argentines did indeed shoot down their own aircraft today, killing the poor pilot. The Argentines are claiming that they badly damaged one of the frigates that was bombarding the airport and drove off two others. London says that damage was minor.

Admiral Woodward [in command of the Task Force] sent a message suggesting that the Argentines might like to offer unconditional surrender, but they refused, saying, 'No, because we are winning.'

After dark, I saw the *Formosa* leave her berth at the East Jetty and head through the narrows. I followed her lights (why is she lit up?) as she changed course at Cape Pembroke and headed south. She's a really good target.

About 9.00pm: There are explosions and flashes south or south-east of Stanley. Probably a second wave of naval shelling, this time under the safety of darkness. This is still going on some ninety minutes later.

Our band of refugees at the Goose has grown with the arrival of Father Austin Monaghan from St Mary's. He's the junior priest there and a very cheery and friendly guy.

We all spent the night in the lounge and Room 17, which is very large and on the ground floor. It is safer than upstairs. I'm dropping off even as I write this. I feel that all the tension that built up over a month has been released. I don't feel good about the situation, but today has ended the speculation and stress about what might be in store for us.

Sunday, 2 May

I'm writing this quite late on what has been a surprisingly quiet day; almost an anti-climax. There was an air raid on the helicopter base at Moody Brook, but apart from that, nothing.

The Argentines seems to be lying low. Perhaps they are licking their wounds. And I suspect that the ships that approached Stanley to launch yesterday's raids have retreated a safe distance to the east. Perhaps both sides are taking stock.

London may also be giving BA time to consider whether they can win a war. I had a tetchy conversation with one of the Argentine journalists up the other end of the hotel. I put it to him that this might be a good opportunity for BA to say enough is enough and that a ceasefire should be arranged. He started spitting vitriol about British aggression. This guy, Nicolas Kasanzew, has been putting out pro-Argentine propaganda since his arrival shortly after the invasion. He's also appearing on the new local TV station reporting dodgy 'facts'. Anyway, he turned away muttering that 'No Argentine would ever surrender the Malvinas.'

He's been wearing a military parka that I know he looted from the barracks at Moody Brook, so I said, 'Maybe not, but you may have to give your parka back to the Marines soon.' A bit childish really, but satisfying.

Robin Pitaluga moved into the Goose later this afternoon. He told a remarkable story. He was at [his farm at] Salvador yesterday, monitoring the usual RT [short-wave radio telephone] frequency of 4.5 MHz, when he heard HMS *Hermes* trying to contact the Argentine authorities in Stanley. The voice in the ship was suggesting the Argentines should discuss surrender terms. They offered to send a helicopter displaying a white flag to Stanley which would take the Governor and three of his commanders to HMS *Hermes* for ceasefire talks. Their safety was guaranteed.

A civilian at Fox Bay East heard the message and passed it on to the commander of the Argentine garrison there. His impressively colloquial English response was, 'Tell them to kiss my arse.'

The local operator at Fox Bay asked Rob at Salvador to pass this message on to the Task Force commander. Typically obliging, Rob called *Hermes* and did so. He probably chose slightly less vulgar language, though.

About two hours after the exchange of radio messages, two large Argentine helicopters approached Salvador, flying extremely low, and landed close to the Pitalugas' house. The choppers were packed with heavily armed troops, who approached the house carefully. Apparently, they had first been to Pt San Carlos looking for Rob. He was immediately arrested and forced to board one of the aircraft. Jene, Nicholas and Saul [Rob's wife and young sons] were left on the farm.

The choppers landed at Moody Brook just minutes before the base came under air attack, so Rob, along with the troops, had to evacuate their aircraft urgently and take cover. He went from there to the police station and was subjected to a couple of hours of very severe interrogation.

He told them about the brief radio conversations with HMS *Hermes* and Fox Bay East, neither of which amounted to much, but the Argentines seemed to be convinced that he had spoken to the Task Force on other occasions and might have been passing intelligence to them.

An officer took Rob across Ross Road to the sea wall. The officer pulled a pistol from his belt. Rob told me that he felt the barrel pressed against his neck, and he was convinced that his time had come. He said he felt calm but was sorry that he had not been able to say a proper goodbye to his family. The officer pulled the trigger but there was only a click, as there was no bullet in the chamber. It was a mock execution.

Soon after this, and with darkness coming on, Rob was pushed into a covered trench next to the Youth Club where two young conscript soldiers were already sheltering. They were told that if Rob gave them any trouble, they were to shoot him. As it happens, they were rather more humane than the officer and they did their best to keep him warm, even giving him some coffee.

This morning, the military police officer Captain Romano (the same guy who calmed the situation during my interrogation) arrived and took Rob to the Goose. Romano told him he had been very fortunate. But he was under house arrest. Apart from reporting to the police station every day, he was not to leave the Goose. Aunt Ning, who is Rob's sister, was understandably delighted to see him, and he'll be in good hands for as long as he stays at the Goose.

Rob's arrival and his story really made us consider our own behaviour. But before that, Robert had come by and persuaded me to join him and Peter for a drink or two at the Victory Bar. Although the Argentines have decreed that all pubs and clubs should be closed, the Victory is allowing some locals in through the private entrance. I didn't take much persuading. We knocked surreptitiously on the back door of the Victory, and it opened a crack. Sue Whitney checked who we were, and we were ushered in. About a dozen people were already propping up the bar, tossing back as many drinks as they could in the short time that the pub was 'open'.

Talk was only about one thing, of course: the attacks on the airport and Goose Green, and what this means for us. Everyone was of the same opinion: that life is going to get a lot tougher and more dangerous. As if to confirm this, there was a huge blast. It shook the building. I noticed that a few people hit the floor still clutching their glasses and cans upright. The blast seemed to be incredibly close, but when we picked ourselves up and looked out the door, a plume of smoke was rising from the Camber on the other side of the harbour. So it wasn't *that* close, but perhaps the blast wave bounced of the rocks of the Camber, sending it in our direction. In any case, it shook me badly.

After about an hour, we slipped out of the pub. It's amazing how many drinks you can get down your neck when time is limited. I haven't drunk that much since the invasion. Someone checked the coast was clear and we headed off along Fitzroy Road. I left Robert and Peter at their parents' house, waved at Gladys in the door and then headed back to the Goose by the quickest route possible. I told Dad I'd been checking out Rowan House.

On the way home I met Tony Chater, who witnessed the Argentine Mirage being shot down yesterday. He said it came in low from the north-west and flew straight into a barrage of anti-aircraft fire. Tony saw it hit first in the right wing, then in the left and then in the belly. It took evasive action and flew on out of sight, obviously in serious trouble.

Back at the Goose, I saw an Argentine doctor who I'm on nodding terms with. I thought I'd see if he felt like a chat, and he did. He said that the airport runway was OK (not sure I believe that) and that Hercules aircraft were continuing to fly in and out. But he said that often as they approach the Islands they are picked up by Royal Navy radar and must turn back before being intercepted by Harriers.

Late afternoon: London is saying that Galtieri spoke to the nation last night, in an attempt to stiffen the Argentine backbone. They would 'fight back with ferocity', he said. BA has admitted losing the two Mirages but is claiming that the British lost more in yesterday's clashes. The Pope has appealed for peace. Good luck with that, Your Holiness.

We had dinner, cooked by Aunt Ning, the girls and Mum. Very nice. If I hadn't sobered up completely from my trip to the Victory, I did so quickly when we tuned into BBC WS after dinner. I could hardly believe what I was hearing and, judging by the looks on the faces of everyone else, they shared my shock.

A British submarine has torpedoed the Argentine cruiser *General Belgrano*. The MoD in London is saying she was 'severely damaged' and they claim she was posing a threat to the Task Force. There is no word about the fate of the crew. Further details will be released later.

I'm shocked, actually horrified, that it has come to this: the first use of submarines and torpedoes in action since the Second World War, and what must be great loss of life among young sailors. We are the centre of this nightmare.

The weather is becoming windy, cold and overcast, which matches my spirits. I went to bed feeling depressed.

The Argentines are taking the blackout regulations seriously. At around 11.00 a patrol turned up and demanded to enter the Goose. They'd spotted a light in one of the east end rooms occupied by Argentine press. Des patched up the blackouts in that room.

Father Monaghan (who I noticed has been reading a book called *Father under Fire* by Neil Boyd) now goes around all the refugees before lights-out, checking on us. I hear him coming some way off: 'Goodnight, God bless; goodnight, God bless . . .' Then he gets to me and I'm ready to be a bit cynical in reply, but his, 'Goodnight, God bless' touches me. God bless him, too.

And God bless any young sailors who might be struggling to survive somewhere in the cold South Atlantic tonight.

Monday, 3 May

I woke early feeling stiff and groggy from a bad night's sleep. I got up once or twice during the night. I looked out on to a very dark Ross Road and noticed their special van with its revolving antenna, which we believe is being used to trace unauthorized radio transmissions. It was parked up outside the hotel.

After that, I tuned my little radio into the BBC, mainly to see if there was news about the *General Belgrano*. But nothing new is being reported. The British probably don't know whether the ship has sunk or not, as the sub would not have stayed around to find out.

BBC WS is speculating that SAS soldiers have already landed and will be guiding aircraft on to targets. If they were responsible for the massive bomb that detonated on the other side of the harbour while we were trying to have a few drinks yesterday, then I think they need to recalibrate their instruments.

There was another incident at about midnight. A British chopper approached an Argentine patrol boat, possibly an armed tug, and came under machine-gun fire. The chopper crew responded, sinking the boat. A second chopper approached looking for survivors but it was attacked by a second Argentine patrol boat. That boat was then attacked and damaged, although it didn't sink. Both choppers were OK.

Robert told me that the new TV station was broadcasting for a while this morning. We don't have a TV capable of picking up their transmissions here. I expect it will be on the air again tonight with propaganda and some old comedy shows. Robert says they close for the night with tub-thumping spiritual/political messages from their senior priest in the Islands. I've never known a nationality that can get nationalism so hopelessly mixed up with the Catholic faith. What a lot of nonsense.

Dad and I went back to the house late in the morning to check that all is OK there – most importantly, to find out if it's been broken into. Three Argentines are digging a defensive trench or bunker among the trees on the edge of the garden. This shook Dad a bit, and he's insisting he'll get compensation for the damage. I said, 'I don't know what the going rate is for a hole in the ground, Dad.' This didn't go down particularly well, but Dad seems to benefit from having something to plan, so he may well go up to see Bloomer-Reeve, demanding money.

The serious side of this is that it shows they are planning for combat not just around Stanley but *in* Stanley. And if they are going to have defensive positions in our garden, Rowan House is even less safe than it was.

In the early afternoon two Air Force men banged on the door and presented us with a signed and elaborately rubber-stamped form saying that they had come to take Dad's Land Rover. Dad was even angrier about this than he was about the holes in the ground. But it was clear to us that we had no choice, so he handed over the keys. They did seem a bit sheepish about it and said that the vehicle would be used as an ambulance. I suspect they say something similar to everyone whose vehicles they take. But we should have anticipated this and disabled the LR days ago.

After the upsetting afternoon spent at home, we were glad to get back to the warmth of the Upland Goose. Dad and I loaded our TV and the video recorder into the Daihatsu along with all the videos we could find. We'll set it up in the hotel lounge. It should help pass the hours after curfew. Supper was early and, as usual, made us all feel a lot better. Two more refugees have arrived: Siggie and Xenia Barnes.

Bill Etheridge at the Post Office called today to let me know there is a letter for me. I picked it up, and as soon as I saw the signature green envelope I knew it was from Pat in Neuquén. She wants me to somehow get on a plane and go over there to stay with her and her family. I'm touched by this because I know that she cares a lot about me and is worried about my safety. But there is absolutely no chance of getting on an Argentine aircraft out, and anyway, I do not feel that I can leave Mum and Dad and everyone else here. I'll write back to her of course and try to explain.[1]

Father Monaghan was out and about visiting his parishioners and the hospital today, as usual, and after supper he told us that an Argentine casualty from a crashed aircraft, probably a helicopter, has been taken to the hospital. He and

Monsignor Spraggon, who also keeps his ear to the ground, believe the man was rescued near Lively Island.

He went on to say that there are twenty-two Argentine casualties in the KEMH. That would take it beyond capacity in normal times. The patients are overflow from the Argentines' own field hospital. Most of the older residential patients and others who are not seriously ill have been moved out of the hospital into local homes. Aunt Lena is still there, though, and I'm glad about that, as she will be safe. Plus, she helps out in the kitchen. In fact, I think her tea-making skills are more appreciated than ever. I must pop up and see her again soon.

We settled in for a session listening to 'Calling the Falklands' and then to the news and 'Radio Newsreel'. Increasingly, we are doing this a little covertly, as we don't particularly want the Argentines in the hotel to know that the WS programmes are so important to us. They could start confiscating short-wave radios or jamming the signals. They have already started doing this to WS broadcasts in Spanish directed at the continent.

It's amazing to think that the *QE2* has been taken over by the government and is about to sail south with an entire brigade of soldiers, including Gurkhas. Two other ships will carry their equipment and supplies.

The submarine that was in action last night has not been named but she is nuclear-powered and what the Navy calls a 'hunter-killer'. BA is saying the *General Belgrano* has sunk, and there is no word of the crew, who number around 1,000 men. Ships and aircraft are searching the area not far from Cape Horn, but low cloud cover has been a problem.

The late-night WS news says that some of the cruiser's life rafts have been spotted from the air. The sea will be appallingly cold, so they'd better move quickly to rescue survivors.

Harold Briley, reporting from BA, says that the submarine attack has caused a wave of resentment against the British and the Americans. But it is likely to destroy the myth of Argentine invincibility which the Junta has been building up domestically since they invaded.

This evening, the mood is the Goose is a bit low. Tomorrow we'll set up the TV and video player, and then we'll look for some less serious videos. It'll do us all good.

To my mattress and blankets on the floor in the lounge an attempt to sleep. I had almost dropped off as I heard Father Monaghan doing his rounds. 'Good night, God bless; good night, God bless . . . '

Chapter 13

Hunting for the Transmitter

(4–8 May)

Tuesday, 4 May

There was another attack on the airport very early this morning (later confirmed to be a second Vulcan raid launched from Ascension Island). The blasts woke me up, but others in the hotel heard an aircraft preceding the blasts, around 5.00am. I couldn't count the explosions as they came in very quick succession.

Captain Romano came to the Goose an hour or two later, looking for Rob. I engineered a bump into him so I could ask him what had been going on. He said that some of the bombs seemed to have time-delayed fuses, meaning they exploded about 20 minutes after impact. He claimed there had not been a lot of damage. But he was looking grim, so although I didn't believe him I didn't push him any further.

A little later, we saw Harriers flying very high overhead, and I'm pretty sure that they were taking photos of the airport area to assess damage from the morning raid.

Later in the morning, Des, Paul and I hitched the trailer to Des's Land Rover and went to the least attractive place in Stanley, the YPF [Argentine state oil company] fuel depot, to buy some drums of oil for the hotel heating system. I couldn't help thinking that there were Harriers lurking around, and the huge fuel tanks are very juicy targets.

Des did not seem to be too bothered, but then he was with the RAF in the Second World War and was based on Malta during the Axis siege. So I guess he has seen worse.

I said to Paul, 'I could think of better things to be doing today. Fancy going fishing?'

He smiled a bit grimy. 'I wish!'

At the depot, Carlos [an Argentine who had been living happily in the Falklands for some years] was glum and not saying much. Very strangely, he was only accepting sterling in payment, which is still our currency alongside Argentine pesos so is allowed. But still, odd. Perhaps this is his little protest at the dumb Argentine military government. So we coughed up, loaded the drums *very* quickly and sped off back to the hotel. Ten minutes later, we were back in the kitchen having coffee.

On the way to and from the YPF fuel depot we noticed a large group of soldiers using a JCB digger to excavate what can only be a mass grave in the cemetery. We could see what looked like bodies awaiting burial. I couldn't count them, as we couldn't slow down for a better look. It is taking more to shock me now, but still, it's upsetting.

Troops broke into the Woodbine [the home of Aub and Sonia Summers] last night. Aub and Sonia are now there checking for damage and what may have been stolen.

I tuned into BBC WS early in the afternoon. There is disquiet in the House of Commons about the sinking of the *Belgrano*. The Government is being asked whether minimum force had been used. The official answer is that the ship had to be sunk as it was a clear threat to the Task Force, but some MPs think it might have been possible to inflict less damage on it. Torpedoes are blunt instruments, though.

The Argentines have rescued about 400 crewmen from the ship, and a further thirty-five life rafts have been spotted from the air. Survivors are being taken to Ushuaia. Not surprisingly, the Argentine press is outraged. They have labelled Thatcher a 'crazy killer'. If it becomes clear the ship wasn't a serious threat, I might have to agree with them.

The wife of a Harrier pilot who shot down an Argentine aircraft was interviewed for one of the papers, and she said she felt very sorry for the Argentine pilot's family. Her husband told her that he 'felt sick' when he saw the Mirage explode.

There is a notable lack of jingoism in the papers. Instead, there's real regret that men are dying because of stupid politicians. I think there is a similar mood here in the Islands. I haven't heard anyone express pleasure at the deaths of Argentines. Everyone seems genuinely shocked that it has come to this.

We checked the house again, feeding the cat (who's always very happy to see us) and checking whether the soldiers are still digging their bunker in the back yard. They were not there today.

I was glad to get back to the Goose before curfew, knowing we would have a good supper and be able to sleep in relative safety. But then, everything unravelled. WS announced that HMS *Sheffield,* a modern Type 42 missile destroyer, has been sunk north of the Falklands. Even the news reader sounded a bit stunned.

Sheffield was apparently hit by an air-launched missile [later confirmed to be a French-built Exocet]. Twelve men are missing and are probably dead.

All I feel is an overwhelming sense of disaster and sadness. I even feel some blame. This is being done in our name, and if we were not here, ships would not be sinking, aircraft would not be dropping bombs and – above all – men would not be dying. I want this to be over, but I know that we are just getting sucked deeper and deeper into it.

Argentine occupation troops march into Stanley on 2 April 1982 following the town's capture by their elite forces.

A Fokker F28 of the Argentine Air Force brings in troops and supplies following the invasion.

LVTP-7 amphibious personnel carriers moving towards Government House during the early stages of the invasion . . . and parked near the Upland Goose Hotel following the British surrender.

The Argentine flag flies over Stanley on 2 April.

Argentina deployed Panhard AML-90 armoured vehicles to the Falklands, one of which is seen here patrolling Stanley.

Pucara ground attack aircraft, such as this one flying low over Stanley, were based at the airport.

Argentine troops are crammed into a commandeered civilian Land Rover during their retreat on 14 June.

An ambulance assists the wounded as Argentine troops retreat through Stanley.

Troops of 3 Para, the Parachute Regiment, astride a Scorpion armoured vehicle examine a captured Argentine FN rifle as they await the order to move into the centre of Stanley on 14 June.

Royal Marines march into Stanley soon after the Argentine surrender.

The Union Flag flies over the smouldering remains of a civilian building on 14 June.

An Argentine Panhard armoured vehicle lies abandoned near the remains of Stanley's burnt-out Globe Store on 15 June.

British troops bring Argentine soldiers under control after they ran amok on the night of 14/15 June. HMS *Plymouth*, the first Task Force ship to enter Stanley Harbour, is visible in the background.

Argentine prisoners of war, floodlit by MV *Forrest*, are gathered on Stanley's Public Jetty for transfer to Task Force ships on the night of 15 June.

Troops of the Parachute Regiment march to Stanley's Christ Church Cathedral for a service of remembrance shortly after the Argentine surrender.

Pucara aircraft destroyed by bombing and shellfire at Stanley Airport, with Argentine prisoners of war in the distance.

Stanley's police station showing extensive damage caused by the helicopter attack of 11 June.

Argentine coastguard patrol craft *Rio Iguazu*, which was based at Stanley but put out of action by British aircraft on 22 May while carrying artillery pieces to Goose Green.

Griff Evans, the farm manager on Pebble Island, cares for a newborn lamb next to an Argentine Beechcraft T-34 ground attack aircraft, which was put out of action when the SAS raided the island's airbase. (This and subsequent photographs were taken in the weeks and months after the end of the war.)

British servicemen who have no known grave but the sea are honoured during a commemorative service aboard a naval ship in 1983.

A member of the Royal Engineers disposes of unexploded ammunition and abandoned weapons on a battlefield near Stanley.

Stanley resident Joe Cletheroe repairs his property, which was damaged in the final days of the fighting.

Margaret Thatcher and her husband Denis arrive in the Falklands in January 1983. She is met by Civil Commissioner Rex Hunt and Military Commissioner Major General David Thorne.

In October 1982 the Defence Secretary John Nott became the first British cabinet minister to visit the Falklands since the colony was founded in 1833. He is pictured meeting troops on West Falkland.

Wednesday, 5 May

Not much sleep last night. I was awake when the sun came up and I held my little radio to my ear to tune into WS without waking anyone up. Of course, there is profound shock in the UK at the sinking of what her crew called 'the shiny Sheff'. Flags in Portsmouth are at half-mast.

The ship's captain, Sam Salt, has already been interviewed by the press, presumably on the relative safety of one of the carriers. He says the crew only received a few seconds' warning, and within 20 seconds of the missile's impact the ship was filling with smoke and fumes. The survivors fought the fire for five hours before the last of them abandoned ship. Twenty men are now missing. The survivors are scattered around the fleet.

BA is saying that the attack took place at around 4.00pm yesterday. They also say that the patrol boat hit by the Task Force a few days ago has made it back to an Argentine port.

Father Monaghan came back from his rounds of the parish with disturbing news. Three houses were badly shot up last night. Stella Perry's boarding house on John Street was hit by rounds from the machine gun at the top of Church House drive. My guess is that these troops are so spooked that they are firing at shadows.

Ally Biggs was sleeping in one room and the bullets passed just a foot or two above him. Old Howard Johnson was sitting in the kitchen, which was riddled. Amazingly, Howard emerged stunned but safe.

Mary Hills' house, also on John Street, received a number of rounds. Again, no injuries (miraculously). Dennis Place's home also came under fire. He and his wife live near the gorse bushes not far from Government House. Dennis said he was up at the time, but had he been in bed he wouldn't have survived.

The Argentine military administrators seem to be trying to do the right thing. They have told the three house-owners to assess the damage and submit a claim for compensation within 48 hours.

The panic shooting continued sporadically throughout today. It's not a safe environment at all. Nevertheless, in the morning we paid a quick visit to Rowan House to check on things and give the cat some food. At some point we may need to bring him to the Goose.

It's tense around town. I saw Robert briefly, and he told me that very early this morning the refugees in the West Store were marched outside and lined up facing the wall with their arms raised. That must have been terrifying. They were asked to explain why so many of them had spent the night there. The Argentine troops involved were clearly not aware that people are allowed to congregate in 'safe' places. Fortunately, the civilians' explanations were accepted and they were allowed to re-enter the West Store. It makes the blood run cold.

I went back to the Goose late morning and had a very welcome mug of coffee. But this was interrupted by Captain Romano. Normally he is fairly relaxed, but today was different. He said he wanted to search my house. He was specific about me, not Mum and Dad, and he waved a piece of paper on which I could clearly see my name.

Romano told me to accompany him and a couple of very professional-looking green-beret-type soldiers to Rowan, where they intended to search.

'We know someone is using a radio transmitter,' he said, looking me squarely in the eye.

I pushed my luck a bit and asked him how they knew that, and he said that there was no other way that the British could have known that the Mirage jet had been shot down by their own anti-aircraft fire. He had a point.

We walked up Villiers Street to Rowan House, and one of the soldiers kept watch outside while Romano and the other guy went through the house room by room, looking for the transmitter. Oddly, they didn't search the garage or the coal shed. They might have become briefly quite excited if they had found my bunker. After that, they said I was free to go, left me and headed back to Ross Road.

I spent some quality time with the cat (who I think appreciated it as much as I did). I sat there, just thinking. Of course, it's not me who's transmitting, but I'm glad someone appears to be doing so. Would I do it if I could? I'm not sure. Even if I had access to a short-wave transmitter, I wouldn't know how to use it. And, frankly, I don't think I'd have the courage.

At the Goose this evening the gossip is that the Argentines are taking over the Fire Service, as the local crew say they need protection from itchy-fingered troops. Some of the military are said to have a 'vague' idea of how the Land Rover fire engines and other kit work, but this is not enough to operate it effectively. I expect they will be forced to leave it in the hands of Neville Bennet and his team and give them the protection they need.

Another talking point is that, from now on, no parking will be permitted on the entire length of Ross Road. I can't see the logic of that, unless they want to keep the road free for the rapid movement of their vehicles

We tuned in to 'Calling the Falklands' in time to hear Peter King's cheerful voice say that the programme has now broadcast 2,000 messages to Islanders from family and friends. That's quite something. CTF relayed a message from Michael [in Oxford] which I know Mum and Dad appreciated a lot. He requested the theme tune from *Rocky*, and they played it. Quite a good choice.

The mayor of Portsmouth, where HMS *Sheffield* was based, has said that the best memorial to the sailors who died on the ship would be for the Task Force to carry out their mission as quickly and with as little bloodshed as possible. *Sheffield* herself is thought to be still afloat, though she is burned out and abandoned.

Tonight, Stanley is surprisingly quiet. Most of the town is blacked out, but the Argentines have been putting the streetlights on along the Fitzroy Road area, perhaps because a total blackout would only help the SAS, who they seem to be convinced have infiltrated the town.

And with that, I'm off to my bivouac behind the chimney breast.

Thursday, 6 May

Early morning news, crackling almost inaudibly through the ether from WS. London has pretty much knocked diplomacy on the head. They say there can now be no ceasefire unless the Argentines unilaterally withdraw. I can't see that happening, so that's it, I think.

One news item that almost made me cough up my tea (thanks, as ever, for that, Aunt Ning) is the report that London has said it will not use nuclear weapons in the conflict. I should bloody well hope not! Presumably, the matter is raised because the Vulcans are nuclear-capable and have proven that they could reach Argentine coastal cities, and because there are rumours that some of the ships may be equipped with nuclear depth charges that they were unable to offload before they headed south. London said that use of such weapons is 'inconceivable'.

It's being reported that two Harriers from the Task Force disappeared yesterday and are presumed lost. There are no details, but the MoD is saying that they were not shot down by Argentine forces. It's upsetting to think of the poor pilots searching in vain for their ships. There are twenty warships and forty-five Fleet Auxiliary or civilian support ships in the zone now. What a shame that the pilots could not have at least found one of these ships and landed on or ejected near her.

Soon after breakfast, I was outside the Goose taking some air when I met the Welsh guy who is the interpreter at Government House. I greeted him and we got chatting. I asked him, more in jest than seriously, how General Menendez is finding Government House.

'I hope the Foreign Office made it nice and comfortable for him,' I said.

'Yes, it is very comfortable, very traditional and nice. But you know the General does not spend every night there.' I raised an eyebrow. 'Yes, I think he is a bit nervous, so he moves around other places for safety.'

He's a very friendly chap, but if I was him I might be a bit more careful what I say to whom. Very interesting, though, and something to share with the others in the hotel. Who knows, it might even filter through to someone who can pass it on to those who might make good use of it.

I was outside the hotel again this afternoon when I saw an Argentine Hercules approaching low over the harbour. It touched down at the airport, which proves that either the runway was not cratered during the bombing raids, or that the

Argentines were able to repair it very quickly. Hercules are very tough planes, though, and they don't need much in the way of a runway. I'm impressed by the courage of the Argentine pilots flying in despite the blockade.

The Herc was on the ground for only about 45 minutes. It took off again and headed to the west, again at very low level. The Argentine troops nearby were ecstatic, punching the air. There was even some celebratory shooting into the air. I hate it when they do that: what goes up has got to come down, somewhere.

The Argentine TV team, who are lodged up the east end of the Goose, were equally ecstatic. Kasanzew the presenter came up to me, and said, 'You see! Your Air Force failed to destroy the airport.'

'Yes, but I think the RAF will be back to finish the job soon.'

We scowled at each other.

I'd heard a rumour that the body of a Harrier pilot who had been killed during a raid was being brought into Stanley for burial, so I spent a little while this afternoon around the Cathedral, where I met Fred Clarke, who was clutching a rolled-up Union Flag. We chatted for a bit, and he said that he intended to unfurl it if the poor pilot was brought into the Cathedral for a funeral service. He wasn't, though.

Padre Bagnall told us later that he had only been allowed to conduct a brief service at the cemetery. An Argentine officer told the padre that as they bury their own men quietly, they could not have a 'full military honours' funeral for a British pilot. It seems more probable to me, though, that they didn't have a proper service because every civilian in Stanley would have turned out to pay their respects, and they did not want a scene like that.

Later, Pete, Robert and I met at Church House. We had a drink or two and a good chat. We left again after a couple of hours and as we were crossing Dean Street, a machine gun opened up with several long bursts. We couldn't tell where the gun was, but it seemed to be almost on top of us. We were on the east side of the road and had no cover at all.

Badly shaken, we pressed ourselves into the side of a house, but realized that gave us no cover. So we ran across the road to the office entrance of the West Store. The door is set back in the concrete wall, and as the machine gun opened up again, the three of us pressed ourselves into this small space. Peter hammered on the door and a nervous voice responded, 'Who's there?'

Peter yelled back, 'It's the Kings and Bound. Open the fucking door!'

Bolts were retracted and keys turned, and we tumbled into the office. We stayed there for about 15 minutes. There was no more firing, so we cautiously ventured out again. Pete and Robert headed back to their parents' house on Fitzroy Road, and I legged it along Ross Rd to the Goose. I still couldn't see the machine gun, but it must have been at the head of the FIC slipway. I hope the gun was pointing into the harbour rather than up Dean Street, but I had no way of telling. I didn't share this experience with Mum and Dad back at the Goose.

Tuning in to listen to CTF has become a ritual for us refugees. Reception on 9.915 MHz is usually good, and as well as the usual messages from stressed friends and relatives there was a good round-up of news.

More light was shed on the latest failed diplomacy. The analysts are saying that London is miffed because BA turned down the plan that was being cooked up between the US and Peru. Francis Pym said, 'There could have been a ceasefire if the Argentines had agreed to it.'

Had the agreement been signed, there would have been an immediate ceasefire and a rapid withdrawal of Argentine forces. At the same time, the Task Force would have withdrawn from the area. A small group of neutral countries would then have moved in to administer the Islands while London and BA talked. That does seem like a good opportunity missed.

I'm pretty sure that we've just witnessed the last gasps of diplomacy. From here on it's going to be no-holds-barred, which is not a nice thought to end the day on.

Friday, 7 May

Yesterday, the Argentines managed to crash a 'box' plane on the racecourse. This is – or was – a small aircraft built by Shorts in the UK, I think, and was based at the racecourse rather than the airport. They were using it to ferry ammunition, men and supplies around the Islands. I guess the plane hit a soft spot on the racecourse on landing or take-off. I don't know if anyone was injured or killed.

Conversation overheard between an MP and some of the Argentine journalists this morning: Yesterday three aircraft, almost certainly Hercules, landed and took off from the runway, which has been repaired. The MP said the planes had brought mail in, but whether that is just mail for the troops or for us as well is not clear. Even when mail does arrive – and that isn't often – the Post Office is so understaffed that it can take up to a week for letters to appear in mailboxes. I wonder if this might also be because the Argentines are reading mail to people of particular interest to them. But to be fair, I have no evidence of this.

Dad decided to test the mail service recently. He posted a registered letter to himself, and it took eight days to return to him. In that time it would have covered no more than 100 yards.

I visited Aunt Lena at the hospital last night. She was her usual chatty self, creating long and complicated stories out of almost nothing, but holding you gripped, nevertheless. I really don't know how she does it. Just as the story seems to be ending, she goes through the elaborate ritual of lighting up another Players Navy Cut, inhaling deeply and saying, 'Anyway, so-and-so said to me . . .' Then the story resumes.

The main thing, though, is that she is still in good spirits and being looked after well by Alison Bleaney and the rest of the medical staff.

I had a look out the hospital's west windows and counted three helicopters parked on the football pitch. It looks like this is now a permanent base, as there's also a large dump of 40-gallon fuel drums. This is a potential target only about 200 yards from the hospital. I wonder if that's by design.

I drove past the cemetery (probably a mistake, as I shouldn't be flaunting the fact that I still have the little Daihatsu jeep) and saw at least nine marked new graves at the east end, as well as a long pit, which may be a mass grave. One of the wooden crosses has a pilot's white helmet on it. I don't think British pilots use white helmets, so this could be the grave of the Argentine pilot shot down by their own AA fire. I know that some of the carpenters at the Public Works Department have been put to work making wooden crosses. It is all very depressing.

Dad and I were back at Rowan House today. He is cheerful if he has things to do. He wandered up to check on the Argentine bunker or trench at the south side of the house. No more work has been done on it, and fortunately no soldiers were there. But Dad noticed some movement around the vegetable patch and found a big mother hen with three little pullets. Dad got them some corn and they clucked around contentedly, as did Dad, really. The birds seem to have made their home in the greenhouse which is fine. They may give us an egg or two in lieu of rent.

This is just the latest bit of our animal welfare work. Yesterday, one of Murdoch McLeod's neighbours said that he had heard a cat in the abandoned house. I couldn't ignore it, so I found a slightly open window and climbed in. I found a big friendly animal that was clearly starving. I took him back to Rowan House, and Dad gave him a good meal. We'll do our best to look after him. No one seems to know where the McLeods are, but we assume they left for the camp in such a hurry that they forgot about the cat. Anyway, we've named him Murdoch, and he seems to be a very happy chap now.

Most days, Mum makes food at Rowan that she takes back to the Goose for supper. The number of refugees there is growing, and they need to be fed. We are now multi-denominational, as Padre and Mrs Bagnall from the Cathedral have moved in. They share spiritual duties with Father Monaghan.

Rob Pitaluga is still with us there, under house arrest. He is only allowed to walk as far as the police station once a day, where he must check in with the intelligence and police unit. Nothing gets him down, though.

'How are you, old chap?' he'll say. 'Bearing up? Jolly good!'

Dinner prepared by Aunt Ning and the girls and Mum boosted morale no end. We listened to CTF at 6.20 followed by the news and 'Radio Newsreel'. We huddle around the radio, keeping the volume low, rather than risk the Argentines in the east end of the hotel hearing it.

London has extended the naval blockade to just 12 miles from the Argentine coast. The Argentine Navy will probably respect it, as with the *Belgrano* sinking fresh in their minds, they know that British submarines are in the area.

A further twenty Harriers are being flown to the Task Force, staging through Ascension Island. They have been rapidly fitted with the latest model of Sidewinder air-to-air missiles. Some very long-range Nimrod aircraft are also being fitted with air-to-air refuelling capability and are deploying to Ascension. They will fly very long missions, presumably to give the Task Force warning of incoming attacks. After the loss of *Sheffield*, they clearly need it.

None of this seems real. There has been a genuine effort to secure peace, but men are already dying, supposedly for us, when just a few months ago we were second-class Brits and London hardly cared about us at all. We don't even have the right to live and work in the UK. So, is this really about hurt British pride and the government fighting for its own survival? I hate to say it, but I think it is.

Saturday, 8 May

Today is warm and calm, but cloudy. As I write this in the early evening, it's been remarkably quiet, with no naval or air action that I am aware of. I haven't even heard any gunfire. I saw one Hercules fly in and out this morning. Those pilots have got *cojones*.

Surprisingly, the shop continues to tick over. Mum and Dad usually open it from 2.00 to 4.00pm. The military say all businesses must be closed by then. A few locals come by, often looking for anoraks and warm clothing as the nights draw in. I have great difficulty finding any enthusiasm to help them, but I do a bit now and again. I expect we'll find one day soon that troops have broken in and helped themselves to the stock.

I went for a walk east and west along the front of town, keeping up a brisk pace so I looked like I was going somewhere rather than having a look around. I'm keeping use of the jeep to a minimum, partly because I hardly have any petrol for it and partly because I don't want it to attract the attention of any Argentines who might want to nick it.

I can see that that the Argentines are building up their defences on the Camber ridge [on the north side of Stanley Harbour]. There are new gun emplacements there.

There are at least two Pucara ground-attack aircraft, maybe more, still operating from Stanley Airport. It's hard to see what they are armed with, but they appear to have rocket launcher 'drums' under the wings. Clearly, they are meant for ground attack.

At 6.20pm it's 'Calling the Falklands' time, of course, so I was back in the hotel in time for that and I joined Dad, Rob, Des and our two spiritual leaders around the radio. It may be quiet here today, but not so elsewhere in the world.

The Harriers which are due to reinforce the Task Force have safely landed on Ascension after a flight of nine hours, which is the longest on record for small attack aircraft. I hope the pilots had thermoses of coffee and sandwiches with them. On the other hand, maybe that wouldn't be such a good idea, as toilet facilities in Harriers can't be up to much.

Red Cross officials have visited the Argentines captured on South Georgia, checking that they are being treated properly according to the Geneva Convention. Other Red Cross people are visiting hospitals in Argentine Patagonia. And apparently, they will visit the Falklands as soon as safe passage can be arranged. I suspect we'll never see them.

There is intensive activity at the UN. Enrique Ros had been representing BA at the UN, and he and the British Ambassador, Anthony Parsons, have been having separate meetings with the Secretary General, Pérez de Cuéllar. He says there has been 'some progress'. This has been the second full day of talks, and he says they will continue tomorrow.

EEC [European Economic Community] ministers have again voiced support for the UK but say they would deplore the use of force that might endanger peace talks. I'm with them there. Brussels will review trade sanctions against Argentina in nine days' time.

Finally, there was a message of sympathy and prayer from Monsignor Ireland and Brother Venacius.[1] They are very kind, but I'm getting a bit overloaded with the spiritual stuff. It doesn't seem to be doing much good.

I tuned into WS again just before hitting the sack. Things have changed a bit since CTF at 6.20pm. The UN delegations will be consulting their governments overnight, but this is against a backdrop of increasing violence. I assume that tomorrow we will know the outcome of the UN talks.

Chapter 14

Shopping and Bombing

(9–13 May)

Sunday, 9 May

Disturbed sleep last night. I'd thought we might not see more major action here until the outcome of the talks is known. But I was wrong. At 1.10am we were woken by the sound of shelling. Hard to tell, even roughly, where the British shells were landing, but they were no direct threat to us. I'd say they were a mile or so to the west, near the edge of town.

Some of us got up and went into the front porch. We kept the lights off and nobody said much; when we did exchange words, they were whispered. Although the shells were falling a good way away, I think we all felt vulnerable. I could hear the distant 'pop' of the shells leaving the guns of the warships, then about three seconds later, they would land with a 'crump'. The shelling stopped at about 2.00am. Interesting intelligence from the girls [Anna, Alison and Barbara]. Yesterday, they were doing some housekeeping when they overheard a conversation between a couple of the Argentine officers lodged at the other end of the hotel. These guys don't know that some of us speak Spanish. Anyway, they said that General Menendez left Stanley on a Hercules the day before yesterday with a couple of other senior officers. We are wondering if he is gone for good or has simply gone back to BA to liaise with the Junta.

Dad remains furious about his Land Rover being taken away. I have seen it being used around Stanley, but not as an ambulance, which is what they claimed they would use it for. On every occasion it's been packed with troops and sprouting guns. Dad decided to go and see Carlos Bloomer-Reeve about it yesterday. Bloomer said that there was nothing he could do, as under military law they have the right to take civilian vehicles. However, he signed a piece of paper saying that they would pay £4.00 a day for the Land Rover. That's almost nothing, of course, but in a way it's a good price: enough to prove they are not getting it scot-free, but not so much that anyone could say Dad is profiteering from the situation. Anyway, they are bound to wreck it.

News from Radio Islas Malvinas is not usually worth giving time to, but they are reporting that aircraft from the Task Force have sunk one of their fishing boats about 70 miles south of the Islands. They said it was 'just fishing'. Fishing for information, I expect.

It's now clear that some of last night's shells fell very close to houses. One landed near John Broderick's house at the west end of Stanley. Kathy and Robert Watson, who live near John Broderick, had a very narrow escape. Kathy told Mum today that they could hear the shells whistling in from the south and landing too close for comfort. At 4.5 inches in diameter, these naval shells are bloody big things.

Some facts about the attack on the Argentine trawler yesterday gleaned from WS early this afternoon: She is the *Narwhal*, and the Task Force is claiming that she was gathering intelligence. A Harrier dropped a bomb on her and then she was strafed, before the crew took to the lifeboats. They were rescued by a British ship, but it's not clear if there were casualties.

It was good to hear a familiar voice on CTF this evening. Claudette Mosely, who worked for our radio station but is now in the UK, had a guest spot with Peter King on the programme. Speaking from a BBC studio in Southampton, she read quite a few messages for people here from friends and families in UK. Her section of the show was introduced with the old FIBS theme tune. She also introduced Rock Berntsen, who sang his song 'Kelpers After All'. One of the lines from the song put a smile on our faces: 'When you get to Heaven and the signpost comes in sight, it'll say all peat-cutting Kelpers to the peat bogs on the right.' Lovely!

The CTF messages can be very moving, and you get a sense of the stress people must be under, not knowing what is happening to us here. I'm sure their imaginations must run wild.

An opinion poll suggests the government is benefiting from a Falklands boost: if there was an election today, the Tories would win comfortably.

A memorial service for the twenty men who died on HMS *Sheffield* was held today. Ministers were there, and the church was so full that about 600 people had to listen to the service outside.

The Argentine account of the trawler attack is very different to the British story. They say the ship was sunk and the crew were machine-gunned in the lifeboats. The MoD has denied this of course, but they do admit that one Argentine was killed in the attack.

Diplomatic uncertainty still prevails as the day ends. Both Brits and Argentines at the UN have been presented with a document detailing the proposal, and they have gone off to think about it. Will we see a positive decision tomorrow? I wouldn't put any money on it, not even a bundle of worthless Argentine pesos.

Monday, 10 May

Last night's sleep was broken by another naval bombardment. It began at 3.25am and went on sporadically for just over an hour. Standing in the dark front porch of the Goose, we could see the flashes of the explosions, and we think that the target was around the Head of the Bay, possibly Moody Brook or the old ESRO [European Space Research Organization] building. From our point of view this is not great, as the shells must have fallen very near our water filtration plant.

Later today, we heard from some of the Public Works Department people that the water supply system was indeed hit, although not the filtration plant itself. It seems that one shell blew a hole in the main pipeline to town. The PWD guys also said that while they were repairing the water main they noticed that a shell had gone through the roof of the ESRO building. These guys are showing real courage, and we are relying on them.

We had got some breakfast in and were going back to Rowan to check on it and feed the cats and our newly acquired chickens, when we were caught by a long burst of shelling. About ten naval rounds thudded in on the south side of town. I also saw a few landing on the airport. This shook us a bit. We did the necessary chores quickly before heading back down Villiers Street to the Goose. If this was the prelude to something bigger, the Goose would be the safest place. But that seemed to be it from the Navy for the day. I'm guessing that the Navy steamed in close, did their shelling and got out again quickly, hoping to avoid an air attack.

After this, it seemed weird to do something as normal as go to the Post Office to check for mail. Surprisingly, though, one of the blockade-busting Hercs must have brought some civilian mail in. I received copies of the *Buenos Aires Herald*. But what I valued most was a touching letter from Pat's sister Anna in Neuquén. Anna echoed Pat's invitation to go and stay with them until the fighting is over. She didn't say it in the letter, but I can imagine how angry she and the family are with the military government. It might have been possible for me to fly out a couple of weeks ago, but I wouldn't have gone anyway, and now it is impossible. Pat and Anna are so kind. I'll write to them thanking them and explaining that I just can't leave.

It's been very foggy all day, which might explain why the Navy felt bold enough to come close in broad daylight and shell the Argentine positions.

The Rowan House bunker is now ready. It's only about 4ft high. It's covered over with bags of coal and timber and, apart from the small door, you wouldn't guess that there is a room inside, with a cooker, some water and tinned food. I've put a tarp on the floor and even fed an extension cable in from a socket in the garage, so there would be electric light as long as there is power. If we are at Rowan and there is shooting or shelling in the area we'll lie low in the shelter.

John Leonard called in at the Goose late this afternoon. As usual when you meet friends these days, we shared our news. John said he'd been told that some of last night's shells were dropped in a circle around Moody Brook. We concluded that they were demonstrating their accuracy or trying to pick off the helicopters in the area, while not destroying the old Marines barracks. I think most of NP

8901 would have been quite happy for the barracks to be shelled. They should have been condemned years ago.

We gathered around the radio in the kitchen this evening for 'Calling the Falklands', and to our surprise found it almost impossible to hear. Reception on 11.82 MHz was initially just about audible, but very soon it was obliterated by a loud oscillating noise. This noise was only present on 11.82 MHz, but the BBC's other frequency, 15.40 MHz, was naturally very bad. It seems clear that the Argentines have started jamming the programme.

As a result of all this, we picked up very little from CTF this evening. But right at the start of the programme, a British Government official said that we are in real danger and they are worried about us. No kidding.

Later this evening, we tried to tune into WS on 15.40 MHz, and there was no jamming. We managed to pick up some interesting information from the general news. HMS *Sheffield* has sunk. She was being towed out of the area when she went down. The Argentine trawler attacked yesterday has also gone down.

The trawler incident strikes me as another possible example of excessive force. I can't see how it was necessary to attack the ship so severely that she was sunk. Of course it's necessary to stop Argentine ships, but presumably the spy-trawler was unarmed.

Tuesday, 11 May

First thing this morning, I noticed the Argentine journalists in the Goose looking shocked and despondent as they were getting a briefing from Mora, the civilian who now runs Radio Islas Malvinas. After Mora had scuttled off, I approached the cameraman, who is friendlier than the reporter.

'It's your Navy,' he said.

'Well, it's not mine; more of the Queen's really, but what of it?'

'They attacked one of our transport ships last night in Falkland Sound and sank it. It was carrying fuel and supplies, some of it for the Islanders. We don't think there are any survivors. The ship was the *Isla de los Estados*.'

I couldn't hide my shock, and I muttered, 'I'm really sorry to hear that,' which I was.

The *Isla de los Estados* was in Stanley just a few days ago, and in recent years she's become a familiar sight here, bringing in fuel, gas and other supplies. The crew often visited the shop and bought lots of perfume, watches and other goods that are expensive in Argentina. She's a naval support vessel but unarmed. Of course, if you decide to break a military blockade you are asking for trouble, but regardless of nationality, it is shocking and upsetting.

The cameraman and I raised eyebrows and shrugged at each other. He wandered off gloomily.

I tuned into the BBC WS and there were early claims that the ship was a tanker (which she was not) and that she blew up spectacularly when shelled by a destroyer or frigate. The Navy is saying that both ships were enveloped in fog, and lives could have been saved had *Isla de los Estados* stopped when ordered to do so by ship-to-ship radio.

Hardly any shelling last night. I counted four shells at about 8.30am, all of which landed some considerable distance away. It was foggy all night and it's continuing today.

Throughout the day, I couldn't get the sinking of the *Isla de los Estados* out of my mind. In particular, I wondered if enough warning had been given before she was blown out of the water. They would have been able to send a message via Channel 16 on the VHF radio system, but language could have been a problem. Apparently, a few flares or star shells were fired over the ship, but these would not necessarily have been interpreted as a demand to stop. It bothers me.

Stanley is looking dirty and broken. We are into winter now, and the wet ground is being churned up by military boots and trucks. The roads are covered in mud, and rubbish is accumulating everywhere. Bless the Public Works Department rubbish disposal guys, who are continuing to work hard, but they can't shift the rubbish faster than it accumulates and are not being allowed into some areas. We used to be proud of our little town's bright and cheerful appearance. But now it's reflecting our mood: neglected, depressed and miserable.

To cheer myself up, I went to the Victory in the late afternoon for a few drinks with Robert. Usual routine: a quick look around to make sure there are no soldiers in the area, then scuttle around to the north side of the building and bang on the door. Sue Whitney pokes a head out to check us, then ushers us in.

There must have been about a dozen people, barely visible through the cloud of cigarette smoke. Rob and I propped up the bar. He downed a few vodka and Cokes and I did the same with some whisky. He'd heard that a military policeman guarding the hospital had been shot and seriously injured. The MP had been on the streets after curfew. Apparently, he was challenged but didn't hear it. So they shot him. I wonder if this was the same young MP who walked me from the hospital to the Smiths' house with some medicines after dark a while back.

More houses have been broken into. Jimmy Watson's house at the top of Dean Street had a particularly nasty encounter with Argentine soldiers. Jimmy and his wife Minnie were sheltering at the West Store when their house was burgled. The couple's possessions were turned out of cupboards and drawers and those that were not stolen were stomped on. This will be embarrassing to the likes of Carlos Bloomer-Reeve, who is trying to convince us that Argentine rule is benign.

After about an hour we slipped out the door again and went back to the Goose, where we chatted with Anna for a while. Both she and Robert are still working mornings at the Treasury.

The foggy conditions stopped flights in and out of Stanley today. The Argentine pilots were probably quite pleased. If I was them, I'd rather stay at base and drink *mate* and smoke Jockey Club fags than dice with death flying in and out of Stanley.

The Argentines were jamming CTF again this evening (we are now sure of this). But we managed to hear some news before the noise reached a crescendo. And we picked up more later from general WS broadcasts.

Peace talks at the UN stagger on. BA says it is still putting forward proposals, and London says they expect the talks to continue tomorrow and perhaps into the next day.

BA is not officially saying anything about the loss of the *Isla de los Estados*, although the MoD has confirmed they sank it, saying she exploded in 'a huge fireball'.

HMS *Sheffield* has been declared a war grave after sinking while under tow. Her precise position is not being revealed.

The news media, the BBC in particular, is receiving a hammering at the hands of Conservative Members of Parliament, who say that news coverage is not pro-British enough. The BBC is insisting that it must report the conflict objectively. Those MPs should hear an edition or two of 'Calling the Falklands', which is blatantly pro-Falklanders. WS can't be faulted as far as we're concerned.

My spirits lifted even further thanks to a hearty dinner provided by Aunt Ning, the girls, Mum and others among the refugees. We are ten now: Aub and Sonia Summers, Father Monaghan, Revd Bagnall and his wife from the Cathedral, Siggy and Xenia Barnes, Rob Pitaluga, Mum, Dad and me.

Most of us check on our houses or do other things during the day, except Rob, as he's under house arrest. The two priests visit their flocks, and we all meet up again at the Goose before curfew. It's not just the thick stone walls of the Goose that help us to feel safe; it's the camaraderie, too. No matter how depressing the day may have been, we end it together, usually finding something to smile and even laugh about.

Wednesday, 12 May

The last 24 hours have been quiet. It was almost as if the *Isla de los Estados* going up in a ball of flame shocked everyone to a standstill. More likely, though, London has throttled-back the Task Force a bit while the talks at the UN reach a crucial stage. Besides, there has been a lot of low cloud, so visibility for air raids and shelling has been reduced greatly.

The sky is much clearer now. It became lively overhead again shortly before midday. Anti-aircraft gunners opened up (hopelessly) on two very high-flying aircraft over Stanley which I assume were Harriers on a reconnaissance mission.

If the pilots have seen anything of interest, I expect they will be lobbing high explosives at it tomorrow.

Anna and I went to the West Store at about 11.15am to buy some food, and while we were filling baskets with baked beans and what-not, a couple of shells landed fairly near. We heard them, of course, but as they didn't seem that close, we carried on shopping. Afterwards we learned that the shells had landed in the harbour, more or less opposite the West Store. On the way out we ran into Melvyn Turner, who said he had seen one shell land on the other side of the harbour near Navy Point. It had appealed to Melvyn's sense of humour.

'A lot of grass and diddle-dee was moved,' he said.

Back at the Goose, Dad saw one of the shells land in the harbour, throwing a column of water high into the air. I'm a bit surprised by this broad-daylight shelling, as the warships are taking a big chance.

Later, about twenty rounds landed south of town. The impacts were loud, but it wasn't possible to see exactly where they landed.

Mum and Dad decided against opening the shop today, even for the few hours allowed, because of the risk of more action. They are right. Best to keep our heads down today.

At about 3.00pm BBC WS flashed the news that two Skyhawks had been shot down with Seawolf missiles in an attack on the Task Force. There were no reports of British casualties. Another Skyhawk escaped. This happened about 30 miles off the Falklands.

Curiosity got the better of me in the afternoon. I decided to ignore the jeep's fuel gauge, which indicates I have very little petrol left, and took it for a quick drive around the south side of town. There was no sign of shell impacts among the houses, but I did drive past a new arrival at the east end of Davis St that made me slow down and stare. This was a huge mobile radar. It is sneakily located in the garden of one of the white bungalows by the Common Gate. Locating something like this among civilian houses must be against the Geneva Convention. But in any case, I think everyone has abandoned these vulnerable houses. The reconnaissance Harriers probably spotted the radar this morning.

Dad dropped by the Post Office today, as much to see [his friend] Bill Etheridge as anything, I expect. There was just one letter for us, from Casio in Japan regarding an order for digital watches. It had been opened very crudely and then sealed again with tape. So it seems they are opening and checking civilian mail.

For my part, I headed to the Victory to meet Robert for a drink or two. I am amazed the Argentines have not cottoned on to this yet and closed the bar. Gatherings of more than a few people are supposedly banned. Someone said twenty-two Argentine soldiers had arrived at the hospital with various illness and injury. They were accommodated in the east end of the building. My source said that there were cases of gangrene and dysentery.

I didn't stay at the Victory long as it is Aunt Ning's birthday today, so I needed to be back at the Goose early. On the way in I encountered two of the Argentine staff officers chatting. They greeted me, and I nodded at them. They seemed to want to chat, so I stopped. I've had these kinds of conversations before, and I'm pretty sure that the Argentines see them as an opportunity to feed misinformation directly into the community, and perhaps even back to London via the rumoured covert radio operator. So I treat everything they say with a huge pinch of salt. They claimed that 'our' little ship *Forrest*, which they took over, was sunk the day before yesterday near Sea Lion Island. If *Forrest* has been lost, that would be a real shame. Uncle Jack is her skipper, although he hasn't been aboard her since the invasion.

The two officers also asked if I had heard that HMS *Herme*s had been badly damaged in an air attack and is limping back to the Caribbean for repairs. I said, yes, I had heard something like this, but it wasn't true. 'I'm certain *Herme*s is OK,' I said. If there was any truth in it, it would have been reported by the BBC. They shrugged their shoulders. We all have our versions of the truth, I suppose.

These guys seemed surprised that we are continuing with our normal lives as much as possible. And they are right; it is amazing.

'People were shopping at the West Store this morning as bombs were exploding,' said one of them. 'It doesn't make sense.'

'Yes,' I said. 'Anna [whom they know] and I were among them. We worry a lot more about the small arms fire from your nervous soldiers. If you can do something about that, we would appreciate it.'

They smiled, a bit sadly, I thought. I left them and carried on into the hotel.

All the refugees were back in the Goose early for Aunt Ning's little celebration. Mum, Sonia and Barbara made a cake, and it was a really nice outbreak of something like normality: lots of smiles and laughter from our disparate little band of refugees.

Still feeling cheerful, we tuned into CTF in the hope that it would not be jammed. It was, but by moving between frequencies we managed to hear a fair bit of the programme.

Three members of a British TV news team were kidnapped in Buenos Aires today. A fourth member of the team managed to escape, and he said that he believed the kidnappers were members of the security forces, in other words the military or the police.

Another British reporter was detained when he was about to board a plane to Montevideo. This is typical Argentine government behaviour of course. Once abducted, many people are never seen again. In this case, the TV guys were stripped naked and left about 30km from BA; not at all nice, but it could have been so much worse.

Dick Baker [Rex Hunt's deputy] managed to get a strange little message through the static. I think he said that someone had received messages from the Falklands. He did not, of course, say from whom or how they had been sent. We suspect – and the Argentines are convinced – there is a radio operator still sending messages out of the islands. I think we all have ideas about who that might be. Perhaps Dick was trying to tell that person that the messages are getting through.

Our spirits were still good this evening, and after a few drinks we all headed for bed. I was lying there on my mattress in the dark lounge as Father Monaghan did his rounds. 'Good night, God bless . . . Good night, God bless.'

And God bless you, too, Father.

Thursday, 13 May

As I lay there last night waiting for the Navy to cruise in and begin shelling, it was almost too quiet. I have an odd feeling about the night attacks. I worry about the risk of shells falling short or overshooting and landing on civilian houses. But I do want the pressure kept up so that, even at this late stage, the Argentines might decide they've had enough of their stupid adventure and sign a peace deal. But when there is no shelling, I start thinking about what else might be going on. Is something far worse waiting for us? I know this doesn't make much sense. But at night my thoughts become darker.

I'm writing this in the afternoon, and so far the day has been peaceful. No sign of action in the sky or offshore. And not even much sign of troops on the streets. It's a calm day with fog and low cloud. Perhaps that is limiting activity.

WS is shedding light on what happened during the air attacks yesterday. They are now saying that three Skyhawks were shot down, rather than the two claimed yesterday. There were twelve planes involved in the attack and they came in three waves. The third wave, though, turned around before making contact.

The BBC's analysts are saying that the destroyers or frigates that shot down the Skyhawks were probably protecting the two carriers, which would have been the main targets. If one of them is put out of action, it might be game over. The commentators think the Skyhawks flew from shore bases, rather than the carrier *25 de Mayo*. They think she is out of action because of problems with her catapult launching system. Let's hope they are right.

Despite the very low cloud, one Hercules flew into the airport and took off again after a very short time on the ground. I saw it come in very low, clearly hoping not to be picked up by British radar.

WS reported a government spokesman saying that they know supplies are getting through to the Islands, but in quantities that hardly matter. I think they are wrong. Just one aircraft sneaked in today, but recently I've seen two or three a day, and Hercs can carry a lot of cargo.

I overheard some of the staff officers talking to the Argentine reporters, and I'm pretty sure they knew I was in earshot. They are taking about HMS *Hermes* being damaged, which I'm sure is bullshit. But the details they have woven around this story are impressive. They reckon that Curaçao in the Dutch West Indies has refused to allow *Hermes* to berth there for repairs.

Bloomer-Reeve made a rare announcement on the rediffusion system today (the transmitter remains off the air). He said he had been checking on the welfare of people in the camp, and everyone, both those who normally live on the farms and those who are refugees from Stanley, are fit and well. But Bloomer-Reeve didn't mention poor Rupert Goodwin, who died of a suspected heart attack at Fitzroy about a week ago. He was buried on the farm.

Lewis [Clifton] invited a few of us to his place for some quiet birthday drinks this afternoon. Pete and Rosemary and Robert were there, plus a few others. We took full advantage of Lewis's liquor cabinet and toasted his health repeatedly. Life is always a laugh with Robert and Pete, and I enjoyed the little gathering a lot. Drinking in the afternoon is becoming a bit of a habit, which may not be a good thing. Oh well, these are extraordinary times.

I sneaked into the Goose by the back door shortly before curfew, avoiding the parents. Happy birthday, Lewis. You'll remember this one as rather special.

Chapter 15

Artillery in the Gardens

(14–18 May)

Friday, 14 May

I slept soundly last night, probably helped by Lewis's drinks, but also thanks to the absence of any action. No shelling and no small arms fire. I woke late, about 8.00am, and could hear some Spanish conversation going on nearby. I cautiously poked a head out from behind the chimney and the chairs piled around my bivouac and saw two Argentine officers sitting comfortably and chatting. I lay back down for a bit, thinking they'd go away, but they didn't.

I listened to their chat about the quality of military rations (bad) and the mail service (even worse). Then, when they got on to some macho bragging about women back in BA, I got bored and rose from my pit. They were a bit shaken to see me emerge, looking dishevelled and dragging my jeans on as I went.

'*Buenos dias*,' I said with some aplomb as I passed them, heading for the bathroom, scratching my backside as I went.

They didn't respond but looked at each other a bit wide-eyed, clearly wondering where on earth I'd come from and worried that they'd just shared some information with me that might cost them the war.

Talking of mail, the Post Office is in a terrible state. Bill Etheridge and Lewis [Clifton] do their best, but it's constantly packed with soldiers, and the whole place stinks. There doesn't seem to be a lot of point in posting mail these days as we don't think it goes anywhere.

The authorities put out a mix of news and propaganda about the loss of the *Isla de los Estados* on local radio today. They confirmed that she went down with all hands near San Carlos. They claimed that BBC WS described the sinking as 'A glorious victory for the Royal Navy'. Well, that's just silly. They wouldn't say that, and I know they didn't.

They also claimed that she had been carrying fuel for local civilians. I don't believe that either. Given the circumstances, we would not have seen much or any of the fuel she may well have been carrying. They were right, however, when they said that the crew had friends locally. They were all civilians, but they must have known they were breaking the blockade.

It's a depressing day overall. Overcast all day. After seven days of talks, still no breakthrough in peace negotiations, so we only have more of the occupation – and probably worse – to look forward to. I mooched around Rowan for a bit and gave the animals some time, while Dad fed the new chickens. He's delighted with them.

I walked along Fitzroy Road to the Victory at about 4.00pm. Robert had got there first. Viv Perkins was standing on the corner of Philomel Hill and Fitzroy Road, looking innocent as she smoked and kept an eye open for troops. She beckoned me over and told me to enter through the snack bar entrance. Viv was keeping an eye open for troops, but she was also watching out for some of the really serious drinkers who could become a problem if they are allowed into the pub.

Rob and I chatted about the *Isla de los Estados* and compared notes about any action we'd seen or heard. We both heard two big blasts today, preceded by the roar of Harrier engines. One was around midday, a little to the south of Callaghan Road, and the other was later, over the harbour. According to some in the bar, the later one was an air burst, which is a particularly bloody nasty thing.

Someone in the bar said he had heard that the *Yehuin*, a small oil rig support ship that has been pressed into military service, had a narrow escape a few days ago. She was being chased by a destroyer or frigate around the south coast and only escaped by going as fast as she could through 'the Jump', which is an extremely narrow gap between Bleaker Island and the mainland. I've been through it on the *World Discoverer*.[1] You would want to be sure that the tide was on your side before having a go, but if there is a ship of the grey funnel line chasing you with a 4.5-inch gun, I guess that would be incentive enough. Anyway, *Yehuin* made it.

I think we were both feeling a bit glum. We headed home, me to the Goose and Rob to his parents' place, before the curfew. There was a final bomb blast at 5.30, as I was reaching the Goose. No sound of jets this time, though.

'CTF' at 6.20 used to be something to look forward to each day. Not so much now, thanks to the jamming. Nevertheless, Dad, Rob, the girls and I gathered around the radio and strained to hear what Peter King was saying. It was more or less audible at the start but, as usual, the jamming signal increased in volume until we could hardly hear anything. Reception was no better on other frequencies. But the main Falklands news is repeated on the news bulletins later, so we are still keeping abreast of what's going on.

At 9.00pm WS news reported that there were indeed Harrier raids around Stanley today. They claimed the airport was attacked, but as I think we saw, the bombs did not drop on target. No doubt that was due to the low cloud.

Galtieri has said on Peruvian TV that Argentina has made concessions in the talks, but he insists that the UK must 'recognize Argentine sovereignty over the Islands'. Fat chance of that.

The Prime Minister gave us a mention at the Scottish Tory party conference today. She paid tribute to Falkland Islanders' loyalty to Britain. She's right, we are loyal, but before the invasion that loyalty didn't seem to count for much. We are not used to being loved.

Saturday, 15 May

Last night, Pebble Island took centre stage. The BBC announced at midday that commandos (meaning the SAS) landed on the island and destroyed an unspecified number of Pucara ground-attack planes and other aircraft based there, using small arms and explosives. An ammunition dump was also destroyed, and a radar installation was damaged. No civilians were injured. This kind of raid was the SAS's trademark operation in North Africa during the Second World War. Strange to think they are reprising it in our islands.

The Task Force commanders would have wanted to neutralize the planes on Pebble before commencing a major landing. There was no mention of Argentine dead and wounded, but two of the SAS force suffered slight wounds. All were withdrawn safely.

Just in case those of us in Stanley were feeling forgotten, a single Harrier roared in about 12.30 and dropped two bombs on the airport. There was a satisfyingly big explosion, and a great pall of smoke rose from the ground. I wonder if they hit an ammo or fuel dump. I would not want to be an Argentine based at the airport, with the constant threat of attack.

I went to the shop with Dad in the early afternoon. We were a bit concerned that it might have been broken into and looted. I wouldn't want Dad to discover this alone. We didn't open the shop but had a good look around to check everything is OK, which it is.

While we were in the shop, a really big bomb exploded. Or if it wasn't large, it was very close. The entire building shook, both of us recoiled and ducked down. Dad let loose a string of bad language, which is entirely unlike him.

I said, 'Dad, I think this is why you and Mum should stop opening the shop. It's just not safe.'

'I know, son, but the shop is really important to Mum and it keeps her happy.'

He's right, of course. Mum is susceptible to depression, and although this is the first time either he or I have alluded to it, it is on our minds.

I think, though, that it's even dawning on Mum that there are hardly any customers and hanging around the shop is not worth the risk. If it goes, it goes. What matters is that we get through this alive.

We'd gone to the shop in the Daihatsu, so on the way back to Rowan House I suggested to Dad that we take the scenic route. He was surprisingly keen, so we drove west up past Government House, where we saw a large helicopter – a Puma,

I think – parked by the 1914 Battle Memorial. The rotor blades have been removed and it's been covered with camouflage netting. We could also see a wing of the crashed Shorts Skyvan on the racecourse. It was pointing up at a very unnatural angle.

Then we headed to Davis Street to see what is going on in that area. We saw something impressive. Wedged into the gardens of the Hodson Villas, very close to Jenny and John McAskill's house, was a huge artillery piece. And I mean huge. It would take a truck to tow it, and the barrel must be about 20ft long. I should think it fires something like four-inch shells. But this was no time to get out with a tape measure.

Locating it near civilian houses must be against the Geneva Convention. And I think there may still be a few people living in those houses.

The soldiers manning the gun looked at us curiously, so I sped up a bit, turned north down Snake Hill and we hotfooted it back to Rowan House.

It's being said around town that the Argentines are having trouble keeping their vehicles roadworthy. PATA [the Government's Plant and Transport Authority] mechanics walked off the job some weeks ago, with the exception of Raymond Poole. Raymond, very reasonably and with courage, said he would stay but he would not work on military vehicles. He only maintains the ambulance, Fire Brigade trucks and any other vehicles that benefit the local community.

It developed into quite a noisy day. Some point around Port William was bombed around 5.00pm. They must have hit something as smoke billowed up from the far side of the Camber ridge. There was some anti-aircraft fire, but less than I'd expect. A Huey chopper took off from the racecourse and flew down the harbour at near zero feet, probably to lift some wounded. I didn't see it come back, but it probably went west on the north side of the ridge.

There were also air raids on Mount Low and the Canache. Perhaps there is an observation post on the mountain. And I think the old Second World War ammunition bunkers at the Canache are being used again. So these may have been the targets.

Five or six dismal-looking Pucara pilots moved into the hotel this evening. The Kings have absolutely no say over this, as the Argentines took over all the rooms at the east end and made it clear that they would do what they liked with them.

No one is happy about this. So far, the rooms have only been used by non-combatants. Mora, who runs the radio station, was asked to clarify. He denied they were pilots. But that's a lie. They were overheard talking and they let slip that they'd come from Pebble Island and had lost their aircraft in the SAS raid. Let's hope they are all shipped back to the mainland on one of the Hercules planes very soon.

WS News at 8.00pm had more information about the Pebble raid. It was a stunning achievement. Eleven aircraft were destroyed or very severely damaged.

Six of these were Pucaras. Their loss will be a big blow to Argentine morale. There are still Pucaras at the airport, though.

Spirits were quite good among the refugees this evening, notwithstanding the arrival of the unwelcome planeless pilots. We've seen very little of them. There was a loud explosion at about 9.15pm, but that didn't really upset anyone.

Aunt Ning, the girls and other ladies are keeping us well fed, and I appreciate it very much. So far, we are not going short of any essentials, other than fuel. That could change if the situation goes on for months, though.

Just before I got my head down tonight I tuned into the BBC for one last time. There was one dramatic piece of news. The BBC quoted an Argentine commander here who said that there are either covert troops ashore sending intelligence to the Task Force or local 'collaborators' are sending information to the British by radio. Of the former possibility, I know nothing, but the second suggestion is probably true. Use of the word 'collaborators' comes with threatening tones attached.

Galtieri has admitted to 400 Argentine dead so far, including those lost on the *Belgrano*, but said he would accept 4,000 or 40,000. He said they will never take down their flag or raise the white flag. What a maniac.

Sunday, 16 May

A beautiful clear and calm day today, and the RAF or Navy took full advantage of it, flying over Stanley at about 8.30 and 10.15am, no doubt to see what damage their bombing had achieved yesterday and what further damage they might cause today. They were too high for effective AA fire. It seems to me that the AA guns are not that good, but there are anti-aircraft missile around here too, some based near the Power Station. So the Harrier pilots had better not become complacent.

I can't just sit around the hotel so I went for a walk at midday. I had a clear view of two Harriers attacking the airport. The sound arrived first, a great roar of jets, and by the time I'd spotted the planes they were already looking very small and approaching the airport at a very low altitude. The first plane dropped its bombs pretty much on target, although I couldn't see exactly what had been hit. The second plane, however, missed and its bombs dropped into Pt William, where they went off with a spectacular eruption of water. It was all over before the AA gunners managed to release a stream of fire.

I kept up a brisk pace so that it looked as if I was out for a purpose rather than mooching around, and while I passed quite a number of Argentines, no one stopped me. At the Public Jetty I noticed that the large mobile radar I spotted a few days ago is still there. It's not clear if it is working; certainly, the dish was not revolving. I'm thinking that it may be parked up here, very near civilian houses, to make it immune from bombing during the day, and then deployed outside town at night. Perhaps it's locating the warships doing the shelling.

Then I headed west to the hospital to visit Aunt Lena and have a chat with other people there. Aunt Lena is in good shape and good spirits. We sat and chatted for a while, enjoying the sun as she crocheted a doily. I asked her if she had enough cigarettes and whisky to be getting on with. She took a big drag on her Players Navy Cut and smiled at me.

'I think I'll get by, dear. Look at this.' She opened the door of her bedside cabinet and revealed several bottles of Johnny Walker Red Label and a couple of hundred gaspers. 'Don't tell anyone,' she said with a wink.

Later, I found Brian Paul in another part of the hospital. He's always remarkably cheerful and happy to have a natter. Over tea, Brian said that yesterday seventeen Argentine patients were evacuated on one, possibly two, Hercules flights that arrived and left again during the night.

There is some concern at the hospital that they are not hearing regularly from the more remote settlements. The RT [government radio telephone system] is working, and the Argentines allow the settlements to come on the air for regular morning medical consultations. But there is very little RT traffic. In particular, no one has heard anything from the Napiers at West Point for almost two weeks. Brian and I agreed that people may be afraid to use the RT. But the danger, of course, is that they may not be getting the medical care they need.

There were some alarming bursts of small arms fire as I walked home, and there was another raid on the airport. I was glad to get back to the Goose. All refugees were back well before curfew and, more in hope than anticipation, we grouped around the radio to hear CTF. Surprisingly, reception was not too bad on 15.40 MHz, but they were jamming it on 11.82.

More and more people being interviewed or quoted on the BBC are saying that the situation must come to a head at some point next week, either through a diplomatic agreement or in a full-scale landing. My money is on the latter.

Two more ships were attacked in Falkland Sound. The *Rio Carcarana*, a large freighter, was strafed and hit with a bomb but not sunk. The crew were seen escaping in lifeboats. Another ship [later confirmed to be the *Bahia Buen Suceso*] was spotted in Fox Bay and strafed. She couldn't be bombed as she was berthed so close to the civilian houses. We know that [my cousin] Stuart and the other locals who were arrested some weeks ago are interned at Fox Bay East, so they may have had a lucky escape.

Father Monaghan was in chatty form this evening. He said that he and Monsignor Spraggon struggled at times to be heard during mass today. The air raids and AA fire were pretty worrying, he said, but no one left St Mary's. He seemed justifiably proud of this. I'm not sure that Padre Bagnall is getting anyone to turn out for his establishment. I must ask him. He's not a very chatty bloke, though.

We almost expect the Navy to steam in and start shelling every night. I was standing in the open front door of the Goose at about 10.45pm when it started.

It seemed to me that the shells were fired well to the east of the airport, flew over Stanley and then landed beyond the west end of town. Judging by the flashes of the explosions, I think the targets were between Felton Stream and Moody Brook. After only about 20 minutes the shelling stopped, but it resumed a short time later, and this time, the shells were landing much closer.

I waited until the shelling ceased again, then went to bed hoping to get a decent night's sleep.

Monday, 17 May

Distressing news today from Father Monaghan, who I assume heard it at his morning service and was clearly upset. The Argentines rounded up dairy cows from the Common yesterday and took them for slaughter. Some people saw between twenty-five and forty cows being driven up the front road towards the slaughterhouse to the west of town. They were all privately owned animals and between them they gave us our fresh milk. Some of the older milkers were probably just living out their days peacefully. The cows were herded along by four or five soldiers riding horses bareback.

There was no appeal to owners who might want to sell their cattle for slaughter, and I'm sure no one would have done so anyway. They were just taken. Stolen. This is the way an Argentine military government would treat us if we were stupid enough to accept them. Do they really wonder why we don't like the idea of being under their thumb?

This wasn't a good way to start the day. But there are not many good days at the moment. Normally, I'd welcome a calm and bright day like today. It's chilly but there's barely a cloud in the sky and hardly a breath of wind. But days with good visibility mean more attacks, and I must admit that I'm getting a bit twitchy about the shelling and the bombing. It's only a matter of time before some of us are caught in the crossfire.

Later today, the Argentines broadcast a notice acknowledging that the milk cows had been taken to feed their troops. There were no apologies, but they said that the cows will be replaced with cattle imported from Argentina. That is a lie. It won't happen.

I may have got it wrong about the good weather heralding more attacks. In fact, it has been relatively quiet today. There were a few recce overflights, greeted with sporadic AA fire. By mid-afternoon there was no news of attacks in other parts of the Islands, but I wouldn't rule that out.

A few blockade-busting planes flew in and out. A Fokker F27 flew west to east (not even the normal approach path) up the harbour at about 60ft. When it took off again, an hour or so later, it again headed up the harbour at an incredibly low altitude and disappeared among the mountains. About an hour later, a Hercules came in using the same technique.

Mum and Dad put in an appearance at the shop for a couple of hours, and I joined them for a bit. A few people came in and bought a few things. Among them was Alec Betts, who was in the company of some Argentine civilians. We haven't seen him around for weeks, as he sided with the Argentines and has made his loyalty quite clear. He moved in with the Argentine Air Force, for whom his local knowledge must be very useful.

He is now very happy spouting Argentine propaganda. He told me that the British ships were (as we thought) shelling the Moody Brook area last night, but they stopped pronto when Argentine gunners began replying with shells from their huge artillery pieces. I doubt this is true. They may well have fired back, but as it was pitch black, it wouldn't have been with any accuracy.

He went on to say that Argentine troops are preparing to face a major attack within the next 24 hours. He's confident it will be driven off. He added that they believe there may well be some British troops ashore already. Alec has made a big mistake and he's not going to be forgiven for this. He's made his bed, though, so he'll have to sleep in it.

I was speaking to Simon [Goss], who is a whizz with radios, and he had been scanning frequencies. He picked up what sounded like a coded transmission in English. It was very brief but could have been from a party on shore. We keep looking for unfamiliar faces around town who might be special forces who have slipped through Argentine lines. Disguise wouldn't be hard: a woolly hat and a snorkel parka would do the trick. We'd know them, though.

Early this evening, the BBC's Brian Hanrahan on one of the carriers reported on the shelling last night. He said that ships moving close to the coast to shell Argentine positions are taking serious risks, as the waters could be mined. He made no mention of the Argentines returning fire last night. The crew of the ship that was involved last night told him that they thought they had started a fire in or around Stanley but they couldn't be sure. As far as we know, there was no fire. But if the ship was close enough for the crew to believe they could see a fire, then it must have been just a few miles off the coast.

I overheard a conversation between Dr Mario (I don't know his surname), the Argentine who is now in charge of the hospital, and another Argentine. No survivors of the ships recently attacked around Falkland Sound have been brought into the Stanley hospital. That is either because there were no survivors or because they are being treated elsewhere. He referred to a military field hospital at Fox Bay.

Tuesday, 18 May

There was one pleasant surprise today. Our little ship *Forrest* returned to Stanley during the night, and when I looked out from the Goose front porch this morning, she was snugly tied up at the Government Jetty. I'd become convinced that she had been lost. She's painted black and grey now and is under the command of the Argentine Navy, but to me she's Uncle Jack's ship and always will be. I wonder what stories she could tell.

We tuned in to WS over breakfast, and according to them, members of the Anglo-Argentine community in Argentina have offered to look after Falklands children and have appealed for a ceasefire so that the kids can be evacuated. I don't think that many, or any, parents will take that up, and with so much else going on, I can't see either Argentines or British arranging an evacuation. It might be a genuine offer but it amounts to no more than a gesture.

The weather today is filthy; little visibility and constant drizzle with a fresh wind blowing. That would suggest that there will be little activity overhead. The blockade-busting planes won't fancy their chances, either.

Last evening, the Task Force lost its third helicopter. The Sea King was apparently trying to detect Argentine submarines and to do that it had to fly low. I guess that they suffered engine failure. Fortunately, the crew was rescued.

I was wrong about the weather keeping people on the ground. There were four air raids between about 10.30am and 2.30pm, including a raid on the airport, which felt comfortably distant.

Robert came by the Goose about 4.00pm and suggested that we go and have a few drinks at the Victory (amazingly, the Argentines have still not cottoned on to the fact that the pub is operating secretly). So off we went, and after the usual covert knocking we were let in. It was really nice to be there. No more than about twelve people, but it was warm and friendly and there was a nice sense of camaraderie and good humour.

At about 5.00, though, that changed. Two hellish bombs exploded. The noise was deafening and the entire building rocked. Robert and I hit the floor, along with most others in the room.

The explosion was somewhere to the north, but as the pub has no windows giving a view in that direction, we couldn't see what was going on. But these were the closest bombs we've yet experienced. Robert was as cheerful as ever.

'That was the first time the wall has hit me in the head rather than the other way around,' he said, before getting us a couple of drinks to replace those that were now soaking into the carpet.

Back at the Goose, Dad was more than a bit annoyed. When the two very large bombs went off, he didn't know where I was but figured I was probably with Rob. He's cottoned on to the fact that we go there. Mum doesn't know, and it's better she doesn't. Dad and I don't see eye to eye on this, but I can understand why he'd be worried if I'm not around when things get nasty. He said the two huge bombs landed on the other side of Stanley Harbour. They were so big that the smoke and debris rose to about 400ft.

We tuned into CTF, not really expecting to hear anything beyond the jamming. But surprisingly, it was a bit clearer this evening. We could at least pick up every second or third word. The Foreign Secretary has warned the Argentines that if the Islands have to be retaken by force, then all concessions offered in the talks (which splutter on) will be withdrawn. Fair enough.

An officer on HMS *Hermes* has denied Argentine claims that air raids and shelling have been indiscriminate. He said that all targets are military and are carefully identified. That sounds reasonable, but that doesn't mean mistakes can't be made. For instance, those big bombs today were too close for comfort.

A very large container ship called *Atlantic Conveyor*, carrying replacement Harriers and helicopters, has linked up with the Task Force to the east of the Islands. That sounds to me like a piece of news that should have been kept quiet.

God bless Aunt Ning and the girls and ladies at the Goose. Supper is always something to look forward to. Even when we've had a rough day, food cheers us all up. Father Monaghan sometimes eats with Monsignor Spraggon before the curfew, but when he returns to the Goose after a day visiting his flock he always shares his stories with us. He's a cheerful and chatty guy and I like him. Padre Bagnall is not quite so gregarious, but to be fair to him he also spends much of his time visiting his flock.

Rob is still having to walk along to the military police and intelligence HQ at the old police station every day, I suppose to prove that he has not absconded back to Salvador.

Before getting my head down for the night I tuned into BBC WS a last time. Argentina has given its 'final' reply to the UN, but we don't know what that is. London's final position is not clear, either. I'm wondering if either or both parties are playing for time. They both benefit tactically from stringing the talks out. The Argentines are spending the time digging in and reinforcing; and the Brits benefit from assembling more ships with supplies, equipment and men.

I don't doubt that the UN is doing its very best. I'm just not so sure about BA and London. Analysts are suggesting that the UK will probably decide tomorrow whether to walk away from talks and launch an all-out assault soon afterwards.

I almost forgot: this afternoon I had a long conversation with one of the Argentine journalists. It was completely impossible to convince him that this conflict never needed to happen. I explained that the Argentines had had the upper hand in the talks before the invasion. In fact, in a weird kind of way, the Brits and the Argentines were on the same side: Argentina wanted to take us, and Britain didn't want us. The only challenge was to find a way by which we could be handed over without London being accused of betrayal. All that was required was patience. But this guy wasn't having it.

'Argentina had to invade,' he said. 'Britain would never give in.'

Well, it doesn't matter anymore. We're in it up to our eyeballs now, and a lot of people are going to die.

Father Monaghan just came by heading for bed. 'Goodnight, God bless.' Thanks, Father. Let's hope he's listening.

Chapter 16

D-Day at San Carlos

(19–22 May)

Wednesday, 19 May

There was more indiscriminate shooting around town last night. Father Monaghan has his finger on the pulse, as ever, and he says that Stan and Daphne Cletheroe, who must both be in their late seventies, got half a dozen rounds through their house. They were sleeping on the floor, which was a good thing, because the bullets passed through the tin and timber only about 14 inches above them. No acknowledgement or apology is expected from the Argentines, of course.

It's a gloomy day, and I don't mean just weather-wise. People seem to be more down than usual. I took my breakfast coffee to the front door of the Goose and had a look over the harbour. The little MV *Forrest* is still safely at the Government Jetty, and I hope she stays there. She's listing slightly to port and looks sad.

WS at breakfast time is saying that a major British landing could come as early as tonight. That figures. The Task Force commanders will not want to have the troops bobbing around at sea for any longer than necessary.

The MoD has said it is taking over a BBC transmitter on Ascension Island to set up its own radio station. It'll be a propaganda station aimed at the Argentines. I think it's a silly idea. Unless the MoD has some turncoat Argentine broadcasters, their stuff is not going to sound credible to any Argentine.

Radio stations are proving to be very important. Here we have Radio Islas Malvinas putting out propaganda with the odd genuinely useful public service announcement. Then there is BBC World Service, which keeps us well informed. The Chilean stations give a nuanced take on what's going on. And now both sides have dedicated propaganda stations.

The BBC stresses it is having nothing to do with the new station, but their broadcasts to this part of the world may be affected, because they will lose a transmitter. But I suppose if MoD wants their transmitter there, they will just take it. In any case, 'Radio Atlantico del Sur' will broadcast on short wave, and very few soldiers here will have short-wave receivers. Not a war-winning initiative, I'd say.

I visited Rowan for a while but was back at the Goose early. It has been a remarkably quiet day. One or two bombs were dropped some considerable distance from the centre of town at about 10.00am. There was a short burst of anti-aircraft fire, but the Harriers zoomed off safely.

Things have been getting Mum down today, and anyway she is not feeling well, with a cold or mild flu. She's spent much of the day in bed, getting up for a while in the afternoon but quickly heading back to bed. She didn't get up for supper. I hope she feels better and is more cheerful tomorrow.

CTF this evening was slightly less effectively jammed than usual. By flipping between frequencies we could hear a fair bit of it. Peter King reported that Galtieri cancelled an interview with British journalists at the last minute for 'a very grave reason' that they will hear about soon. I wonder what that might be. I'd have thought that things could hardly be more grave.

Supper at the Goose, for which I'm always grateful, lifted our spirits a bit, and afterward we got some liquid spirits in us. That helped too.

The 11.00pm BBC news reported that for practical purposes the negotiations are over. Thatcher is to meet with her cabinet in a few hours' time, and there will be a full Parliamentary debate tomorrow.

I went to the front porch for a bit of fresh air and noticed one of the small Argentine patrol boats slipping its moorings and heading off down the harbour. I am certain they are looking for any special forces that might have infiltrated by boat.

I joined the girls, Paul and Xenia in the kitchen. Our chatting ceased when there was some rifle fire very nearby. A round ricocheted off the south side of the hotel. I think we all slipped a bit lower in our chairs. Then, one by one, we all went off to bed.

Thursday, 20 May

I can't sleep. I've been lying on my mattress on the floor tossing and turning, waiting for the Navy to come in close and start shelling. Once those distant 'pops' and nearby 'crumps' start, I'll probably drop off. Very strange.

I'm writing this by torchlight. I've tuned my little Panasonic into WS. I've got to keep it as near to my ear as possible, so I don't wake anyone else up. Perhaps they are awake anyway. Who knows?

Harold Briley is crackling through the ether, reporting from BA about the 'crisis atmosphere' there. He says that the Argentine Government and forces appear to have completed their preparations for war.

The UN Secretary General, Pérez de Cuéllar, sounds desperate. He has phoned both Galtieri and Thatcher almost begging them to back away from the abyss. I doubt if anyone believes they will.

I visited Auntie Lena at the hospital again yesterday. While we were drinking tea in the kitchen, the two Argentine doctors came in. Their doctors are a mix of military and civilians, I think. The one called Dr Mario is nominally in charge, but Alison Bleaney is still in the hospital (thank God), and I feel pretty sure that she is really controlling it. I asked the doctors if the hospital was good enough for their purposes.

'We have all we need, and the operating theatre is very good,' said one.

'What state are the troops in?' I asked.

He looked at his colleague and hesitated before saying, 'They are OK.'

He must have anticipated my next question: 'And they are being fed well?'

I saw him glance at the other doctor, as if to say, 'Back me up here', before saying, 'They are OK.' Soldiers are begging locals for food, so I take whatever they said with a big pinch of salt.

I also asked what provisions are being made to look after the health of the Islanders, particularly those who are on the remoter farms and islands. They all brightened up at that. One of them said he had visited Port Louis a few days ago and found that everyone there was in good health. He said that they had been to or at least spoken to Bluff Cove, too, and all appears to be OK there. But of course, both these farms are near Stanley. What about the really isolated little communities out on the West?

It's twenty-three minutes past midnight, and the Navy has just arrived. They opened up with very rapid shelling (less than two seconds between each shell) of an area to the west. When that subsided, there was some rifle and automatic fire nearer us. A few minutes later, the shelling started again, but closer this time. Twelve explosions, again very rapid fire.

The 'pop' of the guns is very audible, and that must mean that the ships are close. A few minutes later, another volley of twelve shells. A few minutes break, and they do it all again; targets getting a little closer. This cycle continues for about 40 minutes. The weather has been getting gradually worse, with wind building up and rain.

I'm continuing to listen to WS as the shelling comes and goes. The BBC's reporter in Chile has been monitoring 'Radio Atlantico del Sur', the new British station. He describes it as a 'blend of subtle and crude propaganda'. Apparently, they suggested the SAS may have landed already. He quoted the broadcaster: 'Are they here? Are those people Kelpers or are they British soldiers?' I don't think that encouraging paranoia like that helps us very much.

I saw a very bright light outside around 2.00am and went out to the porch to see what it was. The patrol boat was cruising around the harbour, sweeping the shoreline with a searchlight.

I don't know what time I drifted off to sleep last night, but I was feeling very groggy when I dragged myself out from behind the armchairs at about 7.30am. The weather deteriorated during the night and it is dreadful today; strong winds, overcast and rainy.

Anna and I went to the West Store to buy some food this morning. The population of Stanley is about half its peacetime number, if that, and most of them seemed to be in the store. Serious and nervous-looking people were grabbing cans of food and packets of dried food. I spoke to a few people, and everyone said they were stocking up in case the situation gets worse.

WS news this morning revealed that Pérez de Cuéllar has not given up. Jesus, that is one tenacious diplomat. Apparently, he presented an amended set of proposals to both parties late last night. Thatcher is addressing the Commons later today. She'll be preparing them for all-out conflict.

1.00pm: Thatcher has told the Commons that the Argentines' response to Britain's latest suggestions amount to total rejection of peace. 'This is of the utmost gravity,' she said. It seems the UK had wanted a total withdrawal of Argentine forces within fourteen days and a resumption of control by our Legislative and Executive Councils. But BA wanted to flood the Islands with their own nationals.

The Argentines have appealed to Washington to intervene to 'alter Britain's intransigence'. What a cheek. It seems that one of their conditions for peace and a withdrawal is that their flag should continue to fly here, if necessary alongside the British and UN flags. It would be great if people didn't get so wound up over bits of fabric.

This evening, as I write this and listen to CTF, the tension is almost intolerable. Harold Briley says that the mood in BA is 'sombre', as Argentines realize that peace is now out of reach. They are now waiting for an all-out British assault. So are we.

A dramatic news item has just come through from the BBC reporter in Chile. A Navy Sea King helicopter has crashed near Punta Arenas. The chopper is burnt out. The crew has not been found, but it's believed that they made a forced landing due to the bad weather. It's possible, though, that they think they are in Argentine territory and are lying low for that reason. The Chileans are looking for the crew and have assured the British Embassy in Santiago that they will be well treated.

The reporter says there is a lot of sympathy for us and the Task Force in Chile. There is speculation there that the Sea King might have been on a spying mission around Ushuaia or Rio Grande. Perhaps when they realized they were in trouble, they headed west, hoping to put down in Chile.

The mood around the Goose this evening is sombre. I've seen nothing of the Argentine journalists since this morning, when they rushed out and were loaded into one of the Argentines Mercedes jeeps. That's fine by me, as we have a bit of a cold war going on with them.

Supper helped a lot, and we sat and chatted for ages, speculating about what is going to happen and whether we have done enough to prepare for it. We have bags of flour and chicken food in some of the window recesses, and Paul has checked the bunker that he and Des built in case we need it.

At midnight, as I'm writing this, those who had not gone off to bed tuned into WS for the latest grim news. Within the last few minutes Pérez de Cuéllar has spoken at the UN, saying that his peace efforts have come to an end. So that's it, then. War.

BA is saying their troops are now dug in and ready for whatever may come. In London, defence analysts are forecasting a several-pronged attack very soon, one or more of which might be diversionary. Good idea to share that with the enemy.

We're trickling off to bed now. Good night and, more than ever, God bless.

Friday, 21 May

We awoke early and immediately tuned into the BBC to see whether troops have landed. Apparently, there were several landings overnight and the initial objectives have been achieved. Now we must hope that the Argentines will not successfully counter-attack. I'm not noticing much helicopter activity around here, suggesting they are not rushing troops to oppose the landings. No hurry; have a *maté* and a few Jockey Clubs first.

However, at 9.40 an Argentine jet fighter took off from the airport and screamed low over the town with weapons clearly bolted on underneath. It disappeared to the west. Assuming it's heading for the landing site, I think this could be somewhere on Falkland Sound. Two Argentine Air Force guys on the road in front of the hotel got very excited as the fighter flew over. One commented to the other that the plane was an Aermacchi, an advanced trainer, I believe, that is also equipped for ground attack. Let's see if it returns to Stanley safely later. This could be the cue for a mass attack by the Argentine Air Force. It's going to be a dangerous day.

The BBC is reporting that a British Sea King helicopter carrying twenty-one men has crashed. There are no details about survivors and whether the crash occurred over land or sea. The Task Force has now lost seven helicopters.

The MoD is not saying much at all, other than confirming that the landings continue. They don't yet know how successful they've been, and the troops will have much more important things to worry about than reporting back to London. I am not sure whether we are seeing D-Day unfold, or whether these are just raids.

Just as I started to write this, there are some large explosions some distance away. It's naval shells, which we are not used to during daylight hours. It is still going on, and I've counted five, several minutes apart.

I tuned in to Argentine stations on the mainland to see what they're saying. They are not acknowledging any landings; instead, their headline story is the mysterious Sea King helicopter crash near Punta Arenas.

Father Monaghan was visiting his flock for much of the morning, but when he came back he said the RT station was put out of action the night before last. It seems the Argentines panicked and thought there was about to be a full-scale invasion. Some soldiers just went in and cut the power cables and aerials.

That's not good at all, because we now have no way of knowing if anyone is in trouble in the camp.

Steve Whitley [Stanley's only vet] came by the Goose. It's always good to see Steve. He's normally very cheerful, but today he's understandably upset by reports that cattle at the Murrell Farm, just a few miles away, are being injured and killed by Argentine land mines. The Molkenbhur family who live there can't get near the cattle to put them out of their misery with a rifle. It's sickening.

Steve also said that yesterday, from his house up to the west, he saw Harriers bombing positions a long way up Moody Valley, probably near or beyond Two Sisters.

Aunt Ning, who chairs the local Red Cross Society, attended a meeting of her members with Bloomer-Reeve. He told them that three representatives of the International Committee of the Red Cross will arrive on the Argentine hospital ship *Bahia Paraiso* on Sunday or Monday. They will only be staying for 48 hours. Surely they should be staying for the duration of the hostilities. We really are alone.

Bloomer-Reeve told Aunt Ning that Goose Green and Darwin are littered with explosives. He said there is an unexploded RAF bomb near the Hardcastles' house and many unexploded anti-personnel bombs lying around.

Local radio is still not working but the 'box' [rediffusion system] bursts into life every now and again. At midday a strange edict was broadcast: the use of motorbikes is now banned. I think they either want to collect all motorbikes for their own use or they don't like the surly attitude of young bikers. Or, here's a thought: do they think that special forces might be getting around on them, masquerading as local lads?

With so much happening, few of us are wandering far from the Goose, and not far from the radio either. The BBC reports at midday that there may have been up to six landings in the pre-dawn hours of today, involving up to 400 men in each raid. This sounds like information designed to confuse the Argentines. San Carlos and Fox Bay are being mentioned as possible locations for the landings. For their part, the Argentines are reporting a helicopter attack on Darwin and Goose Green and they are claiming to have shot down a Harrier, although they don't say where.

We were not getting any very precise information from the radio, but then an Argentine officer arrived to talk to the journalists. I lingered nearby. I think he knew I was there, but he carried on anyway. He said their forces have twelve British destroyers bottled up in a bay somewhere around Falkland Sound. 'This is the beginning of the end for the British,' he said. He claimed that ground units and fighter aircraft had shot down seven British aircraft.

This is chilling to hear. I'm inclined to think it is largely true, as the Argentines do have some effective defences and they were just waiting to throw their fighter planes into the fray. I'm hoping, though, that it's no more than rumour and bravado. I thought about it gloomily for a bit and decided to disregard this 'news' until it's confirmed by the BBC. But we are all now feeling very nervous.

Dad and I watched as three helicopters flew from the football pitch low over the harbour and landed at the Camber, spaced out just to the west of the oil tanks. They will have put them there for safety. They are well camouflaged and hard to see even though we know they are there.

I walked down Ross Road towards the West Store, which is still opening a few hours a day but is becoming a major shelter every night, and when I got there I was approached by a very nervous young soldier. This is by no means the first time, and it upsets me just as much every time it happens. This guy was very young, perhaps just eighteen or nineteen, and obviously a conscript. He was dirty and with the few words of English he had – I suspect he and his friends have been rehearsing them – he asked me for food: 'Please, mister. I very hungry.' He patted his stomach in case there was any doubt about it and then he held out a bundle of Argentine pesos. I've thought about the moral issues around this situation, but I know what the answer is. These kids are conscripts to an inept army, and they have no wish to be here. They are quite simply Galtieri's cannon fodder and as soon as they have a chance to surrender they will.

'Please, mister!'

'*Esta bien* [it's OK],' I said. '*Hablo castellano* [I speak Spanish].' He said he wanted chocolate, biscuits and batteries for a radio.

'How is it here for you guys,' I asked.

He was not far from tears. '*Muy mal* [Very bad]. We don't have enough food, it is cold and we are always wet. And we are afraid.'

He was certainly afraid, and not necessarily of British troops, shells and air raids. He constantly glanced around to be sure that there were no Argentine officers or NCOs watching him. I asked him what would happen if they saw him.

'They will punish me. Badly. But we are desperate.'

I took his pesos and went into the West Store. I did not buy batteries for him but did buy biscuits, chocolate and Mars Bars. When I left the store, there was no sign of the conscript, but he was watching for me and emerged from hiding across the road near the FIC slip and capstan. He approached furtively and stuffed the food into his coat. But he took the time to thank me. I told him to take care.

What would people think about this? I know what some would think, and it wouldn't be nice. But I don't see this as cooperating with the occupiers. I wouldn't do the same for officers, who always look well fed, well clothed in neat uniforms and fit. But all I could see today, as on previous occasions, was a kid who was hungry, cold and scared. If anyone has a problem with that, then so be it.

Early this afternoon, the Argentines are claiming that their planes have attacked British ships at the north end of Falkland Sound, and if that is true, then they are probably landing in San Carlos Water. This is a natural deep-water harbour, so it makes sense. But boy, will these ships be vulnerable. The weather is what one would normally describe as perfect; mild, just a light breeze and a blue sky. But this is a gift for the Argentine Air Force. Some horrible weather would be welcome right now, but then that would probably delay landings (and it seems increasingly that a full-scale landing is taking place).

By mid-afternoon the BBC is reporting that British troops have established a beachhead in the San Carlos areas and troops are ashore in large numbers. Thank God for that! There are lots of smiles in the kitchen at the Goose, and we all feel that we can now see the end of this nightmare. The BBC is reporting that, crucially, the landings have not been opposed by land forces, which I'm sure is a major mistake by the Argentines. Even I can see that they should have helicoptered troops and artillery into place to oppose the landings, as this is a vulnerable time for the Task Force but will not last. As soon as the invaders have consolidated on shore, the Argentines will have missed their chance.

But it seems the Argentine Air Force is throwing everything it has at the landings. The BBC is saying that five ships have been hit by bombs or strafed, and two of them have been seriously damaged. The Navy crews must be praying for the weather to change for the worse.

It must be like hell out there. I wouldn't put too much store by any claims now, but it's being suggested that nine Argentine Mirage aircraft have been shot down, along with five Skyhawks, three Pucaras and two helicopters. The MoD is admitting that one Harrier has been lost, but it's not clear if it was shot down or crashed. Two small helicopters, possible Gazelles, have also been shot down, and the suggestion is that they were lost to small arms fire from the few Argentine troops who were in the area and who were retreating.

This is carnage. But if the landings have been successful, perhaps it's a necessary price to pay. The Task Force is already reinforcing its positions on land, unloading and setting up artillery and Rapier anti-aircraft missiles. It's believed that they are already constructing a landing facility for Harriers. Getting them off the carriers, which are vulnerable, will be important.

Someone excitedly reported that a Skyhawk had been seen in trouble over Stanley Airport and it crashed on landing. Maybe it was damaged over San Carlos and was unable to get back to the mainland, so the pilot tried to put down here. That would bring the score up to eighteen Argentine aircraft lost.

Our cautious feeling here is that despite the claims of that Argentine officer earlier today who suggested that the British ships were trapped and being picked off, we are winning this battle; but there have obviously been heavy losses.

Late this afternoon: the BBC is saying that the thirty-one people at San Carlos and Port San Carlos have been liberated. They were found sheltering from the gunfire. They will be delighted but perhaps fearing an Argentine land attack and air raids.

Those [Islanders] that we know of in the area are: Diver and Mrs Heathman, John and Mandy McLeod and baby, Freddy Ford and family, Allan Miller and family, Ken and Mrs Summers, Buster Summers and family and six Berntsens. There are almost certainly some refugees from Stanley also.

There is no indication of what the weather will be like tomorrow, but another bright, calm and clear day will only help the Argentine Air Force. Let's hope for low cloud at the very least.

Dad met Jack Sollis today. Uncle Jack has been down to see his old ship *Forrest* and said she's in a bad way. The Argentines told him that she'd come under attack by British helicopters. The superstructure is riddled with bullet holes and several windows have been knocked out on the bridge.

I'm writing around midnight. WS is reporting that fighting at San Carlos went on into the evening. There are claims and counter-claims about aircraft shot down by both sides. BA says ten British planes were lost for just three of their own. That's most probably a wild exaggeration. The British are saying that seventeen Argentine aircraft were shot down but are not mentioning whether any Harriers were lost.

BA is acknowledging that British troops are ashore but claims they haven't been allowed to consolidate. BA says eight ships were damaged by their aircraft and two were sunk. If that is true, then a high price has been paid. We'll have to wait to see if that's true.

London has admitted that the air raids caused casualties on the ships, but about 2,000 men are now said to be on dry land. They'll be relieved, and so are we.

Saturday, 22 May

I thought I'd begin today's notes by reflecting on a few conversations from yesterday. Mum had a conversation with Dr Mario [surname unknown], who is the chief Argentine doctor at the hospital. He seems to be only concerned with his job as a doctor. He said that his colleague Dr Oscar [surname also unknown], a short, bearded guy who we've seen around a lot, is an excellent surgeon. But he's had to send two doctors back to the mainland as they are too prejudiced against us Islanders and the Brits. He said he has great respect for our doctors, Alison Bleaney and Mary Elphinstone. Thanks goodness they stayed in the Islands.

I had a much more disturbing conversation with Father Monaghan. He said he'd been approached by a young soldier who recognized him as a priest. He had some command of English and told Father Monaghan that he had received a letter from his parents, who told him that if he and his brothers in arms do not win this war he would only be welcome home if he was in a box. What madness. Father Monaghan said there was not much he could do to console the boy, and this obviously upset him. He asked me not to share this story, at least until it is all over. That's OK. I suppose it will be a long time before anyone reads this.

It is largely overcast and damp today, which must be a relief for the men around San Carlos. I don't think the weather is bad enough to keep Argentine aircraft on the ground, but visibility will be poor.

It's frustrating to know that such remarkable things are happening on the other side of East Falkland, but we can only know about it by tuning into crackly voices reporting from London. This is why we tune into WS as if it is some religious ritual.

At 9.30am John Nott came on the radio to say that yesterday's landings were successful. All goals were attained. 'Our Paras and Marines are now ashore in considerable numbers. A beachhead has been secured and our troops are now moving forward to harass enemy positions.'

However, Nott confirmed that one frigate has been sunk (no name or details of dead and injured) and another has been disabled, with an unexploded bomb near the engine room. Five warships were hit, but most are not seriously damaged.

London is claiming that eighteen Argentine aircraft were shot down, which is remarkable. I suspect that there may be cases of the same plane being shot down two or three time, but at the very least this suggests that the air raids yesterday were incredibly ferocious.

A little later, the frigate that was sunk has been named as HMS *Ardent*. Twenty of the crew are dead. If the Argentine Air Force can keep this level of damage up, they might just get the upper hand.

But the Paras and the Marines seem to be consolidating on shore. Between 3,000 and 5,000 soldiers are thought to be off the ships now. The total of British men killed today is being reported as twenty-seven, with three wounded. But this figure was reported before the death toll on *Arden*t was released. So we may be talking about nearly fifty men dead.

I find it difficult to process all of this. Massive air raids, warships being sunk, beachheads being established and, of course, men dying. These things are happening in places which I knew as peaceful. The rest of the world had never heard of them at all. It's still hardly believable.

The BBC correspondent who is now on shore in the San Carlos area gave a chilling account of one missile engagement. He described a Pucara flying low over a hill away from the ships with a Rapier missile closing on its tail. Both plane and missile disappeared over the hills, and it wasn't clear if the Pucara had been downed and, if so, whether the pilot had ejected.

Mum had a word with Aunt Alice [her sister, who was a nurse] today, and she said that our hospital is now full of Argentines. She believes that they are spillover from the military field hospital. The medical staff, both theirs and ours, are working flat-out.

The portable radar unit that was at the head of the Public Jetty for several days has now gone. Robert said he thought they had repositioned it in Dairy Paddock on the south side of town.

Reception of 'Calling the Falklands' was bad and became worse, with jamming as the programme went on. But we just managed to pick up that the Post Office in London has stopped accepting mail for the Falklands. That's nice.

Good news at 8.00pm. It seems that the weather (overcast, damp and cold all day) stopped the Argentine Air Force from repeating their performance of yesterday. No air attacks and (still puzzling) no land attacks on the beachhead, either. So the forces, which must now be fully disembarked, spent the day building up their defences, developing a landing strip for the Harriers, unloading stores and setting up the Rapier systems.

This is all really encouraging. The Argentines may now have missed their chance to stop the landings. So the new question on our minds is, how long will it take the troops to get to Stanley?

Galtieri is still spouting propaganda for domestic consumption. The Argentine public are not going to like it at all when they learn the truth. This evening, he's claiming that the British are surrounded and have suffered heavy losses. He's right with that last point, but I doubt if the losses are any heavier than the Task Force commanders would have planned for.

Costa Mendez is due to address the UN Security Council soon. Even if a motion is passed condemning the UK and demanding a ceasefire, the UK or the US will veto it. If it goes the other way and Argentina is condemned, then Russia will veto it. The whole exercise is a waste of time.

About 8.30pm, I joined Rob Pitaluga, Des and Father Monaghan for a drink and to talk the day through. We heard a loud bang followed by some yells from the kitchen. We rushed there and found Anna and Xenia very upset. They had been in the kitchen when a stray 7.62 round hit the stone wall of the hotel, ricocheted through the corrugated iron roof and hit a wall in the kitchen just three or four feet from where the girls were sitting. Both were in tears, understandably.

Aunt Ning was furious and went off to find Mora. He is the only Argentine in the hotel who is even slightly sympathetic. He called an army officer, and they went off into the darkness to see if they could find out where the bullet had come from. They probably won't succeed. It was probably fired by a soldier in what was once the Junior School, just a few hundred yards away, but there are nervous soldiers firing at shadows everywhere.

We don't get weather forecasts on local radio any more, but we are all hoping that it is even more cold, windy, overcast and wet tomorrow. That may be unpleasant for the troops and sailors at San Carlos, but it would be better than wave after waves of Argentine Mirages and Skyhawks trying to blow you to bits.

We all went to sleep tonight knowing that at least one small part of the Falklands is back under British control. And that is a very good feeling.

Chapter 17

Fingers on Triggers

(23–25 May)

Sunday, 23 May

The night was strangely quiet. Dad said he heard sporadic small arms and bursts of automatic fire, but I slept through it. The Navy, though, has throttled back in its bombardments around Stanley, at least for now. Presumably, they are far too busy at the beachhead. That could change very quickly, as we are the ultimate goal.

BBC WS is reporting this morning that, despite the weather, a couple of Argentine aircraft got through the missile and gun screen at San Carlos yesterday. But their bombs fell well short of the ships.

Harriers attacked positions at Goose Green, where a number of those nasty little Pucara ground-attack aircraft are based. They will want to put the grass runways and the planes out of action soon, because the flying time from Goose Green to the beachhead is no more than a few minutes.

It feels spooky around Stanley this morning. The weather is chilly and there is low cloud. So visibility is poor, which is good for the Task Force. It seems tense, and I sense rather than see a lot of nervous soldiers around with fingers on triggers.

Radio Islas Malvinas has just announced that the town's water supply will be turned off from 9.00am to 4.00pm. Effectively, this is rationing. These shut-downs are likely to go on for at least a week, they say, but we fear they won't be able to restore the supply. We've heard that the pipes connecting the filtration plant and the reservoir, which feeds water into the town, have been ruptured by shellfire. We immediately started filling buckets, baths and any other containers we could find with water. This is worrying, to say the least. We can do without electricity but not water.

At 3.00pm WS reported that there was an Argentine air raid on San Carlos early this afternoon, so the poor weather has not entirely dissuaded them. Marines and Paras are now well entrenched, say the reporters there, Brian Hanrahan and Robert Fox. Supplies have been 'pouring in at a hectic rate'. Forward patrols have been pushing out to the north, east and south to make contact with any Argentines in the area.

Islanders at San Carlos have been giving the British soldiers all the help they can. Even the children are helping to build trenches. Some of the Argentine soldiers who were captured have told their interrogators that they had not eaten for three days. Part of me feels sorry for them, but if the Argentines are so poor at keeping their soldiers fed, then morale will be low and they might be less inclined to fight.

Rob Pitaluga believes the Marines of Naval Party 8901 were exercising around San Carlos before the invasion, meaning that they will know the area well. That may have encouraged the choice of San Carlos as a beachhead.

BA is still issuing bullshit communiqués to keep the domestic audience calm. The latest: 'The situation is as expected and the British are being prevented from consolidating their positions.' If the crowds in BA knew the truth about their inept military, they might be storming the Casa Rosada [the President's office].

Some more information is coming through about the sinking of HMS *Ardent*, which was a Type 22 frigate. She was in Falkland Sound bombarding the airstrip at Goose Green when she came under attack by wave after wave of Skyhawks and Mirages. Her last weapon firing was a general purpose machine gun, directed by the civilian NAAFI manager.

There are some indications that Galtieri may at last be seeing sense. He has written to the Pope asking him to intervene, and saying that he would accept a ceasefire that guarantees an honourable peace. I expect it's too late for that, though.

This afternoon, weather conditions improved. This was what the Argentines were hoping for. Waves of Skyhawks and Mirages were launched and they absolutely ripped into the ships and the forces on land. Early WS reports say that HMS *Antelope*, another Type 22 frigate, has been seriously damaged.

Five Mirages and a Skyhawk have been shot down. A Skyhawk and a Mirage were also damaged and may not have made it back to their bases. Details are coming in in dribs and drabs, but we're building up a picture of incredible combat around San Carlos. I doubt if there has been anything like this anywhere since the Second World War.

Some bad news from West Falkland. For some reason, Harriers attacked Dunnose Head yesterday. Tim Miller, the farm manager, managed to get through to one of the doctors in Stanley on the RT system (the RT station must be operational again) to say that he has shrapnel in one eye, and Christine Peck also has shrapnel in her. It seems both Tim and Chris have left Dunnose Head, along with the few others who live there. They are thought to be making their way to another farm, probably Chartres. I hope it goes well for them.

John and Margaret [Leonard] are brilliantly stoic. They asked if we and Aub and Sonia would like to come by their place for something to eat at lunchtime. Seems odd, but it is Sunday and one does that kind of thing on Sundays. When Dad told us about the invitation, I looked at him as if John and Margaret had lost their marbles. But then they've already proved they've lost a few by refusing to leave the Islands when they had the chance. They're American citizens, of course, and their embassy in Buenos Aires offered to help get them back to the US. It would have been relatively easy.

Anyway, the promise of sausage rolls clinched it. I can hardly remember the last time I had one of those delicious things. The Summers wisely but politely refused to leave the Goose. We, however, scuttled along the road to John and Margaret's. We didn't stay long. Before we left, Dad offered to do the washing up. John looked at him wryly: 'And where do you think you are going to get water?'

More Harrier vapour trails going west to east over Stanley as we went home. Also some small arms fire, but a good way off. No anti-aircraft fire.

Nothing much to do back at the Goose other than tune into the WS news. Late this afternoon, there was a major air attack on the army units established on shore. The Argentines say that twenty to thirty planes were involved, and London says that six of these were shot down. These losses, even if exaggerated, have got to be depleting the Argentine Air Force badly. And yet they continue to attack. Air attacks ceased with the fading of the light, thank God.

Harriers patrolling over the Sound encountered two Puma and one Bell Huey choppers. They downed the Huey and one Puma, with the latter exploding in mid-air.

Argentine spokesmen are becoming a comedy act. 'We believe the British are unable to advance beyond San Carlos and they will surrender soon.' Does anyone believe this stuff?

A fuel or ammo dump at Goose Green was destroyed yesterday, ether by naval shellfire or by Harriers. Some Pucaras were also destroyed on the ground. That's no bad thing. But the runway is very near the settlement, so I hope everyone is safe there. We have not heard anything from Goose Green for a long time.

London is now saying that the invasion force was subjected to seventy Argentine combat sorties on 21 May. That almost defies imagination. The Brits have nicknamed San Carlos Water 'Bomb Alley'.

Today, I encountered an Argentine in flying overalls kicking his heels outside the Goose. He's a Pucara pilot I met in the early days of the occupation. He'd fed me a cock-and-bull story then about the Air Force having old Lockheed Elektra planes that they would fill with explosives and crash into the enemy.

He recognized me too. I asked him where he'd been and he told me he'd been based at Goose Green and at 'Isla Borbon' (Pebble Island).

'What happened?' I asked. 'Why are you here now?'

'Your people attacked us at Isla Borbon and destroyed a lot of our aircraft. So then they sent us to Goose Green.' He rolled his eyes and even showed a hint of a wry smile. 'Then a few days ago, your navy destroyed more of our planes. So now I'm here and hoping that I can have another plane.'

He said that, but he didn't look particularly sad to be without one. He'd be aware that he wouldn't stand a chance if he was ordered to throw a Pucara into the British missile shield.

I remembered that when I met him before, he'd been with another young pilot, a darker-skinned guy who looked like he might be from the north of Argentina. What happened to him, I asked.

'He was killed at Goose Green,' came the answer. 'The British dropped a beluga bomb and he was hit.' 'Beluga' is what they call anti-personnel cluster bombs. 'They are outlawed, and yet you still use them.'

'I don't know about that,' I said. 'But I'm sorry your friend was killed.'

I reminded him of the supposed plans for kamikaze attacks. 'What happened to your Lockheed Electra suicide attacks? That wasn't true, was it?'

Now he did smile. 'No, of course not. But I thought you might tell someone who might even pass it on to the British. We know that you have radio communications.'

'Well, I knew it wasn't true. You all say that you would die for the Malvinas, but none of you are stupid enough to commit suicide.'

'I don't think your pilots are that committed, either,' he responded. He claimed that he had met a Harrier pilot who'd been taken prisoner at Goose Green. 'He just wanted to go home.'

The conversation was starting to become confrontational. He said that he and his colleagues know that the local people are helping the British, and there could be a price to pay when this is all over.

I said, 'You don't believe you are winning, do you?'

'Yes, I do. Your BBC broadcasts lie, and I would rather trust what our government says. We will win. Anyway, the British only want the Islands for their money. I've heard that Mrs Thatcher's husband is an owner of the FIC [Falkland Islands Company]. Is that true?'

I smiled, said I was certain that he had no financial involvement here at all and tried to explain that there is a principle at stake: that one country cannot take over another country's territory and put people under suppression.

'But you were second-class citizens under British rule.'

This was tricky territory, because he wasn't far from the truth. I shrugged and said, 'It hasn't been a perfect relationship, but at least our government doesn't torture and kill its own people.'

I realized that I might have gone too far with this argument. It was only a few weeks ago that I was having the bejesus scared out of me in the police station by an Argentine intelligence officer who had a file with my name on it in front of him. If this pilot was a hard-liner, then it might get back to them.

He looked hard at me with a stony expression but said nothing. Instead, he changed the subject.

'Tell me about the little Asian mercenaries that are fighting with your soldiers.'

For a second I didn't know what he was talking about, and then it dawned. 'Ah, you mean the Gurkhas. Yes, they are on their way. And they are very good soldiers. I would not want to meet them on the battlefield.'

His expression was sterner now and disdainful. 'I am surprised that the British stoop so low as to use them. At least we fight our own wars.'

This conversation had run its course. 'Believe what you wish,' I said. 'They are on their way. But I hope this is over soon, for all of us.'

He nodded in agreement. But the initial congeniality of our conversation had gone.

'I hope you will be home soon,' I said. He could take that as he wished. We said goodbye.

It was a quiet evening, and I was pleased to get my head down around 11.00pm. I dropped off quickly but woke up shortly after midnight to a storm of automatic fire very nearby. It sounded like ten or twenty weapons being fired simultaneously. I crept to the porch and looked out cautiously. Judging by the tracer rounds, it seemed that the firing was coming from the dockyard about 400 yards away. Most of the firing seemed to be directed over the harbour. It stopped, and I sneaked back to my pit.

Monday, 24 May

The airport was bombed again at about 9.45am. I was in the kitchen at the time and rushed out to the front to see smoke rising from what may have been the aviation fuel tanks. I think the Pucaras that survived the bombing and shelling at Goose Green have been moved to Stanley, but they are obviously not safe anywhere. That might have been the reason for the attack, and it would certainly account for my strange encounter with the Pucara pilot yesterday evening.

Bad and sad news from San Carlos. The frigate that was badly hit by the Argentine Air Force yesterday was HMS *Antelope*. An unexploded bomb detonated today, and she finally sank. It seems that only one sailor died on the ship. Last night, I felt I was getting used to the incredible level of violence that is going on all around us and in our name. But I'm not. I feel deflated and depressed.

The MoD in London is claiming that sixty Argentine planes have now been destroyed, either by missiles, special forces raids, anti-aircraft fire, Harriers or shellfire. That's estimated to be 25 per cent of their strength. I can't help feeling that this figure is too great to be true. RAF and Navy aircraft losses amount to four Harriers and nine helicopters. At the same time they announced that seventy British personnel have been killed in the campaign so far. It's tragic.

The weather is good day today, remarkably warm for this time of year. That is, of course, the last thing we want. So the Argentine air raids are underway again.

By early this afternoon, twenty to thirty planes are reported to have attacked the beachhead, and seven have been shot down. Not much detail yet released about damage to our ships or troops on shore, but the BBC reporters are saying that there has been *some* damage. The anti-aircraft missiles batteries are now set up on shore, so for the Argentines it must be like flying into a wall of fire.

South African newspapers are reporting that their government is supplying Mirage spares and some weaponry to Argentina. That figures, I suppose: solidarity between equally repellent governments. The SA Government is not commenting, but if it was not true, I think they'd say so.

Harold Briley is reporting from BA that the Argentine public is being given a confused idea of what is going on around the Islands. But he says some people in influential positions are starting to ask how the British were allowed to get a foothold here. If that's the start of dissent there, then it's a good thing.

At about 9.30 this morning someone came into the Goose kitchen saying that smoke was rising from the Mt Kent area [about seven miles west of town]. It sounds like the area has been attacked, although we didn't hear any planes or bombs. We know that Argentine troops have been dug in there for weeks, because the Heathmans at the Estancia managed to tell someone here that Argentine troops from the mountain had visited them looking for food.

At 12.28 two Harriers flew quite low over Stanley, and for once the Argentine anti-aircraft gunners seemed to have their wits about them. They opened up with a deafening cacophony. No obvious success, but they are getting better.

Robert and I visited Pete and Rosemary at Church House. They're spending nights at Pete and Rob's parents, but they check out their flat most days. We were chatting and looking out the front window when two more Harriers came over, quite high this time. The Argentines were again quick to open up, and the Harriers flew off with shells exploding not far behind them. No obvious hits, but close.

On the way back to the Goose I met Jimmy Stephenson [the meteorologist] coming from the met station. His office is very near a missile position, and Jimmy said he watched as the crew scrambled to shoot down the Harriers that flew over at lunchtime.

'They managed to get one away,' said Jimmy. 'But they lit the blue touch paper too late, and by the time the missile took off, the planes had gone.'

We both chortled.

'Could do better, eh?' said Jimmy in his typically droll way.

Late tonight, BBC is reporting that eight Argentine planes are believed to have been shot down today. They can't go on for long taking that kind of punishment.

Some minister whose name I didn't catch was paying tribute to the bravery of British servicemen and the men of the Merchant Navy. Quite right, too: they are civilians, and I don't suppose any of them expected to end up dodging bombs in a combat zone. He said there will be decorations for gallantry and a special Falklands campaign medal. I doubt if anyone on the front line is very concerned about that at the moment. They've got to survive first.

Over supper this evening Father Monaghan told us that Monsignor Spraggon had a very narrow escape last night. We had heard some automatic fire fairly close at about 11.30, but didn't realize that it had gone straight through St Mary's Presbytery, which is only about 150 yards from here. According to Father Monaghan, the Monsignor was trying to sleep at the back of the house when a soldier raked it with bullets. As he was horizontal, the bullets missed him.

This morning, the two priests counted twenty bullet holes in the walls and a lot of smashed crockery. One of the rounds was embedded in a theological book which, fortunately, the Monsignor didn't like much.

'That bloody Argentine got further through that book than I ever did,' he said.

He's a tough guy, the Monsignor. I'm very glad he's OK.

We had a few drinks, and people drifted off to bed. As I write this, it's surprisingly peaceful outside. I can hear some logger ducks making their peculiarly contented noises on the shore 100 yards away. I'm feeling tired but comfortable on the floor behind my pile of chairs.

Tuesday, 25 May

We awoke this morning to the realization that today is Argentina's National Day. This was the day in 1810 when they secured their independence from Spain. It's a holiday, of course, and we fear that BA will want to mark it with an impressive blow against the Task Force. Let's see how it unfolds, but I can't say I'm looking forward to it.

At about 11.15am a couple of Harriers screamed in at low level and dropped two or three bombs on the airport. As the blasts were so close together, I couldn't count them precisely. No signs of fires, but a Huey helicopter with red crosses painted on it flew very fast and low down the harbour, heading for the airport, leading us to conclude that there were casualties.

The Harriers were back at 2.45pm, and a little later, a lone Harrier dropped a bomb near the ammunition dump that we know they have in the Canache. Presumably the bomb landed near and not on the dump, otherwise the thing would have gone off like it was Armageddon.

A matter of minutes later, two Pucara aircraft appeared overhead, flying low, their turboprops whining. At times they flew past the Upland Goose and about 100 metres out over the harbour, flying no more than 20 metres above the water. They flew together down the seafront, north-west to the Narrows and then back again. They repeated this circuit for about half an hour. There is something shark-like about the Pucaras, and although this aerial ballet was compulsive watching, it had a sinister feel.

We quickly realized there was a reason for this odd behaviour. Circling Stanley high and well out of anti-aircraft fire range (although perhaps not missile range) was at least one Harrier. Obviously, the Argentine pilots knew it was there, and knowing they were no match for a Harrier, they figured that they would stay low and close to town, assuming that the Harrier (or Harriers) would not attack them while they were so close to us civilians. Eventually, the Harrier flew off. One of the Pucaras disposed of its single bomb over Port William, and they landed safely at the airport.

I think the Brits are getting frustrated by the airport's continued use – and not just by Pucaras. We're still seeing Hercules transports routinely defying the blockade. I've watched them approach at night, and at the last minute the runway lights are turned on. As soon as the plane has touched down, they are switched off again.

The planes obviously bring in mail for the troops, and sometimes there is even mail for us locals. Today, Bill Etheridge told Dad that there were just two letters for local people, both posted in Argentina.

Radio Islas Malvinas is making a big thing about today being the 176th anniversary of Argentina giving the Spanish a good hiding. They claim there was a ceremony at Government House, but if Menendez was silly enough to waste his men's time flag-waving and marching around, then he is even stupider than I thought. There has, though, been a lot of hand-shaking and back-slapping among the Argentines on the street and in the hotel. I asked one of the Argentine TV team why he was so happy, saying, 'I guess you enjoyed the little air show earlier today?' He didn't get the joke. Instead, he tediously explained the historical significance of today.

'Anything special planned?' I asked, thinking he might say if they had attempted a spectacular raid.

'Yes, we are having an *acto patriotico* [patriotic ceremony] at the jetty.'

'Well, let's hope the Harriers don't spoil it for you.'

He turned and walked away.

I decided to wander down towards the FIC jetty to see from a distance if they really were wasting their time with an '*acto patriotico*'. But the entire area around the jetty, FIC offices and warehouse area is cordoned off. I was told later that they did indeed have a parade on Crozier Place and ceremonially hoisted the Argentine flag.

By mid-afternoon the WS is reporting what might be the Argentines' anticipated National Day spectacular attack. Another Type 42 destroyer has been hit by bombs and is in serious trouble. This seems to have taken place north of Falkland Sound. Six Skyhawks are thought to have attacked the destroyer, and while some were shot down, three managed to get through, and bombed the ship. It sounds awful. I'm sure we will learn more soon. Fingers crossed.

This evening, WS indicated for the first time that they know CTF is being jammed. Presumably, one of the two BBC radio reporters with the Task Force has reported this back to London. As usual, the jamming took a few minutes to wind up to full intensity, and in this time [presenter] Peter King managed to say very clearly that the programme is now being broadcast on a third, new, frequency. This is great news. As long as the Argentines don't twig and start jamming this frequency as well, we should have our programme back. We tuned in to the new frequency immediately, and there it was, perfectly audible.

John Nott broadcast a perfectly crafted string of platitudes, claiming we are very much in their thoughts and implying that all of this is for our freedom. Last year, this guy was planning to do away with our guard ship, HMS *Endurance*, and half the ships now in the Task Force, while pushing us into the arms of Argentina.

More interestingly, the CTF news summary revealed that the three-man crew of the Sea King helicopter that landed near Punta Arenas in Chile had been rescued, handed over to British diplomats and secretly flown out of the country. But we still don't know much about their mission. There is speculation that they may have landed SAS troops on Tierra del Fuego to attack the air bases. If so, it looks as if the raid was called off. We may never know the facts.

CTF picked up on the fact that 25 May was marked with some kind of ceremony in Stanley. Peter King, who has a mischievous sense of humour, said, 'Now here is a list of Falkland Islanders who attended the ceremony . . .' Silence!

I heard today that Simon Winchester of the *Sunday Times* and the other Brit journalists who were here at the time of the invasion are still in jail in Ushuaia, on undoubtedly trumped-up spying charges. The letter that Simon kindly offered to carry to Michael may now be in the hands of his interrogators. I wonder if Michael will ever get it.

Today, the Argentines announced on local radio that a census will be held in Stanley tomorrow. That sounds like a pretty ambitious thing to do in the middle of a shooting war, but as at least half of the population of Stanley are now refugees on the farms, it's not such a huge task. One has to wonder why they are doing it, though. A clue, I think, lies in their intention to give everyone between the ages of sixteen and sixty-five an identity card. They are spooked by the threat of special forces infiltrating Stanley and posing as locals.

In the same news bulletin they claimed that three Harriers were shot down over Stanley today. I'm quite confident that is rubbish. We probably would have seen them coming down in flames, and even if we didn't, someone would have told us about it. Pure propaganda, and probably designed to erode our morale. They also claim that two British helicopters were shot down near Goose Green. No way of telling if that's true or not.

I had been wondering why General Menendez had not got his backside in gear long enough to mobilize a counter-attack at the San Carlos beachhead. Well, according to a WS report this evening, they may have done just that – in a half-hearted way. Argentine forces apparently approached Brit positions at San Carlos last night, having been dropped by helicopter. But they were quickly beaten back with mortar and artillery fire and were last seen heading in the direction of Goose Green. There were no British casualties.

Father Monaghan heard that about forty troops retreating from San Carlos arrived at Douglas Station [about 20 miles from San Carlos] behaving like desperadoes. They locked all the men in the community hall and forced some of the women to cook for them, including one of Mum's old friends, Clara McKay. Then they took the farm Land Rovers and ordered Frazer McKay and Pappy Minto to drive them to Stanley.

They are getting more heavy-handed about property in Stanley. Quite a few houses have been left empty by people who've gone to the farms, and the Argentines have simply moved into many of them. I understand, though, that they are paying rent for some houses. It's made clear to the owners, however, that if they don't accept offers, their houses will be taken anyway. It's becoming very difficult to exercise choice and free will in Stanley.

Padre Bagnall, who I've never really been able to engage with, was looking a bit more miserable than usual this evening. I asked him if he'd had a good day (no irony intended, but I couldn't think of anything better to say).

He looked at me with a mix of sympathy and derision and said, 'Frankly, no.' He said he'd seen two more Argentines being buried in the cemetery. 'I really don't care whose side they were on. They were someone's sons.'

For the first time I felt sympathy for the padre. I expressed my agreement with a sigh, and we sat there silently for a few minutes, before he wandered off looking very tired.

John Nott suggested on CTF that some of the captured Argentine soldiers said they had no idea why they were in the Falklands. I don't believe that. Every Argentine is taught from kindergarten about the 'Malvinas' being Argentine territory occupied by British 'pirates'. They might not like being here but they know *why* they are. Nott went on to say that a special fund is being created which will be used to help the families of those who are killed in the Falklands. That's good.

In the US, Al Haig has said that he expects an early British victory. That kind of optimism might be a little premature. The Argentine Air Force needs to be tamed first.

A pretty miserable evening at the Goose. No one's fault, but I think the situation is getting us all down a bit. I'm writing these final words of the day from my bivouac. I'm going to try to sleep, but the shelling is getting gradually more intense, and sleep might be hard to come by.

Chapter 18

Poised to Move on Stanley

(26–29 May)

Wednesday, 26 May

Heavy shelling last night. It started just minutes after midnight. The first shell landed much closer than was comfortable. I wonder if they realized they'd got the ranging wrong, because the next rounds landed further away, and they gradually moved in two directions, towards the airport and Sapper Hill.

Several of us got up to see what was going on from the front porch. It was chilly and dark, but we kept the light off. Dad, Rob and I were there, having pulled a few clothes on. I heard someone else join us and I turned to see Father Monaghan. It was strange, because for the first time he looked really vulnerable. But now, there he was with no shoes, braces over his vest and no dog collar. He looked nervous. I'm sure I looked the same.

We watched the explosions lighting up the sky, not saying much but when we did we whispered. Dad said he thought there were two ships doing the shelling, as the bangs of the shells leaving the barrels of the guns were coming from two directions. My hearing is not that refined.

The shelling ceased for a while and then resumed, perhaps as the ships repositioned. Eventually, we all went back to bed. That must have been about 2.30am. It was hard to sleep, though.

When the sun came up it revealed a cloudy but calm day. Let's hope it gets even cloudier so that the Argentine Air Force cannot get off the ground. I went to the kitchen early and found Aunt Ning, busy as usual. She greeted me with a smile and said, 'Help yourself to coffee.' She gestured towards the pot percolating on the stove. 'I think we all need it after that racket last night.' I sat there and nursed the coffee as I tried to wake up. Aunt Ning is, without doubt, very special.

I tuned into the BBC as she carried on with the normal domestic chores. Top of the news was the truly shocking report that HMS *Coventry* has been sunk. Aunt Ning stopped in her tracks and joined me as further horrible details unfolded. *Coventry* was north of Falkland Sound, defending the landing area from air attack, when she was hit by wave after wave of Argentine aircraft. She was expected to protect the other ships by taking the brunt of the attacks, so the crew would have known what they were in for. But it must have been terrifying. Twenty men have been killed and a further twenty are wounded, but I suspect those numbers will change – probably for the worse.

A large civilian freighter, the *Atlantic Conveyor*, was also hit and sank yesterday. Four dead and four wounded on her. It seems she was carrying important heavy equipment, including helicopters, so the Argentines will be delighted by this. It's not totally clear, but it seems the ship was hit by an Exocet missile.

Some soldiers came to Rowan House today and took my Daihatsu jeep. They said they wanted it for just three days. Mum and Dad were at the house and I was still at the hotel. They put up some resistance, pointing out to the soldiers that if they were trying to win our hearts and minds, stealing our property will not help them.

Dad lied that he would have to phone me to find out where the keys are (they were, as always, on the hall dresser) but he actually phoned Bloomer-Reeve to complain and ask if he could stop it. Bloomer-Reeve said there was nothing he could do, and that about half of the civilian vehicles in Stanley have now been requisitioned.

'I have very little influence now,' he said. 'And I am having less and less.' He added that the claim of wanting it for just three days means nothing at all. 'They will keep it for much longer. In your own interest, give them the keys.'

The troops had a piece of paper suitably adorned with rubber stamps which they showed Dad. They didn't offer any money to rent the vehicle, which is fine, as I don't want their money. Dad made a big show of taking all tools and other bits and pieces out of the jeep. He was removing the spare wheel when they said, 'That stays.'

I wonder if I'll see the jeep again, and if I do, what kind of state it'll be in.

Late this morning, we saw a very large fire in the area of Long Island Mountain. Huge amounts of smoke. There must be Argentine positions there, and I guess they've come under Harrier attack.

This afternoon, groups of soldiers went from house to house conducting their census and issuing ID cards. I was at Rowan by then. They were not taking any chances. Three soldiers and a pretty ferocious-looking dog remained outside the house, keeping an eye on all sides of the building.

Mum astonished me when she told the soldier who wanted to come in that he must leave his rifle at the door. He spoke reasonable English. Incredibly, he did so, but he still had a pistol. He looked in every room and then started asking us questions. Who lives in the house? How old are Dad and I? Where do we go at night? What vehicles do we have (none now)? Do we have a radio transmitter (not any more), and (curiously) do we have an intercom system? Also they wanted to know if there is still anyone in the house next door (no, as they've gone to Goose Green).

I was issued with an ID card and the soldier filled it in with details of my height, weight, hair and eye colour, languages spoken and whether I have a British passport.

The guy who came in was brisk but not particularly aggressive. The three heavily armed men and the Alsatian dog outside made the point that we had to cooperate.

I am sure that this 'census' is really about building up a list of which houses and vehicles they can requisition. They also now have the details of local men of fighting age, which will help them identify special forces if they infiltrate the town. Most women and men over sixty did not receive the ID cards, although Rosemary told me later today that she and a few other girls were given them. They apparently intend to add mug shots to the cards in the coming days.

'Always carry your identity card; that is an order,' said the soldier as he left. And that does seem to be a wise thing to do.

Jimmy Stephenson stopped for a chat as he loped in characteristic fashion up Ross Road, heading home. He said that he'd briefly been able to see two warships in the far distance from the Met station on the top of the hill.

A senior officer was at the Goose briefing the journos this afternoon. I lurked just within earshot. He said there was a Harrier raid on Port Howard yesterday in which five or six Argentines were killed and more injured. There was, he said, also an attack on Fox Bay, where one person was killed. Stuart [Wallace] and the others who were arrested are, we believe, at Fox Bay. I hope they weren't too close to the bombs.

He also said that local people at San Carlos had been seen directing British troops to Argentine positions. That, he claimed, resulted in helicopter attacks on the soldiers, who were withdrawing. He alleged that they shot the helicopters down. 'This will not be forgotten when we retake San Carlos,' he said, ominously.

If the Argentines had any hope that we would welcome them, then those hopes are well and truly gone. Today's 'census' and an increasingly aggressive attitude show they now consider us to be the enemy.

Mora, the manager of the radio station, knows that we listen to BBC WS more than to his station. He seems to accept this. Occasionally, he even asks us what the BBC is reporting. He's a civilian and therefore we're not particularly worried about him.

Here's what WS is saying tonight both on 'Calling the Falklands' and in general bulletins. Today was quiet compared to the nightmare of yesterday. No more major air attacks on British ships or the landing area. Is that because they are regrouping or because they are finally feeling the effect of losing so many combat planes?

There has been mourning in Coventry following the loss of the ship that bears the town's name. She put up a ferocious fight before succumbing, shooting down five Argentine aircraft, either with her Sea Dart missiles or guns. Other ships and helicopters near San Carlos spent the night rescuing the crews of *Coventry* and *Atlantic Conveyor*.

The *Atlantic Conveyor* was carrying Harriers, but these had been flown off the ship and redeployed to the carriers a couple of days before the attack. However, with the possible exception of one that happened to be in the air at the time, all the huge Chinook helicopters that the ship was carrying were lost. That's serious.

Both Argentina and the UK are, it seems, agreeing to the Security Council request to keep talking to the UN. But the UK ambassador said, 'A ceasefire depends entirely on the withdrawal of Argentine forces.' BA is not going to smoke that. If Galtieri were to withdraw, his government would be finished.

The Queen issues a statement following yesterday's losses. She said her thoughts are with the Task Force and she hopes it will be able to return home soon. You have to feel for her, as Prince Andrew is in the thick of it as a helicopter pilot.

John Nott has been bullish in Parliament. 'British forces are,' he said, 'poised to move on Port Stanley.' He added that ten more frigates and destroyers have joined the Task Force in the last few days. 'Generally,' he said, 'the operation has gone as planned.' I can't imagine that they 'planned' to lose this many ships, but they probably took the possibility into account.

BA is claiming to have captured a Harrier pilot who was shot down. This sounds credible. They say he will be sent to BA. However, London is not confirming that a Harrier has been shot down in the last day or so.

We were drinking coffee in the kitchen shortly before midnight when a huge explosion shook the building. It wasn't followed by any shooting or further explosions. It's hard to imagine what it might have been, but as it was a one-off, I don't think it was a shell. I suppose it could have been sabotage by special forces. That possibility will make the Argentines even more twitchy.

On that note, I'm off to get my head down. Sleep? Well that depends very much on the Royal Navy.

Thursday, 27 May

With the exception of the very big blast, it was a quiet night. I slept quite well. The news over breakfast was that a further five men from the *Atlantic Conveyor* are unaccounted for, which probably means they are dead. That's nine now, including the captain.

It seems likely that the Army might begin its big push on Stanley within the next 24 hours. There are unconfirmed reports that the Paras are fighting 15 miles north of Darwin, which I think would put them around the Sussex Mountains. So the troops are on the move.

Argentina is said to be scouring the world looking for more Excocet missiles. France has said that they will not sell them directly to BA, but another (unknown) country is thought to have offered three at $1,000,000 each. The original price was only $100,000. Supply and demand.

Later this morning, something really big is obviously underway near Darwin and Goose Green. WS is reporting that the Paras are now just five miles outside Darwin. At midday we heard Parliament has been told that 'British troops have gone on the offensive'. It seems that the Marines are moving directly east towards Stanley on the north side of the mountains, and the Paras are heading for Goose Green. The Argentines have Pucaras based there, and they are dangerous.

It's anybody's guess how long it will take the troops to get to Stanley, but it may be a few days. The trip takes about nine hours by Land Rover in the summer, and the tracks will be wet now. Plus, it will depend on how much resistance the Argentines put up. My guess, though, is that they will not find very much in their way.

There's a mood of some excitement in town today, and while no one is looking forward to a shoot-up around the town, I think everyone would like to get it over with.

Mum and Dad are spending very little time at the shop now. They look in on it from time to time just to check all is OK and let the Argentines think someone may be living there. If a local needs anything from the shop, they'll open for them. Some people still need good outdoor clothing.

We're still spending time at Rowan House when possible. This morning, Mum and Dad were there when a very young and miserable Argentine soldier timidly knocked on the kitchen door. He was hungry and wanted food. Mum gave him biscuits and some tinned food. As far as I'm concerned, that was absolutely the right thing to do. In fact I'm proud of her for taking pity on a kid. He will never kill anyone, except possibly himself.

The poor guy was very grateful, but worried about being seen by his own people so he didn't stay around for long. This incident upset Mum badly, and I think Dad felt awful too. These conscripts are just ill-prepared kids.

I had thought the Argentines were handling their logistics better now, but I guess that is not so. It's getting colder as we head into winter, and I doubt if many troops have adequate shelter. Eventually, Galtieri and his cronies in BA will have to answer for inflicting so much suffering on their own young people.

Rob Pitaluga's house in Stanley was taken over today. That means they have destroyed his Cessna plane, taken his Land Rover, his house and even his freedom (as he is still under house arrest at the Goose).

Rob was allowed to go to his house to remove valuables and lock some things in the sheds. I went with him to help. From his house we could easily see as far west as Moody Brook. There is a large hole in the roof of one of the buildings there, a result of either shelling or bombing.

Two Pucara aircraft came in low over Stanley at 5.20pm and landed at the airport. They have probably escaped from Goose Green, which we now know is under attack by the Paras.

I went to the hospital to see Aunt Lena and I noticed helicopters flying in and out of the football pitch. They loaded troops and equipment then flew off to the west. They must be reinforcing Goose Green. Earlier: Some people have seen vehicles full of troops heading west out of Stanley. But they can't hope to get to Goose Green in time. They may be reinforcing a defensive line around the town.

At the hospital they had their own generator running, which is sensible as power cuts are now common. There were several today. Aunt Lena was in good form. When I went into her room, she was sitting there puffing on a cigar. I took her the last of the flowers from Dad's conservatory. She was delighted with these. I asked her where she had got the cigar and she said she has a box of them. She offered me one, and I politely declined. She's still helping out in the hospital kitchen. Aunt Lena is amazing. Tough as nails (much tougher than me), but with a heart of gold.

She told me that earlier in the day an Argentine soldier was brought into the hospital, having stood on a mine somewhere between the Ajax Bay houses and the racecourse. She said the young man died. It's hard to tell with Aunt Lena, but I think she was upset by this. We sat there for a bit in silence. But she eventually reached into her bedside table and brought out a bottle of Johnny Walker Red Label.

'How about a glass of this, dear?'

I said, 'Why not?' so she found glasses and poured a generous tot for each of us. Then she picked up her crochet work and started on it. And again we sat there quietly for a while. Eventually, I gave her a peck on the cheek and said goodbye. I'm pleased Aunt Lena's living at the hospital, because I know she's safe.

On the way back to the Goose, a lone Harrier flew over, very high, presumably having a look over the area. There was some ineffective anti-aircraft fire, but more in hope than expectation.

Back to the Goose and a long evening mainly spent around the kitchen radio. People came and went, and Aunt Ning, the girls and the other ladies prepared food. And yes, I did feel a bit guilty for not helping in any significant way.

The death toll on the *Atlantic Conveyor* has risen to twelve. The ship is burnt out but still afloat, and it may be possible to salvage some of her cargo.

The Americans are said to be supplying arms to the British for use here. They are apparently being flown into Ascension Island. The most important of these supplies are the latest version of Sidewinder air-to-air missiles for the Harriers.

'Calling the Falklands' at 6.20 reported General Menendez saying that the British blockade of the Falklands is causing difficulties for civilians, but his forces are being supplied. Judging by the poor hungry soldier at Rowan House today, I'd say that's a lie. And while we civilians are being cautious with essentials, we are not going hungry.

The junior Foreign Office minister Cranley Onslow spoke on CTF. 'With the Falklands, it is family,' he said. Funny that we never felt the love before the invasion.

Peter King signed off from 'Calling the Falklands' with his customary catchphrase: 'Heads down, hearts high.' It's as good a motto as any.

Later this evening, WS reports that a furious battle going on at Goose Green. The Argentine positions are being shelled, either from the sea or the land. The Paras are advancing but meeting 'stiff resistance'.

Harold Briley in BA is reporting that the Argentines admit the Brits have control of about 60 square miles of East Falkland. But they insist they are planning a major counter-attack. Argentine submarines may also be committed to the conflict soon. This may worry Task Force commanders.

Late tonight, there is still no firm news coming out of Darwin and Goose Green. We are worried for the civilians, among whom are, we believe, a lot of refugees from Stanley. This is nerve-wracking, and I think tonight we are all running on coffee and adrenaline. Sleep is not possible, so I am staying up – with fingers firmly crossed.

Friday, 28 May

The shelling started around 11.55 and went on for over two hours, ceasing every now and again (perhaps while the ships repositioned). Just when we thought it was over, it would start again.

The street lights were turned off, and Rob, Dad, Father Monaghan and I huddled in the Goose front porch watching the flashes of the detonations. Every now and again, a star shell lit up the entire harbour. We wondered if these pyrotechnics might be lighting the way for a commando raid.

No one could get any rest, and eventually most of the refugees from the west end of the Goose, and even the Argentines, including Mora and Kasanzew, from the east end, gathered in the kitchen, where Aunt Ning made coffee. This was comforting, and it seemed both strange and natural for us all to be drinking coffee together as the shells exploded.

I spoke to Kasanzew for a bit. He claimed his sources tell him it's not true that Goose Green is being attacked by the Paras. He claimed there have only been air raids. He's the only Argentine reporter here, and I seriously doubt his objectivity. To be fair, if he was anything other than very sympathetic to the military, they wouldn't allow him to stay. Perhaps his thoughts are different to his words, but I don't trust him.

Eventually, the shelling slowed and stopped, and we all drifted off. I'm feeling very groggy this morning. The weather is miserable; a fresh westerly wind, overcast and drizzle. Visibility would be bad for the Argentine Air Force.

It's not surprising that we know nothing of the outcome of the attack on Goose Green, because if news of the attack's progress was released, it could be like giving the Argentines a free reconnaissance flight over the area.

I expect that bloke with the very dull monotone voice from the MoD [Ian McDonald] will give an update on Goose Green later today. He'll be competing for attention with the Pope, who has arrived in the UK. In his first speech he appealed for peace in the South Atlantic. A bit late, really.

Yesterday, I had a conversation with an Argentine officer who had been briefing Kasanzew and co. He seemed curious about me, I suppose because I am an Islander who can talk to him in Spanish, though far from perfectly. So I thought I'd see what I could learn. He was friendly enough and said that he had arrived in the Falklands a few days after the invasion aboard the icebreaker *Almirante Irizar*. He knew about the invasion about two days in advance and was glad to know he would be involved.

This guy knew that there would be some resistance to the invasion, but he was shocked that Britain had responded by throwing everything it has into retaking the Islands.

The UN is still hammering away at peace talks. That's what they're for, of course. No real sign of progress, but the British Ambassador is quoted as saying, 'We're still in business.' He should see what kind of business is going on here.

I spent a few hours today at the Woodbine, as Aub and Sonia asked me to make it look occupied. I lit the fire and passed an hour or so writing to Michael in Oxford. I told him what's been going on here and stressed we are OK. I'll post it with fingers crossed [see Appendix]. Of course it will have to have an Argentine stamp on it, and at some date that will be of interest to collectors. If Mike receives it, he might make a few quid one day.

Argentina has finally confirmed that there has been a major battle for Goose Green and Darwin. News is still only trickling out from both sides, though. In fact, the BBC is saying that there is a 'news blackout' about the action.

In the absence of fact, rumours are rife, and they are pretty dramatic. The worst of these is that four civilians have been killed at Goose Green. Our mood is subdued. A bloody battle is certainly going on, and a hundred or more Islanders are in the middle of it.

This afternoon, WS is saying that the Argentine positions at Goose Green were taken at about 11.00am today, and the Union Flag is said to be flying over Goose Green. But I spoke to some people who were at the hospital earlier today, and they said that helicopters were continuing to fly to and from the football field, loading troops and supplies and then flying off to the west, in the general direction of Goose Green and Darwin.

One of our number overheard some Argentines in the Goose saying, 'We will counter-attack today.' They may want to but they are probably too late. I wonder if they have the gumption for a counter-attack anyway. But there is so much rumour and uncertainty.

The MoD, as reported on WS, are keeping mum about Goose Green. However, they have said that four Marines and a Royal Engineer were killed and twenty injured in an air attack at 'Bomb Alley'. Two Skyhawks were shot down during the raid. In a separate incident, a Harrier was lost but the pilot was seen to eject.

The fighting at Goose Green seems to have galvanized the mood among the Argentines in town. This afternoon, troops were on the move and more armed vehicles were on the streets. They are removing the soft tops from their fancy Mercedes Benz jeeps and fitting them with heavy machine guns.

Early this afternoon, Mora told a group of us that there has been 'terrific loss of life on both sides at Goose Green'. He appeared to be quite upset. I hope that's not true. Mora is used to putting out propaganda on the radio station, but this time he was believable.

Fortunately, they have not realized that the BBC is broadcasting CTF on two new frequencies. Or if they have, they haven't been able to jam them. So we are receiving the programme well now. We tuned in this evening with particular enthusiasm, hoping for firm news about Goose Green. And we got it. Goose Green and Darwin are safely in the hands of the Paras after a very hard battle. There was no mention of civilian casualties, so we are cautiously optimistic that all are OK. It was also reported that Teal Inlet and Douglas Station, both on the northern route to Stanley, may have been taken. All very encouraging!

BA is acknowledging the British claims of the outcome of the battle at Goose Green, but they are claiming that after their lines were overrun they mounted a strong counter-attack with fresh troops that had been flown from Stanley. We know that reinforcements were being flown out there, but they clearly were unable to change the outcome of the battle.

We've heard that Port Howard was attacked the day before yesterday. Shells from one or more ships were dropped on Argentine positions near the settlement, but at least one detonated on or near the store. Baked beans and tea everywhere, I guess. Robin Lee [the farm manager] sent a message on the 2-metre radio grapevine, asking the fleet to 'kindly adjust your sights'.

Saturday, 29 May

The day dawned bright and fresh. The peace didn't last for long, though: as I emerged from my pit, a Harrier roared in and bombed the Yorke Bay side of the airport. How our normality has changed.

Rende, one of the older Argentines living down the east end of the hotel, shipped out yesterday. Mora told me that he has been 'taken elsewhere', suggesting that he must have some murky role. He had been a very frequent visitor to Stanley before. Mora said that he will come back after ten days or so. We tend to treat Rende with suspicion. He may have been spying during his visits before the war.

Mora also said that Argentine artillery returned fire against the ships that shelled Stanley last night. This is true, I think, as we can tell the difference between incoming and outgoing fire. Last night, some of the shells were certainly outgoing.

It's been confirmed that troops north of the Wickham Heights have taken Teal Inlet and Douglas Station. This means that they are now almost halfway to Stanley. They'll soon be well positioned to put the town under an even tighter siege. Stanley is the real prize, and most of the Argentine forces, including their most professional troops, heavy artillery and Pucara aircraft, are concentrated here. They could feel confident enough to defend the town successfully, meaning that a battle might be long and very nasty. I was speaking to Dad about this, and both of us feel that while liberating Stanley is the objective, the fact that we may be in the way will not stop the attacks. It is going to get a lot more dangerous.

Galtieri's speech to the nation on Army Day was relayed by the radio station here. Tub-thumping macho stuff, but he couldn't hide the truth entirely. He said, 'Argentina's fight is unequal against an extra-continental aggressor and those who support him.' The tone suggested that he is laying the groundwork for explaining away an Argentine defeat.

On CTF this evening it's being reported that an incredible 900 Argentine troops have been captured at Goose Green. That's just amazing. We don't know exactly how many Paras attacked, but I doubt if it was more than a few hundred, and a 900-strong force should have been able to hold out almost indefinitely. No figures for British fatalities yet. I suspect that a high price was paid but I hope I'm wrong. The Paras' commanding officer, Lieutenant Colonel Herbert Jones – known as 'H' – died heroically in the battle. He was shot dead attacking an Argentine machine-gun post. What incredible bravery.

The Navy arrived at about 11.00pm. We heard the first distant 'pops' of shells leaving their gun barrels, followed by the massive 'crumps' of impact. There were a few ranging shots, and then they started pouring in the shells. Most landed near or on the airport and around the Cape Pembroke peninsula. This was not close enough to scare us particularly.

We all went to bed to the sound of shelling. It's oddly reassuring to hear the Navy out there and know that they are trying to end the occupation. But no closer with the shells, please.

Chapter 19

Warning of Severe Consequences

(30 May–2 June)

Sunday, 30 May

The naval shelling was heavy for much of last night. As always, we could hear the pop of the shells as they left the guns and then the crash of them detonating, but unusually, we could also often hear them whistling overhead. That is a disturbing sound. Proper sleep wasn't possible.

These bombardments are effective. Yesterday, we overheard a major who came to talk to their TV people say that a lot of soldiers were killed by shelling on the outskirts of Stanley two nights ago.

We are starting to appreciate how bad it must have been for the civilians at Goose Green, including the many refugees from Stanley who thought they would be safer there. Boy, were they mistaken? The entire population – over a hundred people – was locked up in the community hall about a month ago. The Argentines moved into their homes and took over their vehicles. That was simply criminal.

I've been to that hall, and as I recall it has only a couple of toilets and a rudimentary kitchen. The conditions must have been awful. They remained in the hall as the battle raged around them. That can only have been terrifying. Many of their houses have been wrecked and their valuables stolen.

The fighting is said to have gone on for fourteen hours, and about 1,200 Argentines were captured. They have now been put to work clearing bodies and dangerous material from the battlefield, and cleaning up the settlement which they wrecked.

Robert Fox of the BBC, who was with the Paras, reported that the Argentine commander organized some ridiculously bombastic ceremony to mark the surrender. He paraded his surviving and uninjured troops and made a political speech, before they all sang the national anthem.

Fox said that the British victory was due to the sheer courage of the Paras, because they were badly outnumbered. But the Argentines held on tenaciously from well-prepared positions.

It was being reported that twelve British soldiers were killed, including their commanding officer, H Jones. Thirty-one were injured. No firm figures for

Argentine losses yet, but it's thought that over a hundred were killed or injured. We don't know if any of the civilians locked up in the hall were casualties. Our feeling, though, is that they are probably all OK (physically, at least), as if there had been deaths or injuries, we would have heard about them by now.

I badly needed to get out this morning, so I took a lengthy walk before arriving at Rowan House to check it hadn't been broken into and to feed the cats, including the refugee Murdoch, and our refugee chickens. The sky was beautifully clear as I walked, although it was chilly. I found it refreshing and even a bit cleansing, like a glass of sparkling water.

I left the Goose feeling hopeless and depressed, but by the time I was scattering some grain for the chickens, the mood had gone. Doing normal things reminds me of normal times. I'll keep this remedy in mind in case the situation gets worse.

I saw a few Harriers flying overhead, obviously having a look around to see how much damage was inflicted by the shelling last night and spotting new targets. I felt like waving to the pilots. They wouldn't have seen me, but some Argentines might have, so I didn't.

I was transfixed by the Harriers. Two were flying close together a little lower than normal when there was a puff of Argentine anti-aircraft fire very close to one of them. It veered off course briefly and a moment later there was a ripping explosive noise. The troops occupying the Junior School and Stanley House cheered ecstatically, and I expect they will chalk it up as a 'kill', even though the plane flew on. Later, I mentioned this to Paul. He also saw the incident and wondered if the plane might have fired its rockets and other weapons to lose weight and gain height quickly.

The Harriers continued to overfly Stanley periodically during the day, apparently without much concern. It's obvious they now feel that they have air superiority. They bombed the area sporadically through the day.

I met Jimmy Stephenson walking home from the met station late in the day, and from his vantage point at the station he had watched the Argentines blowing things up (unexploded bombs perhaps?) to the south of town.

Jimmy has got to know some of the young soldiers near the station well. He says their morale is very low. Some of them told him they just want the whole thing to be over so that they can get back to Buenos Aires. Who can blame them? They are ill-equipped and ill-fed, and facing some of the best forces in the world.

According to an edict broadcast on local radio, as from today curfew hours are brought forward to 4.00pm. That's a pain in the backside but a sign of desperation. The same edict ordered everyone living south of Davis Street to move into the centre of town. The edict said this was necessary because of 'British shelling and other such activity'. So those who have held out against leaving their homes are finally making the move to 'safe' buildings. From mid-afternoon sad little groups of civilians walked through the town carrying suitcases and bags.

The earlier curfew means it's no longer possible to go to the pub, which I wasn't doing very often anyway. The occasional drink with Robert and a few others made us feel much better, though.

I ran into David Castle and Michael Smallwood from the West Store. They said that many of those who were ordered to move out of their houses today have gone to the Store. It's very heavily built, and of course they have good supplies there.

'Calling the Falklands' came through very clearly tonight. No efforts to jam the new frequencies. Peter King reported that wounded of both sides from Goose Green are being evacuated to the hospital ship SS *Uganda*. The Navy says that last night, they delivered the heaviest bombardment yet on the Stanley area. That didn't surprise us. It really was alarming at times.

There was a flurry of activity down the Argentine end of the Goose around 7.00pm, and I went down to see what was going on. Casanzew was looking very happy indeed. He told me he was off to Radio Islas Malvinas to announce that a British aircraft carrier had been hit by the Argentine Air Force.

'It was a Super Etendard launching an Exocet,' he told me, smugly. 'This could be the beginning of the end for your people.' And with that he headed off into the dark to announce the news on what was once our radio station.

Is this true? Who knows? As I write this at 9.30pm, the BBC is reporting that there was an air attack on one or more ships but none was hit. All of this worries us.

At midnight WS announced that there had indeed been an air attack on the Task Force, but no ship was damaged, especially not a carrier. One Argentine aircraft, thought to be a Skyhawk, was shot down.

Feeling reassured, it seems safe to go to bed, though no sleep is assured, of course.

'To you, too, Father,' I said, as Father Monaghan made his rounds.

Monday, 31 May

Today, we emerged from the usual disturbed sleep to find a thin covering of snow. It was freezing hard during the night. However, today is one of those winter days that in normal times are invigorating: bright blue sky and a pure white vista.

Last night's bombardment was less intense than expected. I managed to doze through most of it. But there were three extremely loud explosions just before 6.00am. I'm not sure if they were bombs or shells, but we estimated that they landed near Callaghan Road. It's a good thing that everyone has been ordered out of that area.

Father Monaghan returned to the Goose after his rounds, reporting that Jack Abbot's house, just a few hundred metres south of Rowan, suffered some damage, as did Dolly Ford's house on Davis Street. They are getting closer.

It's a good day for flying, and from early on we have been seeing Harriers overhead. A few of them have been flying high and wide circles over the town, obviously taking reconnaissance photos. I think they have discounted the risk from the Argentine Air Force but, as we saw yesterday, the Argentines can fight back with guns and missiles. Even the Argentines must admire the pilots' courage. Flying over Stanley in broad daylight is asking for trouble.

WS reception was very poor this morning. However, I picked up that banks and post offices across the UK are to act as collection points for donations to a fund that will help the families of men killed in the Falklands. 'Money has been flooding in,' according to the WS. When this is all over, I expect we Islanders will contribute to the fund. A lot of families will be having a very tough time.

BA is continuing to claim that one of the aircraft carriers was damaged in an air attack yesterday. The MoD in London is stating categorically that no British ship was hit but a Super Etendard was shot down. Whom do I believe? That's not even worthy of answer.

More credibly, BA is saying that their forces south of Stanley were bombarded and bombed heavily yesterday. The Argentines are interpreting this as a softening-up operation prior to a major attack on the town.

There are reports of an Argentine Air Force Hercules transport attempting to attack a British ship. It seems that the crew lowered the door and just rolled a bomb out. I can't imagine they hit anything.

At about midday, shortly after I wrote the above, my point about the danger of anti-aircraft fire and missiles was underlined. The Argentines unleashed a missile at two Harriers that were reconnoitring high overhead, but the pilots accelerated and flew off to the east. The missile exploded perhaps half a mile behind them.

The planes were back very soon. And this time they were not bothering to take snaps. I happened to be outside the Goose and looking towards the east, when two black dots in the distance became Harriers flying very low indeed over Canopus Hill, near the airport. They dropped a couple of bombs on the airport and strafed it. A missile was launched in response, but too late. The Harriers escaped.

I'm sure they were trying to get the four or five Pucaras that my binoculars revealed are parked on the south side of the runway. They are possibly the only Pucaras still operating in the Islands. They may not be any more, as judging by the billowing smoke and flames, the Harriers hit something.

I didn't see the next attack on the airport area about an hour later. The Argentines seemed to be a bit more prepared this time and they unleashed a storm of gunfire and at least one missile. There was a roar of cheering from Argentines near the Goose, but it's not clear who came out on top in this episode.

Michael and Margot Smallwood are supposed to move into the Woodbine today and look after it for Aub and Sonia while enjoying relative safety. Their house up on Davis Street is no longer safe. The Smallwoods will stay in the Woodbine during the day and go to Tony and Annie Chater's house, just a few yards along the road, at night. The Chaters' place is of the brick shit-house variety, so it should be fairly safe.

Amazingly, Aunt Ning received some rental payment for the Youth Club today. One of the uniformed administrators who kip down in the east end of the hotel arrived at the door of the kitchen with a bundle of pesos which probably amounts to £100 or so. Anna, who is still spending a few hours each day at the Treasury, will take the cash there tomorrow and bank it. It may seem strange that we agreed to rent it to them, but when they approached saying they wanted to have the keys of the building, they made it quite clear that we could either agree to rent it to them or they would take it anyway. The committee thought they might as well get some money for it, but we didn't expect to see any.

That civilized gesture contrasted with an announcement broadcast from the radio station (still on rediffusion only) at 4.30pm. 'Any offence against the military in the Islands will be treated with great severity,' we were told. The tone was sinister, to say the least. They probably left 'great severity' undefined on purpose. From their point of view it's better to let us worry about what it might mean.

It's clear what caused them to issue this threat, though. When a bunch of soldiers went to Kenneth McKay's house intending to take his Land Rover, he ripped a handful of cables out of the vehicle, ensuring it wouldn't go anywhere. Unfortunately, he did this in full view of the Argentines and he was marched off to the police station, where he was chucked in a cell. They initially told Kenneth that he would be flown out to BA, where he would face a military trial. Fortunately, Bloomer-Reeve moved quickly and defused the situation. Within a few hours Kenneth had been released with a stiff warning. We are *very* fortunate that there are some Argentines in senior positions who seem to be humans first and Argentines second.

Tonight's CTF had a lot to report. The Argentine Air Force sounds as though it is getting increasingly desperate. Apart from the ludicrous Hercules bombing raid, two Canberras carried out a night attack on Bomb Alley yesterday. Their bombs fell a long way from British positions. The BBC's man on the ground, Robert Fox, speculated that they are suffering from a serious lack of pilots and planes.

Military analysts are speculating that the Argentines' best artillery and other heavy weapons are being held back for the defence of Stanley.

The MoD has said there was a clash yesterday between British and Argentine troops near Mt Kent, west of Stanley. The King girls, the Keenleysides and I drove out to Mt Kent and climbed it just last summer. It only took us about 90 minutes to get to the top.

It's damned cold outside as I think about getting my head down. There is still snow on the ground, and I can't imagine how horrible it must be up in the mountains.

Tuesday, 1 June

Comparing notes with Paul, Dad and others at breakfast, it seems there was heavy naval shelling of Argentine positions, but all detonations were distant. Anyway, I slept through most of it.

I ran into Mora making his way out of the Goose this morning. I mentioned the sinister tone of the announcement from 'his' radio station yesterday. He said we were lucky, and to take the edict seriously. 'Things are probably going to get a lot worse,' he added, looking glum.

He pointed out that even Argentine soldiers are facing tough justice. He said that three soldiers were discovered robbing a house in Stanley. They faced a summary sentence of eighteen months in jail. He wasn't sure if they were flown back to BA immediately or whether the sentences would apply when the war is over. But he stressed that this occurred before the no-holds-barred fighting had started. He thinks that punishment for both locals and Argentine soldiers will be much more severe now. I feel he's right.

Today is dry with very little wind. There's a slightly overcast sky and it's very cold. I don't feel like moving far from the Goose but I will check on the Woodbine later, as I don't think the Smallwoods have moved in.

I'm now writing in the late afternoon as I sit in the Woodbine, stoking the stove. So I'm warm and lots of lovely smoke is floating out of the chimney, making it look as if the house is being lived in.

I went to see Pete and Rosemary on the way to the Woodbine. We were sitting drinking coffee at 2.40 when there was a very heavy burst of anti-aircraft fire, very close. We ran down the stairs and rushed outside in time to see a jet fighter spiralling down out of the sky to the south of town. Flames were clearly visible from the cockpit area. There was a load of cheering from the Argentine troops all around town.

Of course, we assumed this was a Harrier and we felt miserable. We didn't know if the pilot had managed to eject. Soon after, a helicopter flew low over town, heading in the direction of where the plane went down. Presumably they were looking for the pilot. We were feeling dejected after that.

Later: I just met up with the Jeremy and Martin Smith, and they told me that the shot-down plane may have been one of their own. John [their father] had walked up to the football field and saw a helicopter arriving. It seems the chopper had rescued the pilot. John was close enough to see an Argentine flag on his flight suit. Also, there was no armed guard around him. So, an own goal for the Argentines.

I saw my Daihatsu jeep today. It was parked by the FIC [Falkland Islands Company] jetty transit warehouse. It's thickly covered with Darwin Road-type clay and mud. Apart from that, it looks more or less OK. I'm wondering if they have abandoned it, because it runs on petrol, which is now a very rare commodity.

All of their own vehicles and most of those they have requisitioned run on diesel. I'll keep an eye on the jeep, and if it's still there in a day or two's time I'll have a closer look.

Very disturbing news today from Goose Green. The Argentines had napalm there and a couple of their Pucaras dropped it on the Paras during the battle. They missed, fortunately. Then, after the surrender, the Paras discovered a large dump of napalm tanks. I hope they don't have it here in Stanley, too.

There were only sporadic water and electricity supplies today, with no warning about cuts. This has become routine over the last few days.

My feelings about this whole experience are changing. I have to admit that in the early days I actually felt some excitement. It was an almost unbelievable drama playing out before us. The entire world was watching us, even though we were at the centre of the drama. But now it's depressing, scary and, when I hear about some of the action, sickening. I desperately want it to be over soon.

It seems amazing to me, but the Argentines who inhabit the east end of the hotel (mainly the TV team, a journalist from Uruguay and some officers who have taken over from our civil servants at the Secretariat) still seem to be quite cheerful and optimistic. Of course, their upbeat behaviour could just be a big act for our benefit when they know we are around. Or perhaps they really believe the Argentine propaganda, some of which they are responsible for. In any case, we don't have a lot to do with them.

The troops have been doing a lot of digging around the town in the last few days. Obviously, some of these earthworks are defensive positions, and as they are building them in the middle of town they must be anticipating house-to-house fighting. That wouldn't be a bundle of fun for us.

They are even digging huge holes and burying shipping containers that arrived on the *Formosa*. I'm worried that these are probably full of ammunition.

The Paras captured two almost complete Pucaras at Goose Green, along with thousands of weapons. Apparently, the defences were well laid out, with mortars professionally ranged in advance. The BBC reporter said that a multiple rocket launcher from a Pucara had been strapped to a slide in the kids' play area. It seems incredible that only seventeen Paras died.

Further information emerging from the battle for Goose Green. It was a bloodbath: 250 Argentines were killed and about 140 wounded. Apparently, at one point a group of Argentines waved a white flag, but then as the Paras moved forward to take them prisoner, a position nearby opened on them with a machine gun. Who knows whether that was trickery or a mistake, but the Paras assumed the former.

The BBC reporter said that the troops found evidence that the FIC had been doing business with the Argentines at Goose Green and Darwin. They were pretty angry about this. They found receipts indicating that the farm had sold them engine oil and other goods.

The BBC got on the phone to the Ted Needham, the FIC Managing Director in London, for comment, and he said, 'This could not be true.' Needham also said that the Argentines had asked to rent the *Monsunen*, and this was refused. They took it anyway.

London has confirmed that troops have consolidated their position near Mount Kent. No Brits killed there, but three Argentines died.

As I headed back to the Goose just before the 4.00pm curfew kicked in, I noticed the Argentine hospital ship *Bahia Paraiso* in the harbour. She dropped anchor a little west of the hotel. I'll get the binoculars out later and have a good look at her.

Later, they quickly began unloading cargo into the much smaller *Yehuin*. I wonder what that cargo is. Should be nothing more than medical supplies, but then again . . .

This evening, I had a word with the military police officer Captain Romano, who's still visiting the Goose often to check that Rob Pitaluga is behaving himself under house arrest. He said that the *Bahia Paraiso* will soon be meeting up with the [British hospital ship] *Uganda* and taking 140 wounded Argentines who had been receiving treatment on *Uganda*.

Romano also said that two or three Hercules are flying in and out of the airport most nights. They fly for much of the distance at just about 50ft above the waves, and they take such a circuitous route that it takes five hours to get to Stanley. He said a Hercules was recently intercepted by a Harrier about 50 miles from Stanley and was shot down. I think this is all believable.

This evening, a commentator on BBC WS said no one should assume that British troops will reach Stanley soon just because they are close. They will not want to take the next step until they have consolidated and have worked out exactly what the defences are around Stanley. We can, he said, look forward to many more air raids and much more shelling. So we may have quite a few more weeks under the thumb of the Argentines. That's a depressing thought.

Menendez has been addressing his troops on local radio and TV. He ordered them to inflict a 'crushing defeat on the British'. This, he says, is their 'sacred duty'.

That 'sacred duty' did not seem to help a group of Argentine paratroopers who were dropped behind British lines. They were intercepted and four of them were killed.

That's it: another deadly day in the now famous Falklands.

Wednesday, 2 June

The Navy were dropping shells before midnight. Then all went quiet and I got some sleep until about 4.00am. Most of the detonations were a fair way off, and I suspect they are being directed now by troops around Mt Kent, who probably have a good view of Stanley.

This morning it is calm but drizzling and very cloudy. Not good conditions for air operations.

The Argentine hospital ship left this morning and, from the chatter I overhead among the east-end journalists, she may be meeting with the *Uganda*.

Jessie Booth who, incredibly, is still hunkering down with Stuart in their little cottage up by the racecourse, came into the Goose this morning. They're a tough pair. She cheerfully told us that she'd been watching movements at the helicopter base at the east end of the racecourse. She reckoned that eleven helicopters loaded with troops flew off west towards Goose Green during the fighting there. We told Jessie that she and Stuart really need to find somewhere safer. If shells are not falling around their little house yet, they will be soon. I know they'd be welcome here. As if to emphasize our point, there was a burst of heavy automatic fire.

We passed the day with occasional explosions from incoming and outgoing artillery fire. At about 3.00pm there was a really heavy spell of rifle and machine-gun fire. It was uncomfortably close.

As the day went on, the artillery fire got heavier, most of it incoming. The Argentines have a lot of artillery pieces, mostly to the west of Stanley, and while I'm no expert I'd say that they are not big enough to have much range. There was some fire going out towards the mountains today, though.

The story of the aircraft that Pete, Rosie and I saw shot down yesterday is still confusing. Harry Bagnall returned from his pastoral duties today having had a chat with Bloomer-Reeve. He told Harry that a Harrier was shot down. When two of their choppers flew out to rescue the pilot, two more Harriers were circling the area, so the Argentines headed back to Stanley. Bloomer-Reeve said he thought the pilot was probably rescued by British helicopters. I hope so. But this contradicted John Smith's story. So we are none the wiser.

A couple of local people contacted Mum and Dad today wanting to buy some parkas, so they went to the shop and opened for them. They agreed to sort out payment when something like normality has returned.

The very dirty and miserable-looking little conscripts continue to approach people asking if they will buy food, sweets and whisky for them. It's hard to know what to do. I don't want them here any more than the next Islander, but they are definitely victims. I feel deeply sorry for them and usually get them chocolate, biscuits and things like that. I'm convinced these kids will throw down their weapons and surrender as soon as they get the chance.

This evening, I had a conversation with the Uruguayan journalist. He said that the Pucara pilots who recently flew into Stanley had napalm and wanted to use it. However, General Menendez would not allow it.

All the Pucaras in Stanley are now out of action, mostly destroyed in Harrier raids. He thinks that the Pucara pilots have been flown back to Argentina in the nightly Hercules flights. If we are rid of both Pucaras and their pilots, then that's very good news.

He told me that a Hercules has just arrived under cover of darkness, bringing in a load of their Marines. I should think that a Hercules could carry around a hundred fully equipped troops, so this represents serious reinforcements.

There is an air of expectancy around the town tonight; a feeling that there could be a major attack, perhaps even the final attack, before dawn. At dusk there was a crowd of soldiers at the Town Hall end of Victory Green testing their weapons. A real cacophony of firing, fortunately all aimed out into the harbour.

After supper some of us gathered around the radio to catch up on 'Calling the Falklands', followed by the news. Dad, Mum and I were particularly pleased to hear a message from Michael. He said he'd just come back from Italy and that he'd been talking to friends in the UK who said they were very concerned about us. Really good to hear from him.

Mrs Thatcher seems to be in full Churchill mode. She said there can only be a ceasefire if the Argentines agree to withdraw within ten to fourteen days. That would be nice, but it ain't going to happen.

The MoD is claiming that British troops are now so close to Stanley that they can see Argentine troops at their field kitchens. They have been shelling Argentine positions from the west, and the Argentines are replying with their own artillery. That means that the Stanley area is now being shelled from all directions: the Navy can bring night-time fire from north, south and east, and the Army can do the same from the west.

Three Argentine soldiers were killed and some others wounded yesterday at Goose Green when they were clearing the battlefield. They were moving some ammunition when it blew up.

The BBC's man Robert Fox reported that 140 Argentine bodies have been removed from the battlefield. But he warns that the final count could be higher. That's an appalling number.

Apparently, Denzel Clausen at Goose Green was arrested by the Argentines and badly roughed up. They suspected he had been contacting the British during the battle.

It was quite mild earlier. But the cloud got lower, and eventually Mt Kent was obscured by fog. Our people must have had a damp and uncomfortable day but a relatively safe one. That would be welcome, as they will be bringing up everything they need for the final push.

Chapter 20

Heaviest bombardment

(3–7 June)

Thursday, 3 June

The action started early today. There was a bombing raid at about 6.10am. It wasn't just the bombs that woke us up but the intense anti-aircraft fire. Obviously, the RAF or Navy's intention would have been to catch the Argentines while they were asleep, but they opened up with AA fire immediately.

We looked outside carefully and groggily and saw that it was calm and foggy. Visibility remained poor for much of the day. Despite this, there was a lot of incoming artillery fire from British positions to the west of Two Sisters and Mount Kent. Most shells landed around Moody Brook. The Argentines were firing back with much more enthusiasm than I have seen before. It's an artillery duel.

There were several raids on the airport during the day, but despite all the efforts of the RAF and the Navy, nothing can put it out of action. I saw only one of today's raids. At about 3.30pm a single Harrier dropped a bomb slightly to the north of the runway. A near miss, I think.

Our Met man Jimmy Stephenson dropped by the Goose, as he often does. According to Jimmy, last month was the warmest May on record. This is remarkably good luck for those on both sides trying to survive with very little shelter. I wonder if they know how much worse it could be.

Jack Abbot told Des about the break-in at his house yesterday. He had gone out to see someone briefly, and they took the chance to burgle the place. They stole all his food, a watch, a camera and his binoculars. He thinks the Argentines were watching his house, waiting for him to leave.

Robert [King] told me that his aunt's, Mrs Stacey's, house was also broken into yesterday. All her food was stolen. Rob said that they didn't touch some money that she'd left on a table. That tells us something about their priorities.

A desperately upsetting encounter with a very hungry, maybe even starving conscript today. We were at Rowan for a few hours, and someone knocked on the kitchen door. When Mum answered it, this poor, grubby-looking young boy asked if someone could go to the West Store and buy him some food. He offered Mum money. He said he hadn't eaten for two days. Mum said she couldn't go to the West Store or take his money but would give him some food. She quickly made him some sandwiches and put them in a bag with some biscuits. The kid was polite and tearful and he kept on looking over his shoulder to make sure he hadn't been seen by his own NCOs or officers. It's not the first time this has happened. But it gets more distressing every time. None of us think these kids are going to be a threat to any British troops.

We think there are signs that some of the Argentine civilians at the Goose may be getting ready to sneak away on one of the nightly Hercules flights. Mora was seen buying some suitcases from the Co-Op. And Dr Mario, the chief Argentine doctor at the hospital, contacted Mum and Dad wanting them to open the shop so he could buy a bag. Somehow I don't think they are planning a weekend break birdwatching in the camp.

The *Monsunen* [coastal steamer] has turned up safe and sound at, now free, Goose Green. As she'd been taken over by the Argentines, we thought she had been lost. However, according to a brief (obviously illegal as far as the Argentines are concerned) radio conversation between Brooke Hardcastle [the FIC manager] at Darwin and Harry Milne [FIC Stanley Manager], she was driven up on a reef. The Argentine crew left her, but after Goose Green fell, her old crew managed to refloat her. Fortunately, she suffered only a few dents in her hull. My guess is that she's now joined the Task Force.

There's a good chance that the Argentines monitored the Hardcastle/Milne radio conversation, and while they have allowed use of the RT [radio telephone] system for medical reasons, I'm sure they'll clamp down on it now.[1]

We huddled around the receiver with the volume low this evening. They have still not tried to jam the extra frequencies that the BBC laid on, but perhaps that's because they don't know about them. Best it stays that way.

British troops are reported to be bringing up men, ammunition and supplies for the final push on Stanley. The BBC reporter with them said that some troops are amazed that they have been able to advance so far so quickly. They have even taken some high ground. That can only be Mt Kent, as Tumbledown, Longdon and Two Sisters are very definitely still in Argentine hands. I know this because the Argentine TV team recently visited these positions. I doubt if the Argentines have any fall-back positions, though, which is worrying, because if they are forced from Tumbledown and the other high points they'll be in the streets of Stanley.

The BBC guy said that shelling of their positions has been 'sporadic and ineffective'. Operations have been hampered by fog over the last couple of days, but they don't mind, as it keeps the Argentine Air Force on the ground. 'British troops can choose the time for their big push,' he said.

Harriers were supposed to have dropped leaflets on Argentine positions in and around Stanley today. The leaflets apparently included a 'pass' that any surrendering soldier could use to tell the Brits that he is giving up the fight. In return he would receive food and medical help.

On the same leaflet there is a message to 'Governor' Menendez, informing him of the hopelessness of his situation. 'We do not want to see more blood spilt,' says the message, 'but we will attack Stanley if necessary.'

All this is very nice. But we have seen no sign of the leaflets. If anyone in Stanley had seen them, news would have trickled through to us. I asked the Uruguayan journalist if he knew anything about this. He looked surprised and said no. Anyway, the fog has been so thick today that they couldn't have dropped anything with any accuracy. I suppose they might have a go at it tomorrow. Nice bit of propaganda, though.

Argentine diplomats are sounding a bit windy. They're saying they will accept 'any help offered'. As well they might. But the old adage, 'A friend in need is a pain in the neck' might be applied by Argentina's neighbours.

The MoD has been surprisingly quick in announcing medals awarded for the recapture of South Georgia. DSOs have been awarded to a Marines officer and one of *Endurance*'s chopper pilots. Five medals in total, and six Mentions in Dispatches.

There is an ominous and tense atmosphere this evening. Sporadic incoming naval shelling began at about 11.30pm, just as we were thinking about hitting the sack. I'm now lying here listening to it. Every time it dies down, I close my eyes and think, 'Right, I'm going to get some sleep now.' And then it starts again. It's not close enough to be scary, but not far enough away to ignore.

I think there could be an attack soon after this fog lifts. It feels like a protective blanket but it will lift soon. The imagination always goes into overdrive at times like this. I try to shut it down but rarely succeed. I hope we still have our protective blanket tomorrow.

Friday, 4 June

This morning, the fog has lifted but it's been replaced by filthy weather: low cloud, strengthening wind and rain. But hey, it is winter. Consequently, at the time of writing (late afternoon) there has been almost no air activity over Stanley. The only exception was an aircraft we heard flying above the clouds at about 4.00pm.

Virtually no small arms fire either, and the only sounds of war were incoming artillery rounds from British positions and some outgoing fire. All fairly distant. Last night was relatively quiet, too, probably because during the day fog would have made it impossible for the Task Force spotters (wherever they are) to pick out targets for later shelling.

There seems to be a slight possibility that the UN Security Council will pass a resolution that requires an immediate ceasefire followed by a rapid withdrawal by the Argentines. The UK has the power of veto, of course, but providing the

Argentines agree to immediate withdrawal, they may not apply that. There is a lot of pride and face-saving involved in this. The Argentines would certainly not accept it if it was a demand directly from London, but they might just do so if it comes from the UN. It's still a slim hope, though. However one chose to describe it, it would be surrender, and I don't think the military government in BA would survive. Galtieri and his brainless chums might prefer to fight and lose.

John Leonard still has occasional contact with the US embassy in BA. I believe Bloomer-Reeve enables these calls over the military system. Bill Curtiss, a Canadian citizen, is also regularly checking in with his embassy in BA. John has been urging the Americans to get the International Committee of the Red Cross to send a team to Stanley so they can set up a safe area and maybe even evacuate particularly vulnerable civilians.

According to WS a few days ago, the Red Cross wanted to see the men, women and children at Goose Green, but it is too late to help them. However, we believe there is another group of civilians locked up at Fox Bay, and possibly in other settlements too. There doesn't seem to be much concern about them or, for that matter, about us in Stanley.

In one small respect I'm doing quite well out of this situation. Mum and Alison are spending the long hours of curfew at the Goose knitting. Mum is making me a jumper, and Alison is making me a Starsky and Hutch-like chunky cardigan. Very nice of them!

I made a quick visit to the house to feed the cats (including the refugee, Murdoch) and check that no one has broken in. As I was entering Rowan I noticed some activity around the anti-aircraft gun now located in Bessie Smith's backyard across the road. That would be deafening if it was fired while we were home. No sign of Argentines around the big trench they dug in the trees at the back of Rowan.

No weather for walking, so it was back to the Goose to stock up on tea and an evening WS-listening, while Mum and Alison made steady progress on my jumper and cardigan.

WS is reporting a remarkable gesture towards the Falklands by the people of the Channel Islands. They want to give the Falklands £5 million to be used on rebuilding and development when this is all over. The people of Jersey and Guernsey can identify with us as they were occupied by the Germans during the Second World War.

For every good news story there has to be at least one bad one. At 9.00pm WS reported the failure of the latest Security Council peace proposal. Both the UK and the US have used their veto (one would have been enough!) to defeat a motion demanding an immediate ceasefire and immediate withdrawal by the Argentines. It's disappointing but not unexpected.

I know I've been saying this now for many days, but if the weather improves tonight, the Marines and Paras could begin their final attack tonight or tomorrow. For now, though, I must try to sleep. And as the usual nocturnal shelling has not started, I might actually get some.

Saturday, 5 June

Despite my speculation, this is one of the quietest days for weeks. The day dawned bright and calm, and I was surprised when I realized the British have decided not to move. Could it be that they *want* bad weather?

Later on, it began to cloud over. Around lunchtime, the Argentines launched a missile to the south of town, but I wonder if that was an accident or a test firing, as I didn't see or hear an aircraft overhead.

An hour or so later, an aircraft did scream in from the south, disappearing almost as soon as it arrived. This must have been a Harrier, as I can't imagine that an Argentine pilot would want to come anywhere near his own anti-aircraft sites, knowing their reputation for own goals.

The artillery duel continued sporadically through the day. I think most of the Argentine shelling was from a few huge howitzers that they seem to be moving among buildings on the east and south-east of town. These are really monstrous, and I suspect they fire something like six-inch shells.

The Argentines are claiming they bombed British positions yesterday and also shelled them. I don't know about the bombing, but they certainly have been lobbing shells in that direction. But all Argentine reports are dubious.

At Rowan early this afternoon I tuned into WS. I was shocked to hear that the Army and Navy are preparing to unleash on Stanley the heaviest artillery bombardment since the Korean War, and possibly since the Second World War. That's scary. It seems odd that they are revealing their plans, but perhaps they are trying to scare the Argentines. It scares me.

Mystery still surrounds a Vulcan bomber that got into trouble and landed in Rio de Janeiro yesterday. It may have been on mission to parachute in a new CO for Two Para, replacing Lieutenant Colonel H Jones. In any case, it's being reported that a new 'Sunray' has joined the Paras at Goose Green.[2]

My good news is that – incredibly – I have my jeep back. I can't drive it as there's no petrol left in Stanley. But it is safely home. Dad received a phone call from Bloomer-Reeve this morning telling him that it could be collected from the Secretariat. Without petrol, the jeep is, of course, useless to them.

I scuttled off to collect the jeep. She was in a filthy state inside and out. The exhaust and the front bumper are gone and the bodywork is dented. Inside there were dozens of bullet cases, live rounds and a few hypodermics. So God knows what she's been involved in. I've tucked her away out of sight. I've managed to convince Dad that it's not worth his trying to claim for the damage. We are lucky to have the vehicle back.

I was back in the Goose in time for curfew. Shelling started early and the flashes lit up the sky. The Argentine big guns are now much more active. We can't tell exactly where they are, but they are close. The huge blasts from these howitzers echo through the air, and they are as unnerving as incoming fire.

Tonight is very clear and calm; a perfect night for shelling and for an advance. I have given up trying to predict anything, but still, I wonder if tonight is the night.

We are being nudged out of the news by Israel's attack on Lebanon, which is apparently in retaliation for the attempt to assassinate the Israeli ambassador to London. I think, though, that we'll be back at the top of the news within a day or two.

Most of us at the Goose were feeling restless this evening, so we had a few drinks. We also found a video cassette that hasn't been watched a dozen times, so we sat down and enjoyed *Tinker, Tailor, Soldier, Spy* for an hour or two. It was interrupted by occasional explosions but still it took our minds of what is going on outside.

Sunday, 6 June

The Navy arrived very shortly after midnight. They pounded the west end of Stanley. There are still some civilians living in that area, and they really *must* move into the centre now. The shelling went on until at least 3.30am, and I finally went to sleep. It was nasty and noisy but not the 'heaviest bombardment since the Korean War'. (But I wasn't in the Korean War, so what do I know?)

When I dragged myself out of my pit (a bit later than usual) and looked out the window, I saw that the weather had deteriorated dramatically. A north to north-easterly wind is bringing rain, an overcast sky and almost every other type of unpleasantness.

We were hardly even mentioned in the BBC News this morning. I almost feel hurt. Instead, the world's attention seems to have turned to another illegal invasion, the Israelis in Lebanon.

Sitting here in the kitchen nursing a cup of coffee, as Aunt Ning, Mum and the girls fuss around, it seems to me that the Paras and the Marines are trying to wear the Argentines down with shelling and keep them in their defensive positions enduring this filthy weather. I'd say their morale is extremely low anyway. I hope the waiting doesn't get our people down, too.

Some people are saying that last night's shelling was heavier than I thought. It didn't stop until about 7.00am. I must have slept through the last few hours of it.

Later today, the BBC confirmed that the troops on the *QE2*, the Gurkhas, Welsh and Scots Guards of 5th Infantry Brigade, have landed, presumably at the San Carlos beachhead. It seems they have already begun to move forward.

The correspondent said that they had disembarked in awful weather. I had to smile when he added that two locals on their way to Goose Green had a terrible fright when they were ambushed by Gurkhas. No one was injured, but this story doesn't sound quite right for the San Carlos area. I wonder if the troops landed around Fitzroy, rather than at San Carlos.

Late afternoon: apart from a brief reconnaissance fly-over early this morning there were no Harriers seen today. The weather was against them.

At least one Argentine Hercules managed to sneak under the radar last night. We know because a parcel turned up this morning for one of the priests. From his excited reaction, it was clearly a care package from home.

Rowan is OK. I fed the cats (ravenous as usual). Murdoch appears to be enjoying his new life as a refugee, and Bagpuss is tolerating him. I stoked the fire up, heated some water and had an all-over wash in the basin. That made me feel better.

The water supply has resumed but is very intermittent and I don't think it'll last. We've been warned not to drink it, as it may be contaminated. I'd rather not think what that contamination might be.

The Public Works guys are working heroically to ensure we get at least a little water. The power house people are doing similarly wonderful things to minimize power cuts.

But still, I'm feeling low. The anxiety is constant and getting worse. Not knowing what the future holds is the worst thing. I can't help but imagine the worst.

By evening it was blowing nearly gale-force from the north-east with driving rain. Troops on both sides must be having a very uncomfortable time, but I'm sure that the British are much better trained and equipped to cope with it.

I felt somewhat better after supper at the Goose. Interesting stuff on WS this evening. Reports of 'extremely daring operations that, if successful, could help to bring an early and satisfactory end to the war'. No details at all, but apparently these operations are going on now. What could this be? Raids on fuel and ammo dumps near or in Stanley, perhaps?

Public opinion in the UK is now apparently firmly against negotiation with Argentina, and there is no mood to let them have anything to do with us after the war. Good!

Argentine press communiqués, peddled by what was once our local radio, are just lies. They are saying there was a 'brief' naval bombardment last night, concentrated on positions to the south and west of Stanley. We know, though, that it was heavy and went on for about six hours. They are also claiming that there was an Argentine air attack on British positions. The weather wouldn't have allowed for that, and we would have seen and heard any air attacks.

This evening, for some reason I felt I couldn't get my bedding out and retire to my little corner behind the lounge chimney until the Navy had arrived. I felt almost relieved when we heard the first distant 'pops' at around 11.30pm.

So I got my head down, and was lying there counting the explosions (sheep don't work anymore) when Father Monaghan came past doing his rounds. He asked how I was, and I said I'd been feeling down.

'Never mind, it'll be over soon,' he said. 'God willing we'll be safe, and then we can have our lives back. Good night, Graham. God bless.'

Monday, 7 June

The weather today is calm and quite warm, at around 9°C. It's a very mild winter. As I write this in the early afternoon, the Harriers and the British artillery have been making the most of the clear blue sky. Explosions of incoming shells and bombs have been steady. There was a good deal of AA fire at about 1.00pm, but they definitely didn't hit anything.

The Argentines had one of their very big howitzers just behind Stuart and Jessie Booth's house near the racecourse. It received a direct hit in a bombing raid. I think Stuart and Jessie thought their time had come. I was told that the Harriers came in very low and destroyed both gun and crew. A portable radar station on the south side of Stanley has also been bombed. I'm pretty sure there have been other hits, but these are the ones that I know of. It seems to me that the aircraft are picking off the big targets very accurately, while the artillery from the west harasses the Argentines and wears them down.

One of the guys who is heroically trying to keep the water service going told me that the filtration plant was hit last night. The plant now has a large hole in the roof. He said it is getting harder by the day to keep any water flowing.

Simon [Goss] is continuing to monitor the British Army transmissions. He's a whizz at these kinds of things. He told me today that he was listening to them last night and they said they'd shot down an Argentine aircraft attacking the San Carlos area. A second plane escaped. The BBC confirmed this later today and suggested the two aircraft were Canberra bombers. The one that was hit exploded in a ball of flame.

House break-ins around Stanley are now very frequent. There were five or six last night that we know of. Of course, more houses are being abandoned as people move into safe centres like the West Store. So far, Rowan House has not been broken into. I was chatting to Pete and Rosemary, and we estimated that about sixty houses have been. The figure could be higher.

Non-combatant Argentines such as the priests and journalists continue to buy food for the enlisted men, who are now suffering seriously. The officers seem to be pretty well fed, though. What way to run an army is that? We overheard a conversation at the Goose which suggested one of the journalists is selling food to the poor conscripts at a profit.

The weather deteriorated in the early evening. It clouded over and began to drizzle. I don't think it will be a good night for naval shelling.

'Calling the Falklands' tonight was full of personal messages from people sounding very worried, sometimes even tearful, about their family members here. Sometimes it's difficult to listen to the programme because it's just too emotional.

We are dominating the WS news again. There was a report about how the Gurkhas are being deployed flying around the islands in helicopters, looking for pockets of Argentines who have been overtaken by the British advance and are now isolated. Apparently, they land and persuade them to surrender. The sight of a group of heavily armed Gurkhas approaching could be persuasive, I should think.

The senior officer among the Argentine prisoners of war has had the cheek to complain about their living conditions. He also complained that when they surrendered at Goose Green they were told that they would be able to bury their dead (some 250) within 24 hours, but they had to wait 48 hours.

Approximately 1,000 Argentine PoWs are now aboard a ship (I assume, one of the ferries or liners). They are receiving two hot meals a day along with mugs of coffee. If I was a conscript PoW I'd be feeling a lot happier than I was a few weeks ago.

The commanding officer of the British land forces, General Jeremy Moore, has made radio contact with General Menendez and appealed to him to order his men to lay down their arms. Menendez' reply is not reported.

The BBC's Robert Fox, who's with the troops, said that they welcomed today's fine weather as a chance to dry out and rest a bit after recent wet and windy weather. But he says that bad weather has not affected their fighting capabilities. They're well trained for this.

Last night there was a bloody clash when a Royal Marines patrol located an Argentine force well forward of British lines. In the fight that followed, nine Argentines were killed and one Marine was wounded.

Elsewhere, it is starting to look a little like First World War trench combat. Both sides are in fixed lines west of Stanley, and both send out night-time patrols. An Argentine patrol attacked a British position and the Brits were forced to retreat. Apparently, several Argentines were killed in that incident, with no casualties on the British side.

Encouraged by Simon's success in monitoring the Army's radio conversations, I had a crack at it myself this evening. I tuned in carefully around the frequencies that Simon suggested, and sure enough, up they came. The conversations were cryptic, of course, and they switched frequencies often, so I didn't learn much. But still, it was fascinating and strangely reassuring to hear Birmingham, Liverpool and Welsh accents crackling across the airwaves.

Chapter 21

Missile Attack

(8–11 June)

Tuesday, 8 June

There's been sporadic shelling of Argentine positions throughout the day, and the Argentines were using their big guns in reply. We have seen a few Harriers over the town, but they've been flying high on recce missions. I don't think Stanley has ever been this well photographed.

This afternoon, I took a walk around the south side of Stanley. I was careful to stay well within the limits, because that way if stopped and questioned I could say that I was going about my normal business (whatever 'normal' is these days). I went up Magazine Valley Hill, past the power station. Suddenly there before me was one of their giant artillery pieces. I was transfixed by this, and by the frantic activity around it. Then there were some shouts, someone pulled a lanyard and the thing fired. The sound was overwhelming and terrifying. It wasn't just the explosion but also the 'whooshing' noise as the shell flew through the air. And then the stench of cordite.

When I was thinking straight again, I realized standing there watching them would not look good. It also occurred to me that as this gun was firing out, the opposition might be trying to hit it. Or there could be a repeat of the Harrier attack on the gun near Stuart and Jessie Booth's house. I felt like running, but that would attract attention, so I walked fast and got out of it ASAP.

On Brandon Road I met Duane Andrade, who has a perfect view to the west from his house. Earlier today, he saw a lot of shells, obviously British, landing on the Two Sisters road. He could see Argentines legging it from the area.

I was relieved to get back at the Goose and felt better after downing a cup of tea made by Alison. Jack Abbot had come by and told the Kings a story about Fox Bay being liberated. I don't believe it. Jack's a bit nuts but he's a stoic old chap. He should have moved out of his house on the Hill above Rowan House by now, but he's still there.

It's clear that the Argentine government of occupation is starved of news, as opposed to its own propaganda. Every evening, the radio station manager Mora phones Patrick [Watts], who obviously listens to World Service as much as we do. 'What news, Patrick?' he snaps. That's become a bit of a catchphrase around the Goose. This evening, Patrick told him that the Argentine Air Force launched another amateurish attack on a tanker that they thought was with the Task Force (it wasn't). They simply rolled a bomb out the back door of a Hercules. Clearly, Mora didn't know this, so he hung up and was straight back on the phone to Bloomer-Reeve with a breathless report.

The Argentine authorities have broadcast a message over local radio telling people to report break-ins to the military police immediately, so that the offending soldiers can be caught and punished. I heard yesterday that MPs caught two guys breaking into a house. I don't know how they were punished and I'm not sure I want to know.

Rumours only, and no names, but one home-owner spending nights in a 'safe' building went back to his house this morning, to find a soldier having a scrub in the bathroom. A couple of nights ago, someone who had not yet moved out of his house was woken by a couple of soldiers in his bedroom. They explained they had been through his kitchen, apologized for stealing all his food and then disappeared into the night.

It looks as though some Argentine civilians who were unfortunate enough to still be here when the situation became serious have been drafted into the army. A crewman from the oil rig support vessel *Yehuin* is now wearing military fatigues. Last night, he appeared dejectedly in the Goose with an army officer. The two demanded to see our Argentine-issue ID cards. They were obviously making sure that there were no special forces soldiers hiding among us. Chance would be a fine thing.

The artillery duel continued until almost last light. Later, the sound of explosions from the Navy's big guns rolled down the harbour like thunder. Perhaps the noise is echoing off the low clouds. In any case, it's strange and unpleasant.

BBC WS news this evening was almost entirely about us. The FCO's Cranley Onslow spoke on CTF and said thought is being given to how normal life might resume in the Falklands when the fighting is over. He said that schools have to reopen, wool must be exported, the shops be re-supplied and so on. A statement of the obvious really, but it's curious to see yet another British politician who didn't give a damn about us before the invasion now wanting us to be prosperous and happy.

There was mention of the Liberian-flagged supertanker which is now nursing the unexploded bomb pushed out of the back door of that Hercules. She was steaming along happily, 400 miles north of the Falklands, so the skipper probably assumed he was safe. Some ships have been diverted to help her.

Galtieri is saying that his troops here are in 'good spirits'. But correspondents in BA are saying this is contradicted by the letters that families there have been receiving from sons and husbands on the front line. They speak of poor equipment, awful weather and hunger.

Rose Peart told us today that she was listening on the RT frequency early this morning when she heard Sandy Woodward or a deputy on one of the carriers come up and ask to talk to Menendez or one of his people. Rose said Menendez and an interpreter went to the RT station to listen to what Woodward had to say. The Brits asked for detailed information about where we civilians are sheltering. They probably thought we are locked up in one place, as the civilians were at Goose Green. The Argentines gave them no information, and the conversation ended quickly. Perhaps Menendez thought Woodward was going to surrender.

A mix of good and bad news at 9.00pm. The frigate HMS *Plymouth* was hit and damaged in an air raid. Two of the aircraft were shot down. A major plus, though, is that Fitzroy and Bluff Cove have been taken by the Paras, who encountered no resistance.

The two settlements were taken a few days ago, but this was kept quiet because the Argentines were not aware that the Brits had managed to advance over such a distance (about 45 miles) so quickly. It's a remarkable story. The commander of the Paras at Goose Green realized that the Stanley to Goose Green telephone line was intact as far as Fitzroy. So he called Fitzroy to see if there were any Argentines there. Ronnie Binnie [the farm manager] answered and said, 'They were here yesterday, but not today.'

So the way was clear, and the troops made the helicopter hop from Goose Green to Fitzroy while they had the chance. But the problem of getting ammo and supplies to Fitzroy remained, so *Monsunen* was prepared for sea. A couple of local divers, including Janet Hardcastle, managed to untangle a rope that was around the prop, and a volunteer civilian crew was raised with Finlay Ferguson as skipper. Within a few hours *Monsunen* was being packed with ammo and supplies. After weeks under Argentine control, she was now flying both the Union Jack and the Parachute Regiment's colours. So, one of our little ships has now joined the Task Force. Brilliant!

Sappers repaired the bridge connecting Fitzroy and Bluff Cove, so that settlement was quickly occupied too. No opposition at Bluff Cove either. So British forces south and north of the Wickham Heights now control all approaches to Stanley.

At midnight tonight, as I write, the sky is clear, the wind very light and it's relatively warm. There is an almost full moon. The Navy has arrived on cue and there is very heavy shelling. Standing in the front door of the Goose, it sounded very strange. Perhaps because it is such a calm night, the explosions echoed back and forth around the harbour until they faded out.

I got my head down and lay there with my little radio pressed to my ear. WS is saying that Argentina has acknowledged the Brits have taken Fitzroy, but they claim there was fierce resistance on the ground.

More worryingly, BA is saying that three landing craft or ships and a frigate were spotted and their attack aircraft were called in. The frigate withdrew, but not the landing craft or ships. Three hours later, according to BA, their planes returned and attacked the ships, leaving them in flames. The frigate was located again near Mt Pleasant, and after being hit by rockets and at least one bomb was 'left in a sinking condition'.

BA is also claiming that they launched a fierce attack on troops that had managed to get ashore from the landing ships, and inflicted heavy casualties. They did not say whether the attack on the land forces was by troops or aircraft, but I assume it was an air attack.

After all this time I can pretty much tell what is Argentine propaganda and what is believable. And this story of the air attacks at Fitzroy is in the latter category, unfortunately. I guess the scenario is that the Paras captured the Fitzroy area in their bold leap from Goose Green and then brought more troops up to the area by ship.

Just before I switched the radio off and closed my eyes, the BBC said that the Queen mentioned the Falklands today in a speech at a banquet in honour of President Reagan. 'Once again, Britain has to stand up for the cause of freedom,' she said. It seems tonight that this principle is being upheld at great cost.

Wednesday, 9 June

As I peered out on to the world early this morning I saw clear blue sky and the harbour undisturbed by wind. It is crisp, and I think there was a frost last night. In normal times I would say, 'It's a lovely day,' especially so as we are nearing midwinter. There was no land attack on Stanley last night, that we know of at least.

I visited the Treasury, not because I had any real business to do there but I thought it would be good to have a chat with Tracy Peck, Anna and Robert. They, along with Pete Biggs and Harold Rowlands, have been keeping the Treasury out of Argentine hands. They've worked for a few hours every day, ensuring that everyone gets paid.

Anna, Tracy and Robert didn't have a lot to do, so we had a good chat, and I caught up on their news and gossip. As I was leaving the Treasury at about 11.00am and starting up Ross Road to the west, there was an extraordinarily loud roar of jet engines. I looked to the west and saw two Harriers crossing the harbour at about 150ft. They seemed huge. They had gained a bit of height to cross Wireless Ridge and dipped down again towards the harbour.

Within a few seconds, they'd turned south-east and disappeared out of sight over the power station. They dropped two bombs with almost deafening explosions. I couldn't see the precise targets, but they may have been after the large artillery piece near Dairy Paddock that I saw in action yesterday. It shook me, and I'm still not sure whether I was more thrilled or scared.

According to someone who was in the dockyard at the time of the attack, all the Argentines in the area dived for their defensive positions, while all the locals dived for the doors and windows so they could see what was going on.

I carried on walking for about an hour. Artillery fire started coming in from the mountains but it didn't feel particularly dangerous, so I continued until I had a clear view of the shells exploding beyond the Beaver hangar. Then I turned back towards the centre of town.

I checked out Rowan (cats and chickens all present and correct). Mum and Dad opened the shop very briefly. Someone had asked if they could buy a parka. The Uruguayan TV journalist also came in and chatted to Dad. According to this guy, the Argentine troops are well entrenched, facing the Brits only a few miles away.

Robert told me at the Treasury this morning that Jack Sollis had heard (health warning: this is a third-hand story) that there are 400-plus Argentine dead being stored in the Beaver Hangar. I suppose this could be true, as there must have been many casualties. If the big push doesn't start in the meantime, I will take another walk up that way tomorrow and have a look for myself.

Late this afternoon, the BBC began indicating that there were indeed serious losses during the landings at Fitzroy yesterday. Two ships were involved, RFA *Sir Galahad* and *Sir Tristram*, near Fitzroy. They had carried the Welsh and Scots Guards from San Carlos to Fitzroy, and many troops were still on the ships when they were bombed. We have no numbers for dead and injured, but a horrible story is now emerging.

It seems that four Skyhawks were shot down and another four were damaged. But if two ships have been destroyed and a lot of men killed, then the Argentines will feel they have paid a low price.

The BBC man on the spot filed a vivid and depressing report. He described how helicopter crews flew into the smoke billowing from the burning ships to rescue men in the water and even to use their downdraft to blow life rafts towards the shore. Men who had reached land waded back into the sea time after time to help wounded men to shore.

We shouldn't pass judgement, but why was this operation carried out in broad daylight? It seems to smack of over-confidence. It had been ten days since the last Argentine air attack, so maybe they thought the FAA was a spent force.

Anyway, they are back. There was another air attack at San Carlos yesterday, and HMS *Plymouth*, a frigate, was damaged and five or six crewmen injured. She is not out of action, though. I hope the carriers are still keeping well out of range. The balance of this situation could yet change for the worse.

It was Mum's birthday today. Just after curfew, when everyone was safely under cover, Aunt Ning and the girls surprised Mum with a cake. Everyone was in good voice, probably because we had two priests to lead the singing. I don't know where they got the ingredients for a cake from, as these things must be running low by now. Mum was very touched. It's not been a good news day, but this cheered us up.

Dad had found some chocolates to give Mum, and I gave her a teapot from the Goose gift shop. There was an explosion somewhere and Mum said, 'There, you see? My birthday's gone off with a bang!' A good enough joke, all things considered.

The night is calm, moonlit and dry: a good night for the Navy gunners. Sure enough, they arrived on station and started work at twenty past midnight.

Thursday, 10 June

I'm sitting down to catch up on my notes in the middle of the afternoon. The big event today is the arrival of two men from the International Committee of the Red Cross (ICRC), who are checking on our safety.

The weather has been pleasant enough (again), with clear skies, little wind and comfortable temperatures.

Last night's bombardment was heavier than I thought. Apparently, I slept through most of it. Could I really be getting used to this? Mum stayed awake through much of the night, as the shelling came and went. Sleep was also disturbed by a patrol boat cruising up and down the harbour, playing its searchlight over the waterfront. It was obviously trying to spot special forces that might have infiltrated Stanley.

I woke up at 5.00am to the sound of a helicopter approaching in the darkness. It flew low and slowly along the seafront, passing just in front of the hotel. Also looking for special forces, perhaps?

Three of the Pucaras took off around 8.30am, flew east to west up the harbour very low and disappeared from sight. Some minutes later, there were muffled explosions, probably from the British lines. I wonder if they dropped napalm. About ten minutes after the explosions, the planes were flying back low over the harbour towards the airport. The Brits must now know Pucaras are operating around Stanley, so they'll probably step up efforts to wipe them out. There was a very noisy Harrier attack at about 10.00am, but I don't think this targeted the airport.

I nearly made it to the Beaver Hangar this morning but I thought I'd better turn back when I was near the last of the houses. If I'd been stopped, I'd have had no excuse for being there. The hangar now has large red crosses painted on its roof and walls. Both aircraft have been moved out on to the slip. So it's possible that they are using it as a mortuary. They'd need to have freezer containers in there, though.

On the side of the racecourse there is a crashed or seriously damaged Skyvan aircraft. It'll never get back into the air.

Around 4.00pm, as the Argentine hospital ship carrying the ICRC representatives dropped anchor, there was another raid. The Swiss men told us later that they saw two Harriers come in very low over the Camber, then swerve west and bomb an area this side of Moody Brook. Frankly, the noise of this was frightening. As usual, the soldiers around here opened up with everything they had, including rifles.

In a way we are pleased about this, as it showed the visitors that the situation in Stanley is very dangerous. They checked into the Goose at around 5.00pm, and we managed to talk to them soon after arrival. They looked more than a bit dishevelled and perhaps shaken by the air raid. They said that they had transferred to the Argentine hospital ship from the *Uganda*. Both ships had been in what they call the 'Red Cross Box', an area about 35 miles north of Cape Dolphin. I asked them how long they would stay, and their answer was disappointing: 'Not long. Maybe 36 hours if we are lucky. I'm sorry.'

They disappeared upstairs, presumably to spruce themselves up a bit, and came down again a little while later to talk to us all in the bar. Initially, everyone spoke at the same time, but then we calmed down and, one at a time, told them everything they needed to know about the occupation: the break-ins, the locals who were arrested and taken to Fox Bay, and so on.

Someone raised the issue of napalm, which we think is stored at the airport. They were interested in this and said they will try to discuss it with Menendez when they meet him tomorrow. They'll try to dissuade him from using it. But they pointed out that napalm is not outlawed.

Top of their agenda with Menendez will be the establishment of a safe area in the centre of Stanley where civilians can shelter if the situation continues to worsen. The location of this area would be communicated to the British.

They were asked about the possibility of temporarily evacuating the civilians in Stanley, perhaps using one of the hospital ships. There are only five or six hundred of us left here, so it would be possible. That will be discussed with Menendez too.

We sat there talking until late, which I think was good for us. By the end of the evening I felt the ICRC reps were good guys doing their best, but without the ability to achieve much. Eventually, clearly very tired, they went up to their room.

Tonight is calm, slightly misty and mild. Just one shell was lobbed into Stanley from a ship just after midnight. I wonder if they are keeping things quiet tonight for the benefit of the ICRC guys.

London is saying that details about men killed and injured at Fitzroy will not be publicized for some time, obviously because the information might help the enemy.

According to Argentine radio, there was a large demo in BA today to mark 'Malvinas Day'. Galtieri was there, obviously whipping up passions. Not that it will do him any good. I'd be making plans to leave the country, if I was him.

Maybe tonight . . .

Friday, 11 June

My assumption last night that the Navy might be keeping it quiet for the benefit of the ICRC guys was, almost literally, shot down. Later in the night, there was a very heavy bombardment. I got up and went outside through the kitchen door for a closer look. That's a fairly safe vantage point as the back entrance to the Goose is below ground level. But I could get a look by cautiously climbing the steps outside.

The shells were clearly audible whistling overhead. This would be followed by very loud 'crumps' and flashes. I couldn't see exactly where they were impacting, but it was much closer than normal.

It felt lonely out there in the dark. I knew I was relatively safe but I was nervous, and after 15 minutes I went inside again. I found that a few other people had gathered in the kitchen. They were counting the shells and listening to the radio. Nobody spoke much. After a while I slipped off to my bivouac and I must have fallen asleep while the shelling was still going on. I wonder how much sleep the Red Cross guys got.

At about 8.30am several Harriers came in, typically low and fast, and bombed the airport, just as I thought they would after the Pucaras' sortie. This attack and the Argentines' noisy response had most of us in the Goose heading for the main entrance to see what was going on.

It soon became clear that the airport raid was a diversion. The Argentines had their eyes and weapons trained east. But something amazing, and more than a bit terrifying, was happening to the north.

On the far side of the Camber, almost opposite us, a British helicopter suddenly emerged and immediately launched two missiles. The combined noise of the bombing at the airport and the missiles was overwhelming. As far as I could tell, the missiles were heading straight at us, and I was strangely transfixed. I saw from the corner of my eye that several people who happened to be passing the entrance to the Goose had dived into the ditch, among them John and Margaret Leonard.

By this time the Argentines had turned their fire on the helicopter and the missiles. The helicopter crew were incredibly brave, as not only had they flown covertly to within a few miles of Stanley, but now they were having to remain stationary as they guided the missiles to their target – which at that moment appeared to be us.

It was still twilight, which must have been essential for the helicopter pilots, so the flames from the missiles and the vast amount of tracer fire that the Argentines put up stood out vividly against the sky.

It all happened so fast that it was difficult to keep track of the action. However, one missile went haywire. It turned vertically, climbed and exploded harmlessly over the harbour. However, the second one kept on coming. It slammed into the police station just 50 metres or so from us. The explosion was deafening and the police station's metal roof flew off, with sheets of corrugated iron fluttering down like leaves.

The helicopter vanished. The upper storey of the police station was a smoking ruin, with a gaping hole where the west end of the roof should have been.

It's too soon to say if anyone was killed in this attack, but this is the military intelligence and military police HQ, so I would be very surprised if there were not men upstairs when the missile hit. This was a good target for them, and I wonder how they knew about it.

I joined everyone in the kitchen, where we compared notes about what we'd seen and agreed that this attack had been much closer than was comfortable.

Later, I ran into Kasanzew and his cameraman. I rubbed in the fact that this had been a daring and successful British attack. In response, he claimed that it was ineffective; just one man had suffered a broken arm. I think that's unlikely to be true. In any case, it was audacious and must be morale-sapping for the Argentines.

The fires at the airport continued to blaze for an hour. The incredible attack this morning set something of a pattern for the day. I lost count of the number of low-level bombing raids. The Harrier pilots just get bolder and bolder.

The Argentine artillery was operating sporadically through the day, but far more British shells were coming in than those that were going out.

All of this happened while the two ICRC officials were still with us. I didn't speak to them after last night but I saw them rushing around looking stressed. At about 3.00pm a vehicle turned up to collect them and they headed off, no doubt to rejoin the *Bahia Paraiso*.

Before leaving the hotel, they told Dad and Des that during the meeting with Menendez they suggested two means by which civilians can be protected as the fighting for Stanley intensifies. However, Menendez would only agree to the idea of putting everyone in the cathedral. I doubt that many civilians would like the idea of being cooped up there. There is just one toilet, no kitchen and no washing facilities (other than the font).

In any case, I think it would be dangerous to put us all in one place. One misdirected shell or bomb and most of us would go. Also, I'm nervous about rogue Argentine soldiers. Concentrating us all in the cathedral would make a nightmare scenario like that more possible.

We noticed that some of the large artillery pieces and all of the choppers were moved further away from civilian properties while the ICRC men were here. Some guns had certainly been hidden among houses, and they'll probably go back there now.

There is a rumour going around that they have been unloading supplies, possibly even weapons and ammunition, from the *Bahia Paraiso*. As she's a hospital ship, that would certainly be an offence under the Geneva Convention. There's no way of telling whether this is true. But we have all seen cargo coming ashore.

Our Met-man friend Jimmy Stephenson was arrested today. Dad passed him as he was being led towards what's left of the police station. He shouted to Dad, 'If I don't come out again, my crime was that I was walking around town too much and looking too interested.' They held Jimmy for a few hours and then released him.

Late this evening, the BBC is reporting the *Argentine* account of this morning's missile attack, which is annoying because it's not accurate. They said that naval aircraft dropped bombs on the airport and destroyed 'an empty house'. That was much more than a house; it was the HQ of the men who keep us under their thumbs, and there will have been an impact on their confidence and morale.

Our morale remains high, even though the situation is getting more dangerous by the day. We just want this to be over as soon as possible.

The Navy arrived at 10.30 tonight, earlier than usual. Before that, there had been a lot of rifle and machine-gun fire, with much tracer visible to the north-west, near Wireless Ridge and Mt Longdon.

The shelling got progressively closer and much louder. It's the worst we have experienced. Just after midnight, Argentine radar must have picked up something to the north of Stanley, and anti-aircraft fire opened up deafeningly from all angles. The fire seemed to be poorly directed and was going over the top of the Goose and over the Camber.

Sleep is not possible. We have the feeling that tonight is the night. If it isn't, then it's a very realistic dress rehearsal. At about 12.30am the phone rang. It was a very panicky Alison Bleaney, calling from the hospital. She asked for Bloomer-Reeve or Hussey. They were not here, of course, but Mora spoke to her, and when he came off the phone he was clearly shaken. 'It appears that some civilians have been injured,' he said. 'Or worse.' We had been worried that some of the shells could be detonating among houses. This looks dreadful.

Some people had been trying to rest, but by the time Alison called, everyone was downstairs and Aunt Ning brewed some coffee. We sat around drinking it nervously as the bombardment continued. This situation is deteriorating fast

Chapter 22

Caught in the Final Crossfire

(12–15 June)

Saturday, 12 June

The shelling kept me awake for most of the night. I don't know what time it was, but probably around 3.00am, that I got out of my pit and found a half-size bottle of whisky that I had tucked away in case I needed it. I felt I needed it.

I took the bottle into the front porch, which was in darkness as the streetlights were out. Tracer rounds, flares and explosions were lighting up Mt Longdon. This was not a skirmish, rather a full-scale battle. It looks like this is the beginning of the end. If the Army takes the high ground around that area they will be virtually looking down into Stanley.

I was transfixed by this display five or six miles to the west. I knew men were in close combat. And some were dying. I sat low in one corner of the dark porch hoping that the whisky would calm my nerves and make me feel less guilty. I know it is not entirely rational, but I can't help but feel that this conflict is partly our fault.

After about half an hour I heard someone running up the path. And then a dark figure flung the door open and tumbled into the porch. Feeling safer, I guess, he stood there looking towards Longdon and the pyrotechnic display. He was muttering to himself a bit. He didn't know I was there.

I thought I'd better make myself known, so I said, '*Buenos noches.*'

That gave him a quite a start, but we could make each other out and he calmed down straight away.

'You're Bound, aren't you?' he said.

I was surprised he knew me, especially in the low light. My eyes had adjusted, and I recognized him as one of the Argentine staff officers running the government. He had a room down the east end of the hotel.

'I've seen you around, but we haven't spoken before,' I said.

He introduced himself as Major Hidalgo and said that he was part of the military administration that had taken over the Secretariat. He was clearly very shaken, so I offered him a swig of whisky, which he immediately accepted.

We stood there in the dark looking out to the west, sharing the bottle but not saying a lot.

Eventually, Hidalgo asked if I knew the location of the fighting we were watching. I said I was sure it was Mt Longdon. I added unnecessarily that things seemed to be reaching a climax. 'I'm worried that they are going to be fighting in the streets of Stanley,' I said.

'It's possible', he said. 'In any case, people from your side and mine are already dying here. I went to the house which was hit by the British shells earlier tonight. It was terrible. Two of your women were killed, maybe three. I wanted to help them but there was very little I could do.'

He had confirmed what I thought was likely, but it was still a shock.

'This whole thing is crazy, isn't it? They are up there on that mountain killing each other. And now our people are also dying. For what? You don't think it's worth it, do you?'

I knew I was pushing my luck, but Hidalgo seemed to be a decent guy. He shrugged his shoulders. 'We're soldiers. The same on both sides. We just do as we are ordered. But I now just want this to be over.'

We passed the bottle back and forth a couple more times, and then Hidalgo said he was going to try to get some sleep.

'Good luck,' I said. 'However this turns out.'

'*Igualmente*,' he said. 'The same to you. Thanks for the whisky.'

When I surfaced this morning, I heard last night's rogue shell had hit John Fowler's house on Ross Road West, just to the west of the 1914 Battle Memorial. The women killed were Doreen Bonner and Sue Whitley. They had moved into the Fowlers' very substantial house, with their families, for safety. It seems they died instantly. The shell landed just outside the house.

Mary Goodwin, who is in her eighties, is in a critical condition in the hospital.[1] All the Fowlers, Sue's husband Steve, Doreen's husband Harry and their disabled daughter are thought to be OK, although Steve has a big gash in his back.

According to the information I have been able to put together, at least one naval shell landed in the front garden of the Fowlers. After that, everyone moved to the back of the house, thinking that might be safer. Another shell then landed in the front garden and blew the porch off. And then the shell which killed the ladies landed on the other side of the house.

Everyone at the Goose is very upset, and the incident has made us even more aware of how much worse this situation could become.

The BBC confirmed Argentine official news agency reports about the intensity of attacks yesterday and last night. But London is not commenting. This suggests we are seeing the beginning of the final assault on Stanley.

Mora has confirmed the fighting we saw last night was on Mt Longdon but he will not say whether the Argentines lost the feature. My assumption is that British troops have taken it and now have perfect command of the land all the way to Wireless Ridge, Hearnden Water (will we ever go fishing there again?) and Moody Brook.

The heavy artillery pieces (we believe there are six or seven of them, situated mostly between Davis Street and Callaghan Road) have been pumping shells out towards Mt Longdon. They wouldn't be doing this if their people were still in control of the hill. Around the middle of the day, there was some incoming artillery fire from the mountains, apparently targeting the area around the racecourse. It was much less than the Argentine fire.

The Harriers have been very active again. I couldn't tell precisely what they were targeting. I saw one Harrier leave low over Wireless Ridge with a missile on its tail. The pilot was throwing the plane around, trying to shake it off. He only just managed to do so.

It was tempting not to go to Rowan House to check on it, but late in the morning, when the action slackened off for a little while, Dad and I did dash up the hill. I suppose it's a bit silly, but the first thing we did was look for our cat. No sign of him. We'd left food out but that hadn't been touched. He must have been terrified by the shelling and run off. Murdoch the refugee cat was in the porch, though.

Late this afternoon, the BBC is reporting that the MoD had confirmed last night's action around Longdon, saying that they had advanced about five miles. Argentine troops around town look more nervous. On the way to Rowan earlier, I saw three of their 4WD Mercedes with obvious blast damage and bullet holes.

I listened in to a soldier talking to Kasanzew's TV team. He said he was attacked while driving up to the west. His passenger was injured and he had to beat a rapid retreat.

People with good vantage points in town are saying that they can see the Argentines withdrawing. I saw eight of their small tanks[2] parked up on the hill by Rowan. I assume they have retreated from the west.

The power station took more shrapnel last night. One of the fuel tanks was ruptured but fortunately it didn't catch fire. Les Harris was there at the time. The radiators for the generators were damaged, putting them out of action for some time. Ted Carey [who managed the plant] initially estimated that it would take up to six days to repair the generators, but both were running again by midday. The team there is remarkable.

Danny Borland's house was hit last night. Gas cylinders outside Danny's house exploded. I don't know who is living there now, as Danny left in the early days of the occupation. But I don't believe anyone was injured.

The Public Works team have given up trying to repair the water filtration plant. The pipeline from there to the reservoir above Stanley which feeds water into the town has been broken by shellfire. There will only be water as long as the supply in the tank lasts. That won't be more than a few days. We've filled containers around the Goose in case we need them.

The Argentines allowed the RT station to operate briefly this morning so that Alison Bleaney could check on the health of people on the farms. Alison told everyone listening about last night's tragedy. The Brits will surely have been monitoring this.

Sue Whitley was just thirty and had been married to Steve, our only vet, for about eighteen months. Doreen's husband Harry will now have to look after their disabled daughter Cheryl alone.

Today, the Argentines decreed that all civilians living at the west end of town, effectively beyond the Battle Memorial, must move into the centre of town. I really can't understand why so many people have stayed up there for so long anyway.

This evening, the BBC is reporting that some 300 Argentines were captured last night on Mt Longdon. All British objectives were achieved. There are no hard details about dead and injured, though. The Argentine news agency is playing it down, claiming only 'the first line of defences' was broken. They added that the British advance 'had been checked'. No one believes that.

We received two new refugees at the Goose today. Adrian and Norah Monk have left their house near the racecourse because of the danger that is now undeniable. Norah in particular seems very relieved to be in the Goose. They said that they spent last night in a bunker they had dug in their peat shed. They didn't get much sleep.

Yet again, the night is calm, dry and quite clear, although not so moonlit as it has been lately. I think there will be a hard frost, though, as there was last night. The naval shelling commenced at 11.30. I hope they are more accurate tonight.

Sunday, 13 June

As the day dawned, the Navy handed over shelling duties to the Army. Since then, the artillery duel has been non-stop. Early this afternoon, Wilfred 'Pop' Newman's house on Davis Street was hit and set on fire. Fortunately, neither Pop nor his daughter Joyce were in the house. I took a careful walk in that direction. I could see that there was not much left of poor Pop's house. Shells were still landing in the area. A little earlier, our fire brigade had been there (admirable guys that they are), but the house was too far gone, and all they could do was hose down the neighbouring houses in the hope that they didn't catch.

At about the same time some shells landed near Bob Stewart's house on Davis Street. There was no fire, and although the family were in the house with a few other refugee families, no one was hurt. It helped that this is a concrete-block house. Everyone from that house has now been moved, as has Fred Coleman. The old chap had been refusing to leave his house, but I guess even he saw that it's now too dangerous to stay.

Last night, the old Marines barracks at Moody Brook was hit and caught fire. The camp was still burning this morning. We were speculating in the Goose that some of the Marines from NP8901 probably bribed the artillery to destroy their old home. It was condemned ages ago as inadequate, but the MoD refused to fund a new barracks for them.

Early this afternoon, something large was hit around the racecourse. Probably a helicopter. Great clouds of black smoke were billowing from the area for an hour or so.

British artillery is concentrating on the ridge above the racecourse and on the south side of the harbour. Some of these shells are going wide and landing in the harbour, near the 1914 Memorial. The TV team told me they had been up there and had to dive behind the Memorial for shelter.

I had a noisy argument with some of the TV team about the Argentine big guns, which are definitely concealed among houses. Most of them are in the Davis Street and Callaghan Road area. The Argentines insisted that the guns are at least a kilometre from town.

'You believe your own propaganda if you want,' I said. 'But we've got eyes and ears.' That felt quite good.

As if to confirm our point, a little later in the day, they opened up with one of the big guns from a position right in the centre of town. It's deafening. We are pretty sure it's located in Stanley House gardens, which are just a few hundred yards from here, down Ross Road.

The BBC is reporting that, as well as Longdon, British forces have taken Mt Harriet and the Two Sisters. All three features were attacked at the same time. No details yet of losses on either side, but hundreds of Argentines were captured.

The MoD has accepted Argentine reports of local casualties. London is saying that they agree to the Red Cross's idea of civilians being centralized in 'safe' buildings that would be known to both sides. But they stressed that the progress of British forces would not be held up while such an area is being set up. I'm sure it'll come to nothing. And anyway, I'd rather take our chances well spread out around town.

We were in two minds about checking on the house but went up there briefly. The shells were whistling overhead for most of the time. I had a brief chat with Robert, who said that shrapnel was landing near his house, a couple of blocks along Fitzroy Road. This is the closest the shelling has come to us, and it is scary. We got back to the relative safety of the Goose as quickly as possible.

I brought a new Honda generator to the Goose this afternoon. [Our family had the Honda concession for the Falklands.] There have been power cuts on and off all day, so we'll use the gennie if necessary. We have a couple of other small generators, and I told the guys at the power station that they could distribute these if they thought they would help.

Tonight, the BBC ran a long interview with John Nott, who sounded almost chipper. He confirmed that the casualties on the *Sir Galahad* and *Sir Tristram* were serious but not as bad as had been feared. Forty-three men were killed and four are presumed dead. Forty-six were badly wounded. That sounds like an appalling toll to me. The figures were withheld in the hope that the Argentines would overestimate the losses. Nott claims the ruse worked, and as a result they were not expecting the attacks on the mountains the night before last.

Nott said that many of the Argentines were asleep at the time of the attacks, and the first they knew of them was when British troops appeared among their positions. Highly unlikely, I'd say. But the tabloids would like that gung-ho stuff.

As far as I know, the Harriers did not attack our area today, although there were obvious reconnaissance flights to see what damage had been done. I hope they saw what's left of poor Pop Newman's house.

There was more action near Moody Brook from about 9.00pm. The artillery fire in that area is almost continuous and seems to be directed mostly at the north side of Wireless Ridge. A lot of flares and some tracer could also be seen in the area. It looks like there might be a major attack there.

The girls, Aunt Ning, Mum and others just continue providing food and coffee, almost as if it was nothing was out of the ordinary. Bless them for that. Sleepless nights are bad enough but they would be so much worse if we were hungry.

We feel relatively safe here. We are a motley bunch: Anglican and Catholic priests, a farmer under house arrest, six or seven families, added to every now and again when more refugees come in, which they did tonight. Bill and May Roberts arrived with Peter and Diane. They had been holding out at the top of town but joined us when shells began falling very close to their house.

And down the other end of the building are the Argentine press, their own priests, a few odd civilians like Mora and some uniformed staff officers like Major Hidalgo. The relationship with them is not exactly warm, but there's feeling that we are all in the same boat, so we tolerate each other.

There's no let-up from the huge artillery piece in Stanley House gardens. They can't have any accurate idea of where they are sending their shells, but they pump them out anyway. The Navy arrived at about 11.30 and the racket became incessant. We think that the Argentines are now using their big guns to reply to the Navy. They may deter the Navy from coming too close. Anyway, they are shaking our nerves.

Monday, 14 June

It seems that today is the day we've been anticipating for so long for. At about 6.30am I was lying on my mattress behind the armchairs in the lounge, listening to the shelling, when I heard the outside door open. It was dark, with no street lights. The door of the lounge opened and a couple of men entered. It was Carlos Bloomer-Reeve, with one of his officers. People were soon gathering and someone switched a dim table light on.

It was a remarkable scene. We all stood there in the half-light while Bloomer-Reeve said he had come to collect his men. Mum sounded like she was about to lose it.

'You are going to surrender, aren't you?' she said.

Bloomer-Reeve told her not to worry, but an order to surrender would have to come from BA. He confirmed, though, that they were retreating through the town in the direction of the airport, away from the advancing British forces, meaning there should be no house-to-house fighting. And then he said something I will never forget: 'In about two hours your troops will be here, and you will be free.' There was no more to say.

The journalists, priests, sundry civilians and the military administrators began to gather in the porch, some of them carrying a few things but most leaving with little more than the clothes they were wearing.

Our people shook hands with some of them, including some of the military administrators, Vinelli, Mieri, Angelo etc. I think none of us could bring ourselves to hate them. Captain Angelo wasn't living in the hotel but was there now rounding up his countrymen. He got me off the hook during an interrogation at the police station some weeks ago. He told me once that he did not like this situation at all and was just doing his job. Beneath his wispy moustache, he has an easy smile.

And it was obvious that Bloomer-Reeve was not happy here. During his first, friendly posting to Stanley he'd mixed so well with local people and made genuinely good friends. I'm grateful he was here. He's not driven by Argentine nationalism and has done his best to keep us out of danger. I'm convinced of this.

They clambered into vehicles and drove off to the east. We all stood around. We were all a little stunned, I think. Predictably enough, Aunt Ning made coffee. I dug my camera out for the first time in many weeks. It should be safe to start taking photos again. I was taking some pictures out of an upstairs window when I saw mortar or artillery shells landing in the harbour, just off the Government Jetty.

There were no panicked soldiers on the streets. The big gun in Stanley House continued firing occasional rounds. This suggests that no ceasefire has been agreed.

By 9.00am it is getting lively again. British guns are firing in response to the Argentine artillery. Now, as write this, the shelling from both sides is almost constant.

The trickle of Argentine troops walking down the front road to the east is growing into a throng. They are definitely retreating and they make a pathetic sight. One man who had lost a leg was being pushed down the road in a wheelbarrow by his comrades. I couldn't tell if he was still alive.

The retreating soldiers are mostly the young conscripts. They look dirty, tired and hungry. I think they've been beaten by the cold, hunger and neglect of their senior people, as much as by the British troops. I feel very sorry for them. At least they must now know that it's almost over and they will soon be going home. When they get there, I hope they and their families give Galtieri and his thugs hell.

And then something completely ridiculous. Through the scores of Argentine troops, Les Halliday and Rex Browning are walking to work at the Secretariat. Of course, they have their pensions to think about. But to be fair, most Stanley people will not know that it's almost all over.

I can see smoke billowing from what we think is another house at the east end, but we can't identify it.

At 10.30 the troops are still retreating in a stream along Ross Road. One open-backed Land Rover drove slowly through the crowd, with a wounded man in the back groaning loudly.

We can see two or three buildings ablaze, most probably victims of the artillery. One is just to the south of Joe King's House. I hope the Kings are OK. A great cloud of oily black smoke is coming from somewhere near Government House.

By 1.40 most of the firing has subsided, although the big gun somewhere around Stanley House is still firing sporadically.

John and Margaret Leonard have arrived. They no longer felt safe at home. John had tried to call Bloomer-Reeve at Sulivan House in the hope that he might be able to get a message to the American Embassy in BA.

The voice that answered was not Bloomer-Reeve's. John said in his poor Spanish: '*Esta el Vice-Comodoro Bloomer-Reeve, por favor*?'

The answer: 'Sorry, can't help you there, old chap. You're talking to the British Army. This is Major So-and-So speaking.'

Making matters even stranger, John had been put through to Sulivan House by an Argentine operator at the telephone exchange.

The friendly British officer told John that his troops, the Paras, have paused their advance at the racecourse until a surrender is formally agreed.

By 2.00pm there appears to be a secure ceasefire. A few minutes ago, Argentine troops began moving up Ross Road to the west, the direction they came from. I can't understand why they are doing this, but I hope they stop before they get to the Paras' lines.

Max Hastings, a bedraggled reporter for the *Telegraph*, burst into the hotel looking for a good story, which he got. Des gave him a drink, and Hastings said there is effectively a demilitarized zone of three to four hundred yards between the Paras at the 1914 Battle Memorial[3] and the Argentines, who are moving no further west than the Secretariat. He walked through this neutral zone to get to the Goose.

Thousands of Argentines are now moving west up the front road. Word has come through that it is definitely not safe to move outside, as both sides are twitchy and might open fire. Surrender negotiations are not due to start until 4.00pm.

That's still some hours away. Crowds of Argentines are now gathering around the Town Hall for some reason.

As Max Hastings had managed to cross the lines, Peter [Roberts] and I thought we would also have a go. I grabbed my camera and we headed out through the crowds of Argentines milling around. We tried to look confident, as if we were perfectly entitled to walk through their lines. It seemed like a good idea, but once we were in the open and empty part of Ross Road between the Secretariat and the Battle Memorial, I started to wonder. However, we pressed on and made it up the little hill leading to the Memorial. Suddenly, incredibly, we were among British troops.

They looked almost as dirty and worn-out as the Argentines, but there was something entirely different about them. They were tougher, fitter, well-fed and, while grim-looking, obviously still had the spirit to do whatever might be asked of them. Two small Scimitar and Scorpion tanks were parked by the memorial.

Just a few yards away, by a garden fence, were two dead Argentines. Someone had thrown some sheets of corrugated iron over them, but their legs protruded. The fence had been riddled with shrapnel. It was obvious that this had also killed the men. I didn't want to look, but my gaze kept on returning to the dead Argentines, even as we talked to the Paras around the light tanks.

The Paras were surprised to see us and were interested to know what it had been like in Stanley for the past weeks. We told them the situation had become dangerous and scary in the last week or so, but it was nothing like as bad as their experience. They told us they'd taken Mt Longdon a couple of nights ago and had remained on the mountaintop after that, losing some men as the Argentine artillery pumped shells into their positions. They were glad to have got on the move again, and even more glad to know that they rather than the Marines were the first into Stanley.

A couple of them were checking out and cleaning some Argentine FN rifles. I wondered if these were the weapons that had belonged to the dead men lying just a few yards away.

We carried on walking up to the west and suddenly we heard someone calling our names. The shouts came from a group of Paras in the drive of an abandoned house. We wondered how anyone could know who we were, and then we realized that it was Terry Peck! It was great to see him. We knew that he had got out of town early on in the occupation, but apart from that we knew nothing about him. Terry was in full Para uniform, holding a rifle and hard to recognize because of the camouflage cream on his face. He told us all about his adventures.

He'd found his way to San Carlos, where he volunteered to help in whatever way he could. He ended up guiding 3 Para across East Falkland to the Estancia and then helping their patrols to probe the Argentine lines, before becoming involved in the actual battle for Longdon. It's an incredibly heroic story, and I hope someone writes it down in full some day. Terry asked us about his family in Stanley, and we were able to tell him that everyone is OK. I'd seen [his daughter] Tracy at the Treasury just a few days ago. He said he'd be in town tomorrow.

It was getting late and we didn't fancy going back through the lines in the dark, so we wished Terry well and headed back east along the front road, past the light tanks, the guys with their captured weapons and the two dead Argentines. We had a tense and brisk walk through the empty de-militarized zone, and then we were back in the relative safety and warmth of the Goose.

I managed to get some photos when we were with the Paras, but the light was not good and I really didn't think carefully enough about how I took them. So I hope I get some half-decent results. We're living through history, and I want to record it.

It's now well after dark, and the ceasefire is still holding. We've heard that the Marines of 42 Commando (including most of those who were forced to surrender back on 2 April) are camped around Sapper Hill [to the south-west of Stanley], waiting for the command to enter town.

Mieri returned to the Goose around midnight tonight and he told us that the surrender negotiations reached a conclusion around 7.00pm, when Menendez signed the surrender document. It probably took so long because he was trying to salvage some dignity for the Argentine forces. Mieri cautioned that it only applies to forces in the Islands, so it may not mean that the Argentine air force and navy have thrown in the towel. But surrender is surrender! He says that a proper withdrawal will commence in the morning.

It is definitely too soon to celebrate, because the situation is obviously volatile. The Keenleyside family arrived at the Goose tonight, having been ordered out of their house on Pioneer Row by Argentine officers who told them it was not safe to stay there. They were told that there had been a mutiny, or something like it, by junior soldiers. The officers who evacuated the Keenleysides were clearly on the run.

In the early hours we saw that a building on the other side the Town Hall is in flames. A cautious look revealed it to be the large PWD [Public Works Department] garage. Our fire brigade attempted to put the fire out, but ammunition stored there was exploding, so they couldn't do anything.

Tuesday, 15 June

This is the first day of peace since 2 April. Last night, there was no shelling for the first time in many weeks. There was, however, occasional small arms fire. We understand that the tension among the Argentines boiled over last night and they wrecked some buildings where they were taking shelter. They torched some, including the PWD garage and the old Globe Store, one of our most historic buildings.

Early this morning, I walked down that way to see what it was like. The mess and stench around the wreckage of the Globe, Philomel Hill and the jetty are awful. Kit was scattered all over the street.

Argentines are still milling around, but now so are British troops. They seem to be working with Argentine officers (who I notice are still armed – perhaps for their own protection) to establish some order.

I ran into a couple of British journalists who had been with the troops, and they said that although a surrender was *agreed* last night, the formal document was yet to be signed. They thought this would be done at the airport. I thought this would be good to witness and maybe even photograph, so Robert and I got in my jeep and set off (using the few pints of petrol we found).

Clearly, no ceremony was planned for the airport, and actually I think it *was* signed yesterday. British troops had only got as far as the cattle grid near the airport. We drove on and found ourselves surrounded by Argentines. We must have been the first Brits to reach the airport.

No one seemed to care, though, so we looked around. Six or eight Pucaras were parked near the terminal building, which was badly blasted but intact. The Pucaras looked airworthy. There was a Machi jet trainer/fighter which had been badly damaged and was definitely never going to fly again. The three civilian Cessnas and the [Air Service's Britton Norman] Islander were heaps of mangled metal.

On the way back to Stanley, we saw Captain Romano working with Major Mike Norman, who had led the defence of Stanley on 2 April and was now back. They were supervising the disarming of Argentine prisoners. I thought I should put in a good word for Romano.

'He's a good guy, you know,' I said to Mike Norman. 'He helped get me out of trouble and I think he did the same for others.'

Both Norman and Romano smiled broadly. Mike Norman said, 'Yes, I know. We're getting on fine.'

I said goodbye to Romano. Now he really has something to smile about.

I dropped Robert off at home and went on to the Goose to clear up my things. We won't spend any more nights at the Goose, but what a great place it is, and what a wonderful little community we were.

Aunt Ning said that someone was looking for me; an Argentine officer. I was slightly concerned to hear this but I was curious.

'It's Major Hidalgo,' she said. 'Apparently he's been allowed back to get his things and he asked us if we knew where you were. He's upstairs.'

I knocked on the door of Hidalgo's room and he opened it. '*Me estuviste buscando* [Were you looking for me]?' I said in my not brilliant Spanish.

'Yes,' he said. 'We watched the fighting on Longdon and you shared you whisky with me. The night the women were killed. *Lo recuerdes* [you remember]?'

30th JUNE 1982 No. 20

THE PENGUIN NEWS

THE FALKLAND ISLANDS NEWS MAGAZINE

VICTORY

The date : MONDAY, 14th JUNE 1982

The place : NOT "Puerto Rivero", "Puerto de las Islas Malvinas" OR "Puerto Argentino" BUT PORT STANLEY, FALKLAND ISLANDS

The event : Surrender of all Argentine forces in the Islands

FREEDOM

AND A

FUTURE

The following message reached Prime Minister Thatcher in the early hours of Tuesday, 15th June 1982 -

" H.Q. Land Forces Falkland Islands, Port Stanley.

In Port Stanley at 9 o'clock pm Falkland Islands time tonight 14th June 1982, Major General Menendez surrendered to me all the Argentine Armed Forces in East and West Falkland, together with their impediments.

Arrangements are in hand to assemble the men for return to Argentina, to gather their arms and equipment, and to make safe their munitions.

The Falkland Islands are once again under the government desired by their inhabitants. God save the Queen."

(Signed) J. J. Moore.

The 'Victory' edition of *Penguin News*, produced when publication again became possible.

How could I forget it? It seemed like a lot more than a few nights ago, though. 'I do,' I said. 'I think we both benefited from that whisky.'

'Yes,' said the major. 'Now I have something for you.'

He reached under his coat and produced a Browning pistol. 'I'd like you to have this. I have to surrender it, and I'd rather you have it than anyone else.'

I was lost for words, but muttered, '*Gracias, mayor.*'

'No. I thank you. You showed me kindness that night.'

He began to pass it to me, and then hesitated. I thought he was having second thoughts. Instead, he took out the magazine, flicked out the rounds on to the bed and checked that there wasn't one in the chamber.

'I don't think you need the bullets,' he said. Then he handed the weapon to me. 'I wish you luck.'

'I wish you luck, too,' I said. 'I hope we don't meet again, at least not here.'

'I don't intend to come back for the pistol,' he said. 'I hope we all have good lives from now on.'

'*Estoy de acuerdo* [I agree],' I said. We both smiled and shook hands.

I turned and went back to the kitchen. I didn't tell my aunt about the weapon in my pocket. I thanked her awkwardly for everything she and the family had done. Then I went home.

In the corner of the kitchen, the cat was tucking into a plate of chopped mutton. Even he had sensed that it was all over and it was safe to come home. My mother and father were there too. For the first time in months, they looked happy.

Epilogue

For the purpose of this book, my journal ends on 14 June 1982. But in fact I continued to jot down my thoughts and observations for years. With the surrender, one whirlwind chapter of Falklands history simply gave way to another. I was free to publish *Penguin News* again, and given almost more news than I could cope with, my notebooks filled faster than ever.

As I got *Penguin News* back on its feet, the paper became more important than it had been before the war. The first post-war edition was an incomplete first draft of the most crucial episode in Falklands history. It was published with an appropriate full-colour cover, the 50-point headline reading 'VICTORY, FREEDOM AND A FUTURE'.

While I was preoccupied with *Penguin News*, many others in our community were doing far more urgent work. The Falklands civil service, which had been held together by a skeleton crew through the occupation, re-formed. They had the Post Office, the Treasury and the telephone network functioning again in days. It took just a little longer for government engineers to restore clean running water to the town and to repair the electricity generators and distribution system that had been severely damaged by shellfire.

With most children on the farms, it took longer to open the schools again. Some islanders had lost their homes, so work began immediately to give them shelter until new houses could be built.

Although no one was now shooting at them, there was little rest for the British soldiers and their equally hard-pressed Navy and Air Force colleagues. They were, though, relatively safe, and many were billeted with grateful Stanley families.

The first and most urgent task was to disarm the vast number of Argentine troops and provide them with basic shelter and nutrition. After a difficult few days, the PoWs were embarked on the same ships that had carried British troops to the Falklands just a few months before and taken back to Argentina. There the authorities received them with reluctance. These damaged young men were, after all, angry witnesses to and victims of the Junta's stupidity.

In the early days there was a very real fear that the Junta would continue to prosecute the war remotely, using its depleted but still dangerous air force and its less credible navy. So the British troops who had fought bravely and almost to the point of exhaustion were relieved by fresh men and materiel.The newcomers would set about urgently creating defences to deter Buenos Aires from further action.

The two aircraft carriers HMS *Invincible* and *Hermes* were relieved by HMS *Illustrious*, which had only been accepted into the Navy a few months before, after an accelerated final phase of building and trials. Her Harriers operated air patrols while Stanley Airport was patched up sufficiently to become 'RAF Stanley' and accommodate fighter jets.The RAF's workhorse C130 Hercules freight- and troop-moving planes also began shuttling in and out from their forward base on Ascension Island.

A new fleet of helicopters arrived and the skies above Stanley were almost constantly filled with the beating of rotor blades and the roar of turbines. Within months work commenced on a trio of long-range mountain-top radar stations. Only when this early-warning screen was functioning did both military and civilian communities feel completely safe.

Massive military infrastructure had been put in place with remarkable speed. With good reason, the islands became known as 'Fortress Falklands'. Forty years on, that sobriquet remains appropriate, as Eurofighter Typhoons patrol from the purpose-built tri-service base at Mt Pleasant. (The base doubles as an international airport, allowing scheduled flights from the UK, Chile and Brazil.) At least one destroyer, frigate or patrol vessel operates from nearby Mare Harbour. And those huge radar dishes on three mountain tops still revolve 24 hours a day.

I continued to live in the Falklands for the next ten years, running *Penguin News* for some of that time but eventually handing it over to a new editor and passing ownership to a non-profit trust. *Penguin News* is still published today and is better than ever. I still write a monthly column for it.

I worked for some years developing tourism in the islands but then returned to journalism, moving to the UK, where I worked for BBC World Service Radio, presenting 'Calling the Falklands' and other programmes. I still tell anyone who will listen that World Service is a jewel in Britain's journalism crown; and if they want to know why, I tell them it is because the station broadcasts the unbiased truth to people who need that almost as much as they need bread and water. Why else would the Argentine occupiers of the Falklands have tried to jam their transmissions in 1982?

I went on to spend a number of happy years as a deputy editor and reporter at *Soldier* magazine, which involved travelling the world with the Army. British soldiers impressed me in Afghanistan, Iraq and the Balkans every bit as much as they did in the Falklands.

I then began a ten-year career with the Ministry of Defence's Public Relations and Media Directorate, which took me perilously close to the dark arts of information management. But it also took me intriguingly close to the centre of government, when I was seconded to the Afghanistan Communications Team, answering directly to 10 Downing Street.

Now, as I write, it is October 2021. I am happily retired with a wife, Nadia, a dog and a cat and a home in West London. We live contentedly here, but I return to the Falklands as often as possible. Whenever I am home (and the Falklands will always be that), I spend a little time thinking of the events of 2 April to 14 June 1982. That period was the most challenging, frightening and even enlightening time of my life (so far). Frightening and challenging, obviously. But enlightening? Indeed, I learned some important lessons.

For example: never underestimate the ability of unscrupulous leaders to stir up nationalism in support of causes that are stupid and outdated. Conversely, don't offend the pride of others unnecessarily. They are likely to come out swinging.

And, when the chips are down, it's often hard to tell who are the 'good guys' and who are the 'bad'. Neither come from Central Casting. Those lessons from 1982 still ring true forty years on.

Finally, when I am back in Stanley, now a neat and prosperous town which has doubled in size over the years, I make a point of meeting my surviving friends from 1982, especially those who sheltered with my family and me at the Upland Goose Hotel.

Their numbers have, of course, diminished with the passing of the years. So, for those whom I can no longer enjoy meeting, I repeat the dedication with which I started this book: good night, God bless. Wherever you are.

The author Graham Bound in the Falklands in 1982, and in London in 2022

Appendix

Letter dated 27 May 1982 from Graham to his brother Michael in Oxford, UK

Dear Mike,
I don't know whether you will get this letter, as we don't know if local mail for the UK is being taken on the Argentine planes that get through the blockade. But we know from people in the Post Office that they at least taking their own mail.

Mum and Dad are quite concerned that they have not heard from you for a long time. We have heard that the Post Office in London is not accepting mail for the Falklands, and as we have not received anything for weeks, that might be true. Telegrams too are out of the question. But there is no harm in trying to send a letter.

The one sure way to get a message through to the Islands is to send it via *Calling the Falklands*. The BBC are broadcasting the programme to us every day now. If you phone them at Bush House, they will be pleased to record your voice or read the message for you. I think it would be a good idea if you could do this.

At the moment, things are a bit quieter around Stanley than they have been for some days. There are still daily bombing raids by Harriers, and there's the replying anti-aircraft fire. And a few nights ago Task Force ships were shelling positions near us very heavily. But the worst of the action is probably going on in other parts of the Islands.

We're doing our best to keep safe. We spend every night from when the 6 o'clock curfew begins at the Upland Goose, which, as you know, is made of very thick stone. Even so we managed to get a bullet in the kitchen a few days ago. Luckily it was just a ricochet that didn't hit anyone. But some houses have been riddled by rifle fire, either accidental or fired on purpose by nervous soldiers. The stone houses are so much safer than the tin and timber ones. We go back to Rowan House almost everyday to check on it. I've built a pretty safe bunker in the garage just in case we're caught there when anything starts.

Mum and Dad still open the shop for an hour or two some days, and I help them out when necessary but with at least 50 per cent of Stanley people now on the farms, there is not much business.

I see Pete King most days.Some of us regularly meet at his place as there really isn't anywhere else to go, except the Victory bar which we also frequent. It's open via the back door from 4.30 to 5.30 but the Argentines don't know about this.

Pete is still working at the secretariat as are Harold [Rowlands] and some others. It's better to keep the government offices in local control as much as possible. The offices are only open for a few hours in the mornings. Shops like the West Store and the Co-Op also open for a few hours daily, so that we can buy basic supplies. They are starting to ration some items.

Despite everything, we're living well enough. For the moment we have enough food and we are comfortable. We feel reasonably safe at the Goose. The long evenings after curfew get boring but that's a small thing. The crowd of refugees at the Goose (16 of us including a Catholic and an Anglican priest!) get along pretty well.

A lot of houses have been requisitioned by the Argentines, and they're helping themselves to vehicles too. Dad's Land Rover and my Daihatsu Jeep have both been taken by them.

I hope you're managing to record the TV coverage of the crisis. If necessary, just buy more videocassettes.

I'm going up to the hospital to see Aunt Lena in a little while. She is as well as ever. Dad has managed to find some flowers for her in the front porch, and he's made them into a nice bunch, so I'm taking those up to her, plus a few packets of those Players Navy Cut fags that she lives on. By the way, don't forget to mention her if you send a message via the BBC. Everyone does that, by the way, so there wouldn't be anything strange about you giving them a message.

The McLeods just along the road went to camp and we found ourselves looking after their cat. In addition, a family of hens and pullets have moved into our backyard, so we might have the rare treat of some eggs soon.

That's all for now Mike. We're looking forward to hearing from you soon.

Love from us all,
Gray

Notes

Chapter 1: Pawns in the Game

1. Under the Communications Agreement of 1971, Lineas Aereas del Estado, a branch of the Argentine Air Force which provided air services to more remote parts of Argentina, operated a weekly, latterly twice-weekly, flight between Comodoro Rivadavia and Stanley, using Fokker F27 and F28 aircraft.
2. The Polish fishing fleet was very active around the Falklands, although London's refusal to introduce a licensing regime meant that it did not generate any revenue for the Islands. When martial law was introduced in Poland to counter the rise of the Solidarity movement, some crewmen jumped ship and applied for asylum in the Falklands.
3. Briley, the BBC's South America correspondent, became an important media figure during the Falklands War and a popular person in the Falklands, thanks to his determined and often brave reporting from Buenos Aires, particularly his questioning of official propaganda.
4. The English language *Buenos Aires Herald*, under the editorship of Robert Cox, was one of the few media outlets in Buenos Aires which reported the Junta's abuse of human rights. *Penguin News* had a reciprocal arrangement with the newspaper, by which each supplied copies to the other free of charge.
5. The family ran successful retail and tourism businesses in Stanley.
6. 'Camp', derived from the Spanish word *campo* and inherited from the gaucho population of the nineteenth century, refers to rural areas of the islands, effectively anywhere other than the capital, Stanley.

Chapter 2: Tit for Tat

1. The Argentine state gas company had an exclusive deal to supply bottled gas to the islands. Later, on the eve of the invasion, it was feared that they might be a fifth column, and they were arrested.
2. South Georgia was officially a dependency of the Falklands and the Governor's authority extended the 800 miles or so to the island.

Chapter 3: Invasion

1. Gilobert had completed his time as manager of LADE in Stanley just a few weeks before and had been replaced by another Argentine Air Force officer.
2. The Falkland Islands Broadcasting Station, with its ironic acronym FIBS, was the only local radio station. It would be taken over by the Argentines and renamed 'Radio Islas Malvinas'. The station broadcast on the medium waveband, and programmes were also distributed to speakers in Stanley homes, but not outside the town, by a cable rediffusion system. In the weeks ahead, radio transmissions would often cease, but the rediffusion system continued.
3. My brother Michael was in the UK, and I didn't know where my parents were, but I hoped they were safely in Montevideo, Uruguay.
4. Later, I did spend some time at the radio station, but I was contributing nothing. Rather than go back to an empty house, I went to my friends the Kings at the Upland Goose Hotel. I was worried, particularly about the Defence Force, as many of them were my friends and they had neither the training nor the equipment to cope with this. They had, however, bravely turned out that night.
5. No such 'atrocities' occurred. There have been claims in recent years that the Marines killed many more Argentines, but these are not substantiated. There is evidence for just one death, that of Pedro Edgardo Giachino.
6. Simon Winchester and his colleagues were deported that day but continued reporting from Patagonia, where they were arrested on spying charges. They spent the rest of the war in jail. Simon managed to keep my letter and eventually delivered it to my brother.

Chapter 4: Careful What You Say

1. Secondary school-aged children of farmers attended school in Stanley, living in two hostels. In the uncertainty that prevailed after the invasion there was an urgent need to get them back to their families.
2. Stuart worked for the communications company Cable and Wireless and was in a position to know that the Argentines were monitoring phones.
3. Gilobert, LADE's former Stanley manager, was well known in Stanley and friendly with the governor and his deputy. His help negotiating a ceasefire was vital. It has never been established whether he was aware of the invasion plans before 2 April, but it was certainly fortuitous that he was there.
4. Compact two-metre radio transceivers were vital for communications before 1982, as the telephone system outside Stanley was rudimentary. Most homes in the camp were fitted with two-metre sets, as were many vehicles.
5. Terry Peck was Chief of Police until shortly before the invasion. He left the post after a disagreement with senior members of the administration. During

the occupation, he made his way out of Stanley and eventually joined the Parachute Regiment as a guide. He is remembered as one of the foremost local heroes of the conflict.

6. 'Calling the Falklands' (often referred to as CTF in the text) was a BBC World Service programme specifically for the Falklands. In normal times it was a weekly music request and messages show, but after the invasion it became a news programme and was broadcast daily. The Argentines attempted to jam it, with some success.

Chapter 5: To Fitzroy with a Friend

1. Bloomer-Reeve, a career officer in the Argentine Air Force, served as the Stanley manager of LADE, the Argentine Air Force airline, for several years in the late 1970s. He spoke fluent English, was an anglophile and with his easy-going nature, made many friends in the islands. During the occupation, he often intervened to defuse dangerous confrontations between islanders and the Argentine military.
2. The aircraft were Pucaras, slow but lethal ground-attack aircraft, designed and built in Argentina, mainly for anti-insurgency combat. A large number would be based at Stanley Airport and on grass strips at Goose Green and Pebble Island.
3. Falklands occupation postal items became of great interest to philatelists. Thirty years on, envelopes posted in the first few days of occupation bearing Falklands stamps ruled through with biro strokes would sell for well over £100.
4. Venie Summers never returned to her home in Stanley. Shortly after the surrender, she died, with her family around her. She was buried at Fitzroy.

Chapter 6: Bunker Building

1. It later became clear that the hospital meeting did take place and such a letter was drafted and smuggled out to London.

Chapter 7: No Chocolate Eggs

1. Luxton, who owned Chartres farm on West Falkland, was a councillor, although not at the time of the invasion, and was hawkishly outspoken in his criticism of Argentina's Falklands ambitions and all Argentine involvement in the Islands, enabled by various agreements with the British Government in the 1970s.
2. In the decades leading up to the invasion, the Falkland Islands Government Air Service operated several De Haviland Beaver float planes for passenger, freight and mail services around the islands. The aircraft did not survive the war.

Chapter 8: Fuel Runs Low

1. Under an agreement between Buenos Aires and London, Yacimientos Petroliferos del Estado (YPF), the Argentine state fuel company, had a monopoly on supplies to the islands.
2. I have no recollection of approaching Bloomer-Reeve. We may have decided it would better to wait and see if there was any fallout from the search.

Chapter 9: A Stormy Meeting

1. The Tussac Islands in Port William are just a few miles from Stanley and even closer to the airport. They are wild habitat completely covered by the tall native tussac grass.
2. Colville edited the *Falkland Islands Times*, but the rivalry was friendly, as we shared enthusiasm for music and played in the same band.
3. Alison Bleaney was one of the three British doctors at the King Edward Memorial Hospital. When the Senior Medical Officer Daniel Haines was arrested and imprisoned at Fox Bay, she became the senior doctor. She was awarded the OBE for her work during the occupation.

Chapter 10: The Gloves Come Off

1. Cindy Buxton and Annie Price had spent the summer in South Georgia filming a wildlife documentary for Anglia Television. We knew them well from their previous work in the Falklands.
2. Bill Curtis and his family emigrated to the Falklands from Canada, where they had lived in fear of nuclear war. They were not to find peace in Stanley.
3. Bill Luxton (see note 1, Chapter 7) was deported soon after the invasion. Councillor John Cheek had been in the UK at the time of the invasion.
4. The wheeled armoured cars were Panhard AML 90s, French-built and generally considered to be very effective.
5. My cousin Stuart Wallace was an elected councillor, but not at the time of the invasion. Velma Malcolm was the local coordinator for the influential lobbying group the Falkland Islands Committee, while Gerald Cheek, Brian Summers and Owen Summers were officers or NCOs in the Defence Force.

Chapter 11: Interrogation

1. Capitan Alfredo Astiz, sometimes known as 'The Angel of Death', became internationally known for his involvement in the military government's campaign of murder and torture. However, London refused to hold him and allow access to the Swedes. Astiz eventually faced justice in his own country and was jailed.

Chapter 12: Shock and Horror

1. I had met Pat about two years earlier, when she came to Stanley for a study holiday, hoping to improve her English. Later, I visited her and her family in Neuquén, in the foothills of the Andes. Her family was kind and fiercely opposed to the military government. They did not agree with the invasion and had good reason to know how dangerous the Junta could be. A close friend of the family was kidnapped and murdered by the military. His only offence had been printing anti-government posters.

Chapter 13: Hunting for the Transmitter

1. Monsignor Ireland was the Falklands' former senior Catholic priest, and Brother Venancius was his assistant.

Chapter 15: Artillery in the Garden

1. *World Discoverer* was a pioneering small cruise ship which operated around the islands and the Antarctic in the late 1970s and 1980s. My father and I travelled aboard her often, hosting her passengers on Bleaker Island, which we operated as a wildlife tourism destination.

Chapter 20: Heaviest Bombardment

1. The Argentines did move to silence the Radio Telephone system. The Stanley station was closed, although cautious use probably continued between the farms and outlying islands.
2. A new commanding officer for Two Para, Major Chris Keeble, was parachuted into the sea from a Hercules and subsequently picked up by helicopter.

Chapter 22: Caught in the Final Crossfire

1. Mrs Goodwin subsequently died of her injuries.
2. These were not light tanks but armoured cars (see note 4, chapter 10).
3. The imposing granite memorial at the west end of Stanley commemorates a major naval battle on 8 December 1914. A squadron of German cruisers attempted to attack Stanley, unaware that a superior British force was in the harbour. In the ensuing battle the German squadron was almost totally destroyed, with the loss of thousands of lives. The British ships escaped with minimal losses.